CONTENTS

Targeting English Homework
Year 6

ISBN: 978 1 925726 63 3

Published by Pascal Press
PO Box 250
Glebe NSW 2037
www.pascalpress.com.au
contact@pascalpress.com.au

Author: Susan Wilson
Publisher: Lynn Dickinson
Editor: Marie Theodore
Cover Designer: Janice Bowles
Typesetter: Stacey Grainger
Images & Illustrations: Dreamstime (unless otherwise indicated)

Acknowledgements
Thank you to the publishers, authors and illustrators who generously granted permission for their work to be reproduced in this book.

Introduction

Targeting English Homework aims to build and reinforce English skills. This book supports the ACARA V9 Australian Curriculum for Year 6 and helps children to revise and consolidate what has been taught in the classroom. ACARA codes are shown on each unit, and a chart explaining their content descriptions is on pages v and vi. The inside front and back covers show the topics in each unit.

The structure of this book

This book has 32 carefully graded double-page units which are divided into three sections:

- ★ Reading and Comprehension – includes a wide variety of literary and cross-curriculum texts
- ★ Grammar and Punctuation
- ★ Phonic & Word Knowledge.

Each unit also includes a Comprehension Reflections segment for children to rate their comprehension experience. This encourages critical thinking.

Comprehension Reflections

Look at the top of the opposite page. This text is an I__________ text – N__________.

Write one thing you learned or found interesting:

____

Write one question you have or something you want to find more information about:

____

____

Rating

Assessment

Term Reviews follow Units 1–8, 9–16, 17–24 and 25–32 to test work covered during the term and allow parents and carers to monitor their child's progress. Children are encouraged to mark each unit as it is completed and to colour in the traffic lights at the end of each segment. These results are then transferred to the Marking Grid. Parents and carers can see at a glance if their child is excelling or struggling!

- **Green** = Excellent — 2 or fewer questions incorrect
- **Orange** = Passing — 50% or more questions answered correctly
- **Red** = Struggling — fewer than 50% correct and needs help

SCORE /18 0-6 8-14 16-18

Score 2 points for each correct answer!

How to Use This Book

The activities in this book are specifically designed to be used at home with minimal resources and support. Helpful explanations of key concepts and skills are provided throughout the book to help understand the tasks. Useful examples of how to do the activities are provided.

Regular practice of key concepts and skills will support the work your child does in school and will enable you to monitor their progress throughout the year. It is recommended that children complete 8 units per school term (one a week) and then the Term Review. Every unit has a Traffic Light scoreboard at the end of each section.

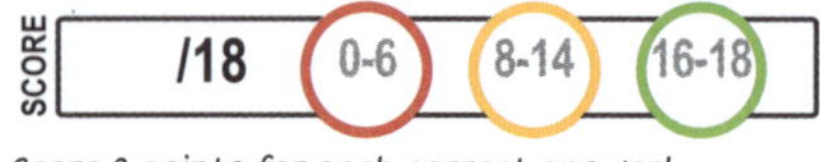

Score 2 points for each correct answer!

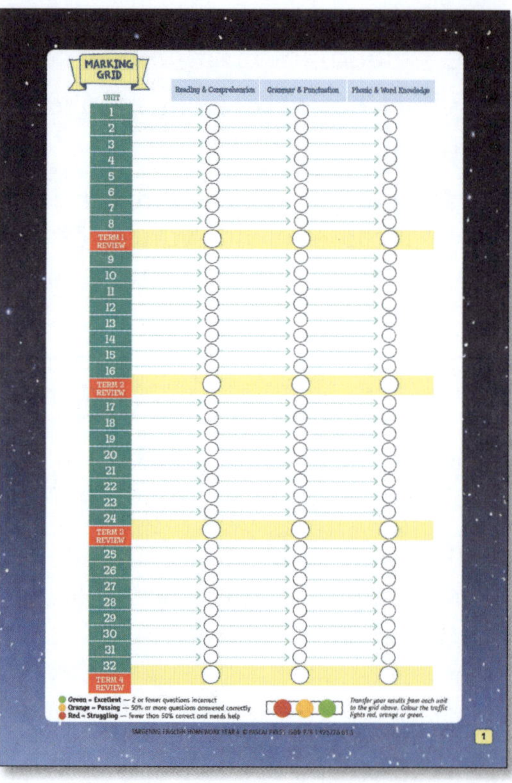

You or your child should mark each completed unit and then colour the traffic light that corresponds to the number of correct questions. This process will enable you to see at a glance how your child is progressing and to identify weak spots. The results should be recorded at the end of each term on the Marking Grid on page 1. The Term Review results are important for tracking progress and identifying any improvements in performance. If you find that certain questions are repeatedly causing difficulties and errors, then there is a good reason to discuss this with your child's teacher and arrange for extra instruction in that problem area.

My Reading List

The Reading List on page 146 provides a handy log for your child to record and rate the books they have read each week. It can be photocopied and shared with their teacher or kept as a record. If your child is an avid reader, then photocopy an extra copy before they start to fill it out.

Answers

The answer section on pages 147–164 can be removed, stapled together and kept somewhere safe. Use it to check answers when your child has completed each unit. Encourage your child to colour in the Traffic Light boxes when the answers have been calculated.

TARGETING ENGLISH HOMEWORK YEAR 6 © PASCAL PRESS ISBN 978 1 925726 63 3

Australian Curriculum Correlations Year 6 English		Reading & Comprehension	Grammar & Punctuation	Phonic & Word Knowledge
CODE	**CODE DESCRIPTION**	**UNITS**	**UNITS**	**UNITS**
LANGUAGE				
AC9E6LA01	Understand that language varies as levels of formality and social distance increase		23, 28	
AC9E6LA02	Understand the uses of objective and subjective language, and identify bias	1, 2, 8, 10, 11, 18	2	
AC9E6LA03	Explain how texts across the curriculum are typically organised into characteristic stages and phases depending on purposes, recognising how authors often adapt text structures and language features	1, 2	2	
AC9E6LA04	Understand that cohesion can be created by the intentional use of repetition, and the use of word association			
AC9E6LA05	Understand how embedded clauses can expand the variety of complex sentences to elaborate, extend and explain ideas		2, 3, 6, 8, 17, 26, 27, 30	
AC9E6LA06	Understand how ideas can be expanded and sharpened through careful choice of verbs, elaborated tenses and a range of adverb groups	7	2, 4, 5, 11, 12, 18, 19, 23, 24, 27, 28	
AC9E6LA07	Identify and explain how images, figures, tables, diagrams, maps and graphs contribute to meaning.	30		
AC9E6LA08	Identify authors' use of vivid, emotive vocabulary, such as metaphors, similes, personification, idioms, imagery and hyperbole	1, 3, 7, 11	1, 7, 9, 10,12, 15, 25, 29, 31	
AC9E6LA09	Understand how to use the comma for lists, to separate a dependent clause from an independent clause, and in dialogue		3, 6, 8, 13, 14, 16, 20, 21, 22, 27, 30, 32	
LITERATURE				
AC9E6LE01	Identify responses to characters and events in literary texts, drawn from historical, social or cultural contexts, by First Nations Australian, and wide-ranging Australian and world authors	17, 19		
AC9E6LE02	Identify similarities and differences in literary texts on similar topics, themes or plots	1, 2		
AC9E6LE04	Explain the way authors use sound and imagery to create meaning and effect in poetry	19		
LITERACY				
AC9E6LY01	Examine texts including media texts that represent ideas and events, and identify how they reflect the context in which they were created	27		
AC9E6LY04	select, navigate and read texts for a range of purposes, monitoring meaning and evaluating the use of structural features; for example, table of contents, glossary, chapters, headings and subheadings	All units		
AC9E6LY05	Use comprehension strategies such as visualising, predicting, connecting, summarising, monitoring and questioning to build literal and inferred meaning, and to connect and compare content from a variety of sources	All units		
AC9E6LY08	use phonic knowledge of common and less common grapheme–phoneme relationships to read and write increasingly complex words			1, 2, 5, 7, 9, 10, 12, 15, 16, 24
AC9E6LY09	Use knowledge of known words, word origins including some Latin and Greek roots, base words, prefixes, suffixes, letter patterns and spelling generalisations to spell new words including technical words			All units

Australian Curriculum Correlations Year 6 English		Reading & Comprehension	Grammar & Punctuation	Phonic & Word Knowledge
CODE	**CODE DESCRIPTION**	**UNITS**	**UNITS**	**UNITS**
CROSS CURRICULAR COMPREHENSION TEXTS				
SCIENCE				
AC9S6U01	Investigate the physical conditions of a habitat and analyse how the growth and survival of living things is affected by changing physical conditions	3, 4		
AC9S6U02	Describe the movement of Earth and other planets relative to the sun and model how Earth's tilt, rotation on its axis and revolution around the sun relate to cyclic observable phenomena, including variable day and night length	9, 15		
AC9S6U03	Investigate the transfer and transformation of energy in electrical circuits, including the role of circuit components, insulators and conductors	12, 13		
AC9S6U04	Compare reversible changes, including dissolving and changes of state, and irreversible changes, including cooking and rusting that produce new substances	21, 24		
HISTORY				
AC9HS6K01	Significant individuals, events and ideas that led to Australia's Federation, the Constitution and democratic system of government	14		
AC9HS6K02	Changes in Australia's political system and to Australian citizenship after Federation and throughout the 20th century that impacted First Nations Australians, migrants, women and children	20		
AC9HS6K03	The motivation of people migrating to Australia since Federation and throughout the 20th century, their stories and effects on Australian society, including migrants from the Asia region	22, 28		
GEOGRAPHY				
AC9HS6K04	The geographical diversity and location of places in the Asia region, and its location in relation to Australia	5, 6, 32		
AC9HS6K05	Australia's interconnections with other countries and how these change people and places	5, 6		
CIVICS & CITIZENSHIP				
AC9HS6K06	The key institutions of Australia's system of government, how it is based on the Westminster system, and the key values and beliefs of Western democracies	16		
AC9HS6K07	the roles and responsibilities of the 3 levels of government in Australia	23, 30		
ECONOMICS & BUSINESS				
AC9HS6K08	Influences on consumer choices and strategies that can be used to help make informed personal consumer and financial choices	11		
HEALTH & PHYSICAL EDUCATION				
AC9HP6P01	Explain how identities can be influenced by people and places, and how we can create positive self-identities	29		
AC9HP6P03	Investigate how the portrayal of societal roles and responsibilities can be influenced by gender stereotypes	8		
AC9HP6P09	Investigate different sources and types of health information and how these apply to their own and others' health choices	10, 31		
AC9HP6P10	Analyse how behaviours influence the health, safety, relationships and wellbeing of individuals and communities	10		

TARGETING ENGLISH HOMEWORK YEAR 6 © PASCAL PRESS ISBN 978 1 925726 63 3

MARKING GRID

UNIT	Reading & Comprehension	Grammar & Punctuation	Phonic & Word Knowledge
1			
2			
3			
4			
5			
6			
7			
8			
TERM 1 REVIEW			
9			
10			
11			
12			
13			
14			
15			
16			
TERM 2 REVIEW			
17			
18			
19			
20			
21			
22			
23			
24			
TERM 3 REVIEW			
25			
26			
27			
28			
29			
30			
31			
32			
TERM 4 REVIEW			

Green = Excellent — 2 or fewer questions incorrect
Orange = Passing — 50% or more questions answered correctly
Red = Struggling — fewer than 50% correct and needs help

Transfer your results from each unit to the grid above. Colour the traffic lights red, orange or green.

AC9E6LY04, AC9E6LY05, AC9E6LA02, AC9E6LA03, AC9E6LA08, AC9E6LE02

TERM 1

Imaginative text – Narrative

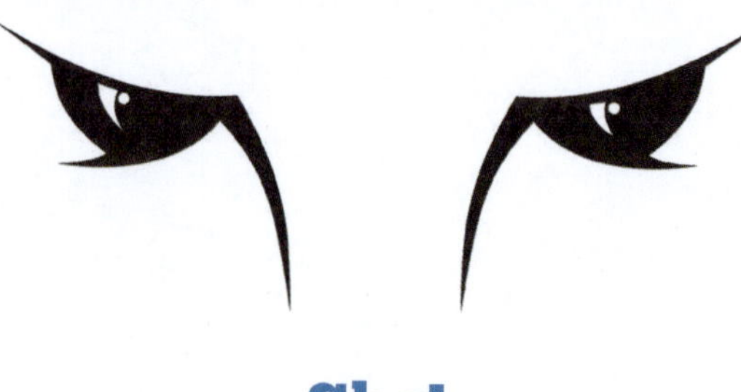

She!

The murderer lay waiting in the dark. The footsteps of her intended victim grew louder. He was only seconds away. Her black eyes were still and glittering like black diamonds when shards of streetlight penetrated the darkness where she waited. She stared down the path to the newcomer who was totally unaware of her presence. He drew level to where she lay. She could hear him breathing ... so close, so close.

She drew herself up to a terrifying height, looming above the startled and increasingly anxious newcomer like a gathering storm. She swayed back and forth in the glow of the streetlights, a hypnotic and dangerous dance. For a long moment, the two looked at each other, the newcomer and the ruler of the path. Then movement returned to the intended victim, and he darted back from the path and turned and ran. Half sobbing in terror, he made for the corrugated iron fence that followed along the path, its rusty uniform ribs jutting to the sky. She was fast, faster than he was, but she had to reach him before he had a chance to climb his way to freedom and out of her grasp.

His short legs, working as hard as engine pistons, scurried over the terrain. The rocks tore the skin from his feet, but he scarcely felt it. There, in front of him, looming out of the darkness, was the rust-encrusted fence. Once, it had been painted a dark green, but lack of care and the ravages of time had reduced it to a sad and stooping remnant of its old self.

She lunged forward, encircling his waist and holding onto him with a vice-like grip, suffocating him and coiling tighter at the end of each breath. She had won. She was still the ruler of the path, and no newcomer would pass freely. She would manoeuvre his head towards her gaping mouth and devour him, headfirst. Or so she thought.

Looking up at the noise above her, she saw her intended victim climbing the fence – his feet pads sticking to the iron surface until he scaled the top and fell in a bruised heap onto the path on the other side of the fence. In complete surprise and bewilderment, she looked at the thing wriggling in her strong grip. It was his tail!

As a gecko, he had the ability to drop his tail if attacked and eventually grow a new one. She still devoured what was left of the gecko and slithered back to where she had been hiding before, hoping for a better snack than the tail of a very lucky-to-be-alive gecko.

Beware those who tread the path as a newcomer. She lies in wait for you ...

TARGETING ENGLISH HOMEWORK YEAR 6 © PASCAL PRESS ISBN 978 1 925726 63 3

Reading & Comprehension

TERM 1

Write the answer or shade the bubble next to the correct answer.

The answers to these questions are in the text.

① **Who was considered the faster of the two?**

○ the newcomer ○ 'She'

② **Why did the gecko not slip downwards when climbing the fence?**

Think about these questions and search for the answers in the text.

③ **What time of day did this occur?**

○ midday
○ night-time
○ mid-morning

Find two clues in the text that support your answer.

④ **How did 'She' stop her victims from being able to escape?**

Use inferencing skills to answer these questions. The answers are not in the text. Think about what you know and what the author says.

⑤ **What animal is 'She'?**

Find two clues in the text that support your answer.

⑥ **Why would 'She' be called ruler of the path?**

⑦ **After reading the text, why do you think geckos lose their tails?**

⑧ **Find devour in the text. Use context clues to choose the correct meaning of devour. Context clues are hints and extra information in a sentence that help you understand the meaning of an unknown word.**

○ eat greedily ○ regurgitate
○ scare ○ skin him

Use your experience and opinions to answer these questions. The answers are not in the text.

⑨ **The newcomer fell in a 'bruised heap' on the other side of the fence. What does bruised heap mean?**

Describe a situation when you have fallen in a bruised heap.

⑩ **Think of the description of the fence, the terrain and where 'She' was hiding. Where in your neighbourhood could this path exist? Give two reasons for your answer.**

Comprehension Reflections

Look at the top of the opposite page. This text is an I__________ text – N__________.

Write one thing you learned or found interesting:

Write one question you have or something you want to find more information about:

Rating

Score 2 points for each correct answer! SCORE /20 0-8 10-14 16-20

Grammar & Punctuation

AC9E6LA08

Context clues

Context clues are hints that the author gives to help define a difficult word. There are different types of common context clues. One type of clue is when the author uses a synonym. This is when a word with the same meaning is used in the sentence to help you understand the word you are unfamiliar with.

Circle the synonym for the word in bold in each sentence.

Example: In complete **surprise** and bewilderment she looked at the thing wriggling in her grip.

1. **Looming** above the startled newcomer, she overlooked his frightened form.
2. The fence was encrusted with rust and **covered** in red streaks.
3. She would manoeuvre his head towards her gaping mouth, **moving** it into position.

Antonyms

Antonyms, or words with opposite meanings, can also be context clues. Look for certain cue words like but, however and although.

Example: The newcomer was totally **unaware** but became **conscious** of her presence very quickly.

Circle the antonym for the word in bold in each sentence.

4. The fence was affected by the **ravages** of time; however, the owner was planning its restoration.
5. The newcomer had **scaled** the fence without trouble although he descended with a thud.
6. She **lunged** at the newcomer, but he retreated towards the fence.

Figurative language – Personification

Figurative language adds description to your writing. One example of figurative language is personification, which is when you give human characteristics to something non-human. For example, in the text, the newcomer and 'She' are not human, yet they are given human feelings and thoughts. The newcomer is anxious and sobs in terror. 'She' feels surprised and bewildered at being beaten and is labelled a murderer, a label we do not give to animals.

In the text, the fence is given human qualities. Find two examples where descriptions of the fence give it human qualities.

7. ______________________
8. ______________________

Similes

Another form of figurative language is similes. This is where you compare two things using the words like or as.

9. **Find three examples of similes in the text.**

____

____

____

10. **Write your own similes. Be creative in selecting what you want to be compared to.**

Example: I dance **like** a cat on a hot tin roof.

I dance ______________________

______________________.

I sing ______________________

______________________.

Score 2 points for each correct answer! SCORE /20

TARGETING ENGLISH HOMEWORK YEAR 6 © PASCAL PRESS ISBN 978 1 925726 63 3

Phonic & Word Knowledge

AC9E6LY08, AC9E6LY09

Complex words – Uncommon letter patterns

English has borrowed many words from other languages, so some words have uncommon letter patterns. Man**oeu**vre (pronounced muh-noo-vuh) is borrowed from the French language and is spelt in Australia and England with three vowels in a row. Americans spell it with only two vowels in a row (man**eu**ver). It means 'movement requiring skill or care'.

① – ⑩ Using the table, how many new words can you make adding prefixes and suffixes to the base word manoeuvre? Leave off a letter for those marked with a •. Can you get to 10?

Prefixes	Base word	Suffixes	New words
out- un-	manoeuvre	-able• -ed• -ing• -s -ability•	

Greek-derived words with 'aero'

Have you ever spelt **aero**plane as airoplane? In Australia and England, the Greek prefix 'aero' is used, meaning 'air or lower atmosphere'. 'Aero' also forms many other words in the English language.

Choose the best 'aero' words to fit into each space. Use context clues and a dictionary if needed.

aerosol aerobics aeronautic aerodynamic aeroplane

⑪ The newcomer would have wished for an _______________ to help him escape the ruler of the path.

⑫ Of course, he would have to know how to fly and have _______________ skills.

⑬ After all, his body was not designed for speed. He was not _______________.

⑭ Perhaps if he had gone to _______________ classes, he would have been fitter and might not be gasping for air.

⑮ If only he had an _______________ can of repellent spray to deter her from chasing him.

Silent 'p'

Pneumonia comes from the Greek word for 'wind, breath or air' and refers to a disease of the lungs. Pneumatic means 'relating to or using air', such as tyres on a car. These words have a silent 'p' before the letter 'n'. Other words that have a silent 'p' can be in these letter patterns: pn, ps and pt.

Match the scrambled words that start with a silent 'p' with their correct spelling.

⑯	t e n p a m c u i		pneumonia
⑰	p c c s y i h		psychiatrist
	a e u i o m n n p	→ pneumonia	psychology
⑱	t h i s i c s p r a t y		pneumatic
⑲	g o o s h y c p l y		psychic

Score 2 points for each correct answer! SCORE /38  0-16  18-32  34-38 

Imaginative text – Recount

Hero's Courageous Battle

Reporter: Sally Skink | The Gecko News

Late evening, local time, a newcomer to our parts, Mr G, survived a nasty conflict with our feared, 'Ruler of the Path'!

Mr G was interviewed after the conflict and has provided his account of the fray and how he survived such a fight.

"I was minding my own business, making my way up the path to visit a friend who lives in the back garden. Suddenly, a villainous pair of eyes spotted my movements and blocked my path. I did not cower or back away. I stood my ground and demanded that she move out of my way.

"With a menacing hiss, she launched herself towards me. I am very nimble, so I easily sidestepped her brutal onslaught. Time and time again she hurled herself towards me, and each time I was too quick for her.

"After some time, she lay panting in the grass, too confused and tired to continue. I positioned myself to annihilate this problem in my journey and hurl her over the fence. I approached closer and closer to her exhausted frame.

"I seized her in my grasp, and, with a mighty scream, I tossed her over the fence. However, with the rush of excitement and the valiant effort to pick up such a large creature, I accidentally caught my tail as well.

"So, not only did I see the ex-ruler of the path go sailing over the fence, but my tail went with her. I was flabbergasted! It took me completely by surprise."

Mr G has since been voted in by the local council as the official 'Protector of the Path'. In this position, Mr G would be expected to continue his heroic efforts to keep the path safe for all who live in the area and for any future newcomers.

Mr G has yet to make a formal statement. We have not been able to contact him but hope to bring you a report as soon as we can locate him.

TARGETING ENGLISH HOMEWORK YEAR 6 © PASCAL PRESS ISBN 978 1 925726 63 3

Reading & Comprehension

TERM 1

Write the answer or shade the bubble next to the correct answer.

The answers to these questions are in the text.

1. **Mr G sees himself as nimble because he:**
   - ◯ is a good dancer.
   - ◯ sidestepped the attacks from the 'Ruler of the Path'.
   - ◯ has been voted in by the local council as the official 'Protector of the Path'.
   - ◯ could pick up a large creature.

2. **In Mr G's account, who or what goes over the fence?**
   - ◯ the Ruler of the Path
   - ◯ Mr G
   - ◯ the Ruler of the Path and Mr G's tail
   - ◯ Mr G's tail

Think about this question and search for the answer in the text.

3. **How has Mr G portrayed himself to the paper?**
   - ◯ heroic and shy
   - ◯ brave and confident
   - ◯ brave and humble
   - ◯ strong and silent

Use inferencing skills to answer these questions. The answers are not in the text. Think about what you know and what the author says.

4. **The word fray is used in the second paragraph. Using context clues, choose the best meaning of 'fray' below. Look for synonyms to help you.**
   - ◯ meeting
   - ◯ interview
   - ◯ discussion
   - ◯ dispute

5. **The word flabbergasted is used in the seventh paragraph. Using context clues, choose the best meaning of 'flabbergasted' below.**
   - ◯ out of breath
   - ◯ amused
   - ◯ shocked
   - ◯ scared

Would the Ruler of the Path read this newspaper? Provide one reason why she would and one reason why she would not.

6. Reason she would:

   ____

   ____

7. Reason she would not:

   ____

   ____

8. **Why do you think the newspaper has not been able to contact Mr G? Why did he disappear? Explain your answer.**

   ____

   ____

   ____

   ____

Use your experience and opinions to answer these questions. The answers are not in the text.

Reporter Sally Skink found a secret witness, and it turns out that Mr G has exaggerated and even invented the events! Have you tried that when retelling a good story?

Is exaggeration lying? Give one reason why it is and one reason why it is not.

9. Exaggeration is lying.

   ____

   ____

10. Exaggeration is not lying.

   ____

   ____

Comprehension Reflections

Look at the top of the opposite page. This text is an I__________ text – R__________.

Write one thing you learned or found interesting:

____

Write one question you have or something you want to find more information about:

____

____

Rating   

Score 2 points for each correct answer! SCORE /20 0-8 10-14 16-20

Grammar & Punctuation

AC9E6LA02, AC9E6LA03, AC9E6LA05, AC9E6LA06

TERM 1

Personal recounts and noun groups

Part of the text has Mr G providing a personal recount of the incident. A personal recount is where the author tells about an experience that they were involved in, providing their thoughts and point of view. This is 'subjective writing' and may not be an accurate representation of what truly happened. Mr G uses noun groups to paint a picture in the minds of readers. Noun groups add description to your writing.

Look through the text and write the adjective that describes the noun to form a noun group.

Adjective – describes noun	Noun – name of person, place or thing
Example: nasty	conflict
①	hiss
②	onslaught
③	frame
④	scream
⑤	effort
⑥	creature
⑦	efforts

Imagine you are Mr G. Change the adjectives to make yourself sound more like a hero.

Reporter's adjectives	Mr G's adjectives	Nouns
round	*Example:* observant	eyes
thin	⑧	legs
chubby	⑨	body
nervous	⑩	attitude
meek	⑪	voice
dull	⑫	skin
small	⑬	creature
unsteady	⑭	walk

Precise verbs

Your ideas can be expanded by putting thought into the verbs or action words you choose. Using precise verbs rather than general verbs can improve your writing.

Match each precise verb from the text with a general verb.

Example: cower or back away	jumped
⑮ demanded	beat
⑯ launched	asked
⑰ hurled	took
⑱ annihilate	shrink
⑲ seized	threw

Exaggeration for humour

The text uses strategies such as exaggeration to create humour. Mr G exaggerates the story to represent himself as being better and braver than he really is. Unit 1 portrays a more objective view.

⑳ **Use exaggeration to retell an incident at school. Stretch the truth to create a humorous subjective recount.**

Score 2 points for each correct answer!

SCORE /40    

TARGETING ENGLISH HOMEWORK YEAR 6 © PASCAL PRESS ISBN 978 1 925726 63 3

Phonic & Word Knowledge

AC9E6LY08, AC9E6LY09

Vowel alternation

The vowels a, e, i, o and u have short and long sounds. The vowel in 'hop' is short compared to 'hope' where it is long due to the 'e' on the end of the word. However, vowels can change from short to long when adding a suffix. When this happens, it is called vowel alternation.

Examples:
crime (long vowel) – add a suffix to form criminal ('i' is now a short vowel)
cave (long vowel) – add a suffix to form cavity ('a' is now a short vowel)

Change the words in bold by adding a suffix so that the word fits the meaning of the sentence. You are changing a long vowel to a short vowel.

1. Mr G is good at sport and is very ______________. **athlete**
2. I have a great deal of ______________ for his ability. **admire**
3. Mr G made a ______________ that he would only play one sport. **decide**
4. The factory decided to increase ______________ of chocolate for Mr G. **produce**

Look at the word pairs. Work out which word has the short or long vowel and write it under the correct heading in the table.

Example: wise / wisdom
5. reduction / reduce
6. inspiration / inspire
7. divide / division
8. president / preside

Short vowel	Long vowel
Example: wisdom	wise
5	
6	
7	
8	

Consonant alternation

Consonants are all the letters of the alphabet that are not vowels. When consonants change from being silent to sounded out, it is called consonant alternation.

Example: sign (silent 'g') – add a suffix to form signal ('g' is sounded)

First, match the following words to make pairs. Then write the words in the correct column depending on whether they have the silent or sounded letter. Finally, write the silent letter.

Example: sign	muscle
9. designate	resignation
10. muscular	design
11. bombard	doubt
12. resign	signature
13. dubious	bomb

Silent	Sounded	Silent letter
Example: sign	signature	g

Use these words to fill the spaces in the text so that it makes sense.

designate
resign
doubt
muscular
dubious

Mr G wanted to (14) ___________ as 'Protector of the Path' as he was very (15) ___________ that he could defeat 'She' if he met her again. 'She' was much too (16) ___________ and would no (17) ___________ beat Mr G again and even eat him. Mr G thought of a genius plan. He would (18) ___________ She' as 'Protector of the Path'.

Score 2 points for each correct answer!

Reading & Comprehension

AC9E6LY04, AC9E6LY05, AC9E6LA08, AC9S6U01

TERM 1

Imaginative text – Narrative

Trapped!

It happens, you know. One minute you see the outside world and then, poof, back into the darkness once again. I could use an idiom to say that this was the straw that broke the camel's back. I had had enough! I wanted freedom! Little did I know that I would change and grow to love my prison. Change and grow I did.

My life started out in a brightly lit place where I was lined up with the others like soldiers on parade. I was a star, glowing white and fresh-faced and new, waiting for the world to open my eyes. My new owner took me home and lay me on what I learnt was a kitchen bench. My outer wrapper was opened, and I was spread with delightful ingredients and then put into another wrapper and into total darkness. Here I have stayed and have not been released from my prison. Then 'they' made their presence known and grew. I am now part of the colony. I am part of 'them'.

It was dark and no air escaped or came into where I lay. Even though it was dark, I sweated, so my prison became damp, dark and somewhat warm, just how 'they' like it. They had come in the air and were trapped here with me. I didn't see them at first because they were too small. Then they started to grow. I could feel them making their way into the spaces along my surface, sinking little feet into every crevice. Thousands covered me in the space of what I thought was a day, and after a short time there were millions. They were hungry and started to consume me as they grew upwards from my surface. And so, I changed.

I became part of the growing colony, no longer glowing white and fresh-faced. I was furry, with glorious colours of white, yellow, green, grey and black. A multicoloured hairy colony with pods waiting to break open to release more of 'them' into the air. I gave birth to the colony. I was the colony.

*****

Sam, it's the start of term tomorrow and I need you to clean out your schoolbag, ready for school. OH NO! You haven't left your lunch from the last day of term in your bag all this time? That's disgusting! You have a horrible mouldy sandwich in there. Don't open the sandwich bag. It's full of mould spores and they are dangerous for you to breathe in. You know mould spores are tiny, microscopic fungi that float on every breeze. They were obviously in the air that was trapped with your sandwich. I'm throwing this into the bin now! At least you didn't leave any homework in your bag. Or did you?

TARGETING ENGLISH HOMEWORK YEAR 6 © PASCAL PRESS ISBN 978 1 925726 63 3

Write the answer or shade the bubble next to the correct answer.

The answers to these questions are in the text.

1. **The prison was:**
   - ◯ damp, dark and somewhat warm.
   - ◯ a brightly lit place.
   - ◯ a kitchen bench.
2. **When did the narrator start to see 'them'?**
   - ◯ when 'they' were a star, glowing white and fresh-faced and new
   - ◯ when spread with delightful ingredients
   - ◯ when 'they' started to grow
3. **What are mould spores?**

   ____

   ____

Think about these questions and search for the answers in the text.

4. **What was the prison?**

   ____

5. **What was the narrator of the text?**

   ____

   Write two clues from the text that led you to this answer.

   ____

   ____

6. **Who were 'they' and 'them' in the text?**

   ____

Use inferencing skills to answer these questions. The answers are not in the text. Think about what you know and what the author says.

7. **This line is in the text: My life started out in a brightly lit place where I was lined up with the others like soldiers on parade. Where could this be?**

   ____

8. **What happened to the narrator of the story while in prison?**

   ____

   ____

   ____

   ____

Use your experience and opinions to answer these questions. The answers are not in the text.

9. **The narrator says they could use the idiom, the straw that broke the camel's back when they were put back into darkness. What do you think they meant by this?**

   ____

   ____

   ____

10. **Describe a situation where it was the last straw for you, and you had had enough.**

   ____

   ____

   ____

   ____

   ____

   ____

   ____

   ____

Comprehension Reflections

Look at the top of the opposite page. This text is an I__________ text – N__________.

Write one thing you learned or found interesting:

____

Write one question you have or something you want to find more information about:

____

____

Rating   

Score 2 points for each correct answer! SCORE  /20  0-8 10-14  16-20

Grammar & Punctuation

AC9E6LA05, AC9E6LA09

Complex sentences – Commas

TERM 1

A complex sentence contains an independent clause that would make sense if it was a sentence on its own and at least one dependent or subordinate clause that could not form a sentence on its own. These two clauses are joined together by a conjunction or joining word. The conjunction can go in the middle or at the beginning of the sentence.

Example: **I sweated** even though it was dark.

You can reverse the positions of the clauses and put the conjunction at the start of the sentence and the independent clause at the end.

Example: Even though it was dark, **I sweated.**

There is a comma after the dependent clause if it is first in the sentence.

OR

If it is first in the sentence, **there is a comma after the dependent clause.**

Reverse the positions of the clauses in these sentences by placing the conjunction at the start of each sentence. Notice where the commas are.

1. **I did not see them** until they started to grow.

   Until ______________________________,

   I ______________________________.

2. **The colony started to grow** after we were locked in the prison.

   After ______________________________,

   the ______________________________.

3. **I resented the colony** before I became part of it.

   Before ______________________________,

   I ______________________________.

Reverse the positions of the clauses in these sentences by placing the conjunction in the middle of the sentence. This time you do not need commas in the sentences you write.

4. Even though I was part of the colony, **I missed my old self.**

   I ______________________________

   even though ______________________________.

5. Once they started to grow, **I was covered by millions of them.**

   I ______________________________

   once ______________________________.

6. If you leave your lunch in your bag over the holidays, **you will create your own colony.**

   You ______________________________

   if ______________________________.

Reverse the positions of the clauses in these sentences. You will need to move the conjunction and decide whether to use a comma. Some clues are provided.

7. There was a horrible smell in my room because I left a banana in my bag all holidays.

   ______________________________,

   ______________________________.

8. While Mum gave me a lecture, Dad made me clean out my bag.

   ____

   ______________________________.

Reverse the position of the clauses in this sentence. This time there are no clues.

9. Whenever I take it to school, the teacher makes me leave my bag outside.

   ____

   ____

Score 2 points for each correct answer! SCORE /18

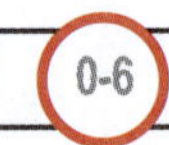

TARGETING ENGLISH HOMEWORK YEAR 6 © PASCAL PRESS ISBN 978 1 925726 63 3

Phonic & Word Knowledge

AC9E6LY09

Syllables

To help you spell words, you need to break them into syllables. An easy way to determine a syllable is to count how many times your chin moves downwards when you say a word. However, English can be difficult in that some syllables are stressed and some parts of words we do not say at all.

Stressed syllables

Stressed syllables do not need a holiday! They are the part of the word that has a longer, louder, higher sound than the other syllables in the word.

Example: present

If used as a **noun**, the **first syllable** is **stressed** – I gave my friend a **PRE**-sent.

If used as a **verb**, the **second syllable** is **stressed** – I will pre-**SENT** my speech tomorrow.

Both words are spelt the same but are pronounced differently. Placing stress on the wrong syllable can lead to mispronounced words and unclear speech.

I'm stressed!

Circle the stressed syllables in the bold words.

1. Don't touch that **ob-ject**. (noun)
2. I **ob-ject** to the way you spoke to me. (verb)
3. I **dis-like** your tone of voice. (verb)
4. Sorry, but it was a **pres-ent** from a friend. (noun)
5. You were lucky to **re-ceive** such a gift. (verb)
6. They found it in the **de-sert**. (noun)

Unstressed syllables

Unstressed syllables can contain vowels that we do not say. These are called schwa vowels. The schwa sound is the most common unstressed syllable in the English language. Because we do not say the whole word, it can be tricky when it comes to sounding out syllables for spelling.

The schwa is the lazy way to say the word and often sounds like 'uh' where your mouth barely moves. The 'uh' sound is only found in vowels (a, e, i, o, u).

Examples: The schwa or 'uh' sound is the 'a' in asthm**a**, the 'er' in wat**er**, the 'ar' in li**ar**, and the 'or' in fact**or**.

Say each word out loud and circle the stressed syllable.

7. fam-i-ly
8. ex-tra
9. sal-ad
10. hea-ven
11. be-low
12. for-mal
13. a-maze
14. free-dom

Circle the schwa sound in these words. You are looking for the unstressed vowel/s that make an 'uh' sound.

Examples: fam-(i)-ly ex-tr(a)

15. for-mal
16. a-maze
17. be-low
18. free-dom
19. doc-tor
20. hea-ven

Score 2 points for each correct answer! SCORE /40

AC9E6LY04, AC9E6LY05, AC9S6U01

Informative text – Description

Swim Back in Time

Put on your wetsuit and get ready to dive in. The time portal is activated and waiting for you. You and your classmates will travel back in time to see for yourself the evolution of our oceans. There have been many changes to our oceans that have impacted the life within them. However, our impact on oceans today is just as dramatic.

Dive in and swim with time. The timeline below will guide your way.

4.5 billion years ago – The Earth forms.

4.4 billion years ago – The oceans form.

3.5 billion years ago – Single-cell microbes appear, but the atmosphere and oceans lack oxygen. You need your oxygen tank for land and sea exploration.

2.3 billion years ago – Bacteria emerge. Oxygen is starting to be produced.

542 million years ago – There is more oxygen in the water, and the climate is warmer. This leads to an explosion of life although most of these animals lack a backbone. You swim among animals like sponges and worms, as well as many animals with shells. Look out for the largest predator of the time. It is one-metre long and has sharp, jagged teeth and crushing jaws.

360 million years ago – Extinction event causing global change – The balmy ocean temperatures turn ice cold. Glaciers form so the sea level drops. Be careful because approximately 75% of Earth's species become extinct.

252 million years ago – Extinction event – This is the largest extinction in the history of the Earth. Approximately 90–98% of all ocean life disappears. The Earth's atmosphere changes due to volcanic eruptions sending out toxic gases. There is less oxygen in the atmosphere and in the oceans. The oceans become acidic and temperatures rise. Good luck!

230 million years ago – Reptiles appear in the sea and on land. Giant sea lizards that are eight metres long and have dagger-like teeth roam the oceans. Keep your eyes open and don't get eaten!

146–66 million years ago – The oceans are warm, dinosaurs rule on land and marine reptiles swim in the oceans.

66 million years ago – Extinction event – An asteroid collides with Earth and causes mass extinction. Sunlight is blotted out by dust and soot, the Earth's temperature drops, and the oceans become more acidic. Dinosaurs become extinct but mammals survive. I hope this includes you! A variety of species in the world's oceans, including large sharks, survive the mass extinction. Major groups of fish species develop after the dinosaurs disappear.

Today – Extinction of many species due to human impact – Coastal developments and overfishing cause a loss of ocean life. Pollution from run-off, oil spills and plastic waste is killing species at an alarming rate. Global warming causes the melting of glaciers and, with that, rising sea levels. The extra carbon dioxide that humans make is dissolving into the water and causing the seas to become more acidic.

Hope – Marine conservation and the sustainable use of our oceans can be achieved. This can be through agreements between countries and through actions and rules made within countries and at the local level. The United Nations has declared marine conservation to be one of the major development goals for the future – a common goal for humanity.

Future – Swim on to the future. What do you see?

TARGETING ENGLISH HOMEWORK YEAR 6 © PASCAL PRESS ISBN 978 1 925726 63 3

Reading & Comprehension

Write your answers on the lines provided.

The answers to these questions are in the text.

① What animals would you have swum among 542 million years ago that did not have **backbones**?

② What percentage of Earth's species became extinct **360 million years ago**?

③ How did an asteroid cause the extinction of dinosaurs?

④ How many extinction events happened in the past?

Think about this question and search for the answer in the text.

⑤ What is causing the **extinction** of ocean life today?

Use inferencing skills to answer these questions. The answers are not in the text. Think about what you know and what the author says.

⑥ 360 million years ago, temperatures dropped, the sea turned ice cold and glaciers formed. Why did this cause the **sea level** to drop?

⑦ 542 million years ago there was an explosion of life, **the seas were warmer** and there was **more oxygen in the water**. Why would these two things help life to develop?

Use your experience and opinions to answer these questions. The answers are not in the text.

⑧ Plastic waste ends up in our oceans. What is something you could do at school to stop your plastic waste ending up in the oceans?

⑨ The last line says **swim to the future**. What do you think you will see in 50 years' time? Describe this using two sentences.

⑩ How would we be affected if all **plastic disappeared**?

Comprehension Reflections

Look at the top of the opposite page. This text is an I__________ text – D__________.

Write one thing you learned or found interesting:

Write one question you have or something you want to find more information about:

Rating   

Score 2 points for each correct answer! SCORE /20   
0-8 10-14 16-20

Grammar & Punctuation

AC9E6LA06

Past tense

TERM 1

The tense of a verb (doing word) in a sentence gives you an idea of when the action happened. It could be something happening in the present, in the future, or it could be something that happened in the past. If an action has already happened, it is past tense. The timeline in this unit takes you into the past. There are four ways to use past tense. Don't let the tense names in the table confuse you.

Simple Past	Past Continuous	Past Perfect	Past Perfect Continuous
verb + **ed** or **irregular form** of the verb	Auxiliary (helping) verb **was/were** + **main verb** + **ing**	Auxiliary verb **had** + **past participle** with **-ed** or **irregular form**	Auxiliary verbs **had been** + **main verb** + **ing**
Dinosaurs **walked** the Earth. (-ed) I **swam** with them. (irregular verb 'swim')	Dinosaurs **were walking** the Earth. I **was swimming** with them.	Dinosaurs **had walked** the Earth. I **had swum** with them. (irregular verb 'swim')	Dinosaurs **had been walking** the Earth. I **had been swimming** with them.

Some verbs are irregular and a little tricky by not using 'ed' in the simple past or past perfect tenses.
Examples: swim – swam – swum / fly – flew – flown

Change the verb in each sentence as you move through the tenses. Can you get all 21 verbs correct?

Simple Past	Past Continuous	Past Perfect	Past Perfect Continuous
Example: I **checked** my scuba gear.	I **was checking** my scuba gear.	I **had checked** my scuba gear.	I **had been checking** my scuba gear.
I **watched** for predators.	① I ____________ for predators.	② I ____________ for predators.	③ I ____________ for predators.
I **stayed** clear of danger.	④	⑤	⑥
I **enjoyed** the dive.	⑦	⑧	⑨
I **fought** (fight) for my life.	⑩	⑪	⑫
I **sank** (sink) to the bottom.	⑬	⑭ *(Not 'sank'. Use 'swim' as a clue.)*	⑮
I **pretended** to be lifeless.	⑯	⑰	⑱
I **threw** (throw) away my gear.	⑲	⑳ *(Not 'threw'. Use 'fly' as a clue.)*	㉑

Score 2 points for each correct answer! SCORE /42    

TARGETING ENGLISH HOMEWORK YEAR 6 © PASCAL PRESS ISBN 978 1 925726 63 3

Phonic & Word Knowledge

AC9E6LY09

Prefixes meaning 'no' or 'not'

From the text, we know that many species have disappeared over time. The word disappear is made from the base word appear and the prefix 'dis' that goes at the beginning of the word. The prefix 'dis' changes the meaning of the word to mean 'not to come into view'.

There are many prefixes that can mean 'not'. But which one do we use? The table has some clues.

Write each word with its prefix.

Prefixes	Base Words	New Words
non	verbal	*Example:* non-verbal
un	likely	①
anti	social	②
in (cannot go in front of words starting with 'i' or 'u')	accurate offensive	③ ④
il (goes in front of words beginning with 'l')	logical literate	⑤ ⑥
im (goes in front of words beginning with 'm' or 'p')	moral possible	⑦ ⑧
ir (goes in front of words that begin with 'r')	responsible	⑨
dis de	mount construct	⑩ ⑪

Using the information in the table, rewrite each word with the correct prefix.

⑫ perfect ____________ ⑯ organised ____________ ⑳ mature ____________

⑬ legible ____________ ⑰ rational ____________ ㉑ fair ____________

⑭ helpful ____________ ⑱ healthy ____________ ㉒ sense ____________

⑮ believe ____________ ⑲ honest ____________ ㉓ legal ____________

㉔ – ㉘

Poor Sam has become very muddled in using the prefixes. Can you circle his mistakes and write the correct spelling on the line underneath the word.

It's (nonlikely) I would be (irsane) enough to go swimming back in time.

unlikely insane

What if I am dissuccessful and get eaten? It's not that I am imgrateful for

____

the chance to dive with flesh-eating animals, it's just disbelievable that I would

____

survive. Mum thinks it's an inpossible task, yet she has given permission for me

____

to go. I think I caught her smiling. I think she is unresponsible if she lets me go.

____

Score 2 points for each correct answer! SCORE /56 0-26 28-50 52-56

Reading & Comprehension

AC9E6LY04, AC9E6LY05, AC9HS6K04, AC9HS6K05

Informative text – Report

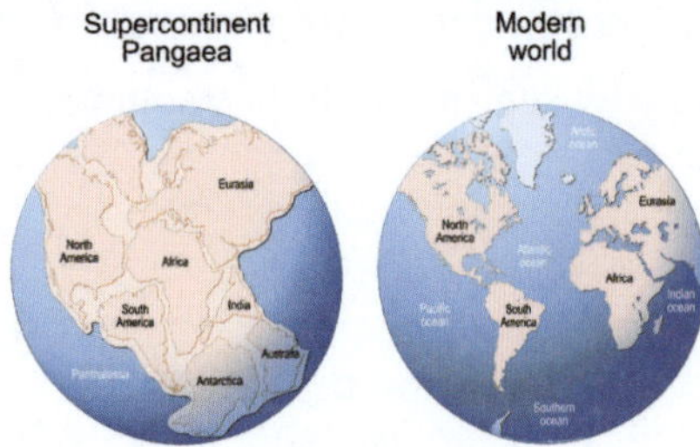

Continents

Scientists believe that 200 million years ago all the land on Earth was connected as one single landmass surrounded by water. This single landmass slowly broke up and different parts or plates moved apart. Their movement was generated by forces under the crust of the Earth. These landmasses have taken millions of years to move to where they are now, moving centimetres every year. This process is called plate tectonics. These landmasses have been divided by man into different continents. Most people agree that there are seven continents: Africa, Antarctica, Asia, Oceania/Australia, Europe, North America and South America. Australia is often grouped with New Zealand and countries in the Pacific Ocean into a continent called Oceania.

The closest continent to Australia is Asia. Asia is the biggest in land size and the biggest in population of all the continents. It holds over 60% of the world's population as it holds two of the most highly populated countries in the world, India and China. Asia also holds the largest mountain range in the world, the Himalayas. Asia is our closest neighbour. Let's compare!

Asia
• **Biggest** continent (out of 7) in land size • **Largest** population • Lies mostly in the **Northern Hemisphere** • Largest desert – Gobi Desert, **5th largest** in the world • Has **48 countries** • Has the **three biggest cities in the world:** Delhi, Tokyo and Shanghai. **Biggest city is Tokyo** – over 37 million people • Has some of the **richest countries in the world:** Qatar and United Arab Emirates
Oceania
• **Smallest** continent in land size • Australia is **6th** in population size and Antarctica is **7th** • All in **Southern Hemisphere** • Largest desert (in Australia) – Great Victoria Desert (not in Victoria), **12th largest** in the world • Has **14 countries** • **Biggest city is Sydney** – over 5 million people • **Australia is the richest** country in Oceania.

Australia is part of the Asian region, and our history has ties with Asian nations. For example:

- The Afghan cameleers brought camels to Australia in the 1830s. They began a transportation business that helped with the settlement and development of inland areas of Australia.
- The Japanese and Malaysian pearl divers in Western Australia were important in the development of the Australian pearling industry which helped to support the colony.
- Many Chinese people came to Australia to look for gold in the 1850s. They set up many small businesses and helped pioneer the banana industry in Queensland.
- Many people from Asia have migrated to Australia, making our country a rich and diverse multicultural place to live.

In another 250 million years, scientists predict that all the continents will come together once more into a giant supercontinent. Just wait and see!

TARGETING ENGLISH HOMEWORK YEAR 6 © PASCAL PRESS ISBN 978 1 925726 63 3

Reading & Comprehension

Write the answer or shade the bubble next to the correct answer.

The answers to these questions are in the text.

① **Plate tectonics** is the process where:

- ◯ all the land on Earth was connected into one single landmass surrounded by water.
- ◯ people divided landmasses into continents.
- ◯ Australia is often grouped with other Pacific nation countries into Oceania.
- ◯ land parts or plates are moved by forces under the crust of the Earth.

② **Continents:**

- ◯ have always been where they are now.
- ◯ are landmasses that have been divided by people.
- ◯ is another name for countries.
- ◯ hold over 60% of the world's population.

③ **India and China are on different continents.**

◯ True ◯ False

Think about these questions and search for the answers in the text.

④ **Which continent is the biggest in land size and has the largest population?**

____

⑤ **In which hemisphere does most of Asia lie?**

____

⑥ **Name two ways Asian nations have become a part of Australia's development and history.**

____

____

____

____

⑦ **How are Oceania and Asia similar? Write one observation.**

____

____

⑧ **How are Oceania and Asia different? Write one observation.**

____

____

Use inferencing skills to answer this question. The answer is not in the text. Think about what you know and what the author says.

⑨ **Why do you think the camels brought to Australia by the Afghan cameleers were important in inland Australia?**

____

____

____

Use your experience and opinions to answer this question. The answer is not in the text.

⑩ **Why would Antarctica be the lowest ranked of all continents in population?**

____

____

____

Comprehension Reflections

Look at the top of the opposite page. This text is an I__________ text – R__________.

Write one thing you learned or found interesting:

____

Write one question you have or something you want to find more information about:

____

____

Rating   

Score 2 points for each correct answer! SCORE /20  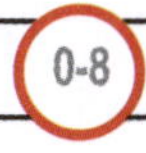  

Grammar & Punctuation

AC9E6LA06

Noun–verb agreement

It's all about the verbs! Verbs are doing words that describe an action and show the tense. Verbs (singular or plural) must match their subject (the person or thing performing the action). This is called noun–verb agreement.

Example: The student **attend** school and she **study** hard. This just does not sound right. The student **attends** school and she **studies** hard. This is correct, but why?

A singular (one person or thing) subject has a matching singular verb. The singular verb has 's' or 'es' at the end.

Subject (Noun)	Present Simple Verb
She (singular)	studies (singular) **add 's' or 'es'**
They (plural)	study (plural) **no 's'**

Circle the correct form of the present simple verb in these sentences. The subject is in bold and the verb is purple. Ask yourself if the subject is singular or plural.

1. **India** belong / belongs to Asia.
2. **Continents** move / moves a few centimetres per year.
3. **Fred** live / lives in Australia.
4. **Camels** live / lives in outback Australia.
5. **Thousands of Australians** fly / flies to Asia every year.

Collective nouns

A collective noun is a label for a group of people or things, such as a crowd, committee or class. A collective noun usually has a singular verb if it is acting as a single group.

Example: The **class** (singular collective) **meets** (singular verb) in the classroom.

If there is more than one class, then it is plural.

Example: The **classes** (plural collective) **meet** (plural verb) regularly.

Circle the correct form of the present simple verb in these sentences.

6. The **school** accept / accepts new students.
7. The **schools** in the area accept / accepts new students.
8. The **team** play / plays on Saturdays.
9. All **teams** play / plays on Saturdays.

Here are some trickier examples. If all the individual parts or members in the group need to be identified, then you use plural.

Example: The **class meet** (plural noun and verb) their friends at recess. Here, we are talking about each individual member of the class.

Example: The **class goes** (singular noun and verb) on excursions with their teacher. Here, we are talking about the class as a whole, not each individual child.

10 – 17

Now put all this information together and circle the correct form of the present simple verb in these sentences.

Sam love / loves to play school chasey, but **teachers** take / takes a different view on the game. The **school** ban / bans school chasey. **Schools** often ban / bans this game due to it involving too large a group. **Sam** take / takes pride in his ability to organise students although teachers wish / wishes it was for a different purpose. **Sam's family** has / have different opinions about his organisational abilities, but on the whole **the family** supports / support him. He can just be a little bossy!

Score 2 points for each correct answer!

TARGETING ENGLISH HOMEWORK YEAR 6 © PASCAL PRESS ISBN 978 1 925726 63 3

Word origins – Asia

All languages have loan words which they have borrowed from other languages. English has borrowed many words from many languages which makes it a more complex language.

1 – 17

In the table are loan words from India and China. Sort the words into the right group. You may need a dictionary to help you.

Loan words	
bandana	ketchup
bangle	kung-fu
bok choy	pyjamas
cheetah	shampoo
chopsticks	tea
cot	thug
dinghy	tycoon
judo	typhoon
jungle	verandah

Country of origin – China

Country of origin – India
Example: bandana

The schwa sound

The schwa sound is very common but can make spelling tricky, especially with words like 'neighbour' which comes from the text. The first syllable in neighbour is stressed, so it is pronounced more loudly or strongly. The last syllable is unstressed. This last syllable has a schwa sound that sounds like 'uh'.

Example: **NEIGH**-bour sounds like **NEIGH**-buh. (The 'our' makes the schwa sound.)

Circle the schwa sound in these words.

18 armour 19 colour 20 humour 21 flavour

Words ending in 'ous'

Words with an 'ous' ending can also have a schwa sound. In these words, the 'ou' makes the schwa sound.

Example: **HID**-e-ous (pronounced **HID**-ee-uhs)

Circle the schwa vowels in these words.

22 enormous 24 hideous 26 nervous
23 famous 25 jealous 27 serious

28 – 47

Find these 20 tricky-to-spell words in the table and circle them. They all have a schwa vowel sound highlighted in green.

bargain	jealous	cupboard	humour
captain	colour	China	famous
villain	enormous	astronaut	hideous
potion	nervous	dinosaur	neighbour
thorough	armour	serious	flavour

e	r	o	h	m	t	h	f	p	e	x
o	m	i	b	o	b	u	a	t	z	w
n	l	u	o	w	r	m	m	a	g	u
p	e	o	j	u	j	o	o	i	i	n
b	y	i	u	c	s	u	u	n	z	e
f	x	q	g	r	h	r	s	g	p	r
t	w	k	h	h	x	i	s	r	h	v
v	w	i	t	y	b	e	n	s	s	o
e	a	l	o	u	s	o	h	a	l	u
n	o	r	m	o	u	s	u	s	z	s
o	t	w	e	x	g	z	b	r	o	m

Score 2 points for each correct answer! SCORE /94  0-44  46-88  90-94

Reading & Comprehension

AC9E6LY04, AC9E6LY05, AC9HS6K04, AC9HS6K05

Imaginative text – Description

TERM 1

School Trip

Hi Family [who are stuck at home while I am away on this amazing school trip]

I could say I miss you, but I would be wrong. Sorry, but I am having too much of a good time in Singapore this week. It's a city and country all in one place. How cool is that? It isn't just one island. There are 63 islands that make up the country of Singapore, but the biggest is Sentosa Island. You can drive along a bridge that connects Sentosa Island to another country, Malaysia. We are going to do that before we fly home.

You could fit Singapore into Australia 11 159 times, so it's not that big compared to home. It is a lot more crowded as nearly six million people live here. That's a little more than Sydney, but Sydney is 17 times bigger in area. The teacher called it population density. I think it means a lot more people live in the same space in Singapore than they do in Australia. Apartments and homes are much smaller in Singapore and there are many high-rise buildings. Singapore is considered the third-richest country in the world and Australia is 25th, but, like anywhere, there is a big difference between those with money and those without.

The food is delicious! I am eating so many wonderful rice and noodle dishes that I may have to go up a size in my school uniform. Many Singaporeans eat out at food courts or centres in the city, and we were lucky enough to go out as a group and eat at one of these for dinner yesterday. I am addicted to chicken satays and peanut sauce. I can't stop eating them. I'm showering a lot because it is quite steamy and humid here. I'm not used to this much humidity, and yes, I am using deodorant. Well, most of the time.

Singapore is one of the busiest ports in the world, and trade with other nations is extremely important. Tourism is also very important to Singapore's economy, and there is a lot to see. I want to go to WaterWorld at Universal Studios, but the teacher said we must do educational things. We have gone on many excursions visiting temples in the city as many Singaporeans are Buddhist. There are many Christians in the country as well. We are going to visit a school because education is very important, and Singapore sets a very high standard in their testing of students. In Year Six, students sit for an exam that can affect where they go to high school, so studying is very important. I hope they don't give me the test!

I learnt that Singapore means 'lion city'. The story is that about 600 years ago, a prince came across a strange animal while out hunting and thought it was a lion, but there are no lions in Singapore. It may have been a tiger as tigers could be found in the wild 100 years ago. Anyway, he named the city after the lion. One symbol of the city is a merlion, a creature with the head of a lion and the body of a fish.

I am having lots of fun, but I hope you miss me. I don't miss the family, but I do get a little homesick at night. Only three more days and you will have me back. Not that I'm counting.

Lots of love,

Your favourite child

TARGETING ENGLISH HOMEWORK YEAR 6 © PASCAL PRESS ISBN 978 1 925726 63 3

Reading & Comprehension

Write your answers on the lines provided.

The answers to these questions are in the text.

1. What is the biggest **island** in Singapore?

2. A bridge connects Singapore to what other country?

3. How many times would Singapore fit into Australia?

Think about these questions and search for the answers in the text.

4. What is **population density** and what does it mean for people who live in Singapore?

5. Why would the **merlion** be chosen as a symbol of Singapore?

Use inferencing skills to answer these questions. The answers are not in the text. Think about what you know and what the author says.

6. What do you think this statement from the text means? **There is a big difference between those with money and those without.**

7. Why do many Singaporeans live in apartments and not in separate houses?

8. Describe one big difference between Singapore and where you live.

Use your experience and opinions to answer these questions. The answers are not in the text.

In Year Six, students in Singapore sit for an exam that may influence where they go to high school.

9. Give one reason why this exam **should** also be introduced into Australia.

10. Give one reason why this exam **should not** be introduced into Australia.

Comprehension Reflections

Look at the top of the opposite page. This text is an I__________ text – D__________.

Write one thing you learned or found interesting:

Write one question you have or something you want to find more information about:

Rating   

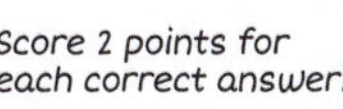

Score 2 points for each correct answer!

SCORE /20  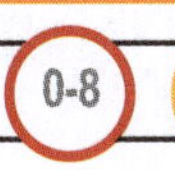 

UNIT 6

Grammar & Punctuation

AC9E6LA05, AC9E6LA09

TERM 1

Complex sentences

A complex sentence has one independent clause that makes sense on its own and one or more subordinate (dependent) clauses that do not. The two clauses are joined by a conjunction that can go in the middle of the sentence or at the start.

Adding a subordinate clause to a simple sentence to provide more information, changes that sentence into a complex sentence. Complex sentences make your writing more sophisticated and interesting.

Example: I'm showering a lot because it is quite steamy and humid here.

(The subordinate clause is underlined.)

You can also reverse the position of the clauses and start with the subordinate clause (underlined).

Example: Because it is quite steamy and humid here, I'm showering a lot.

(Notice the comma at the end of the subordinate clause.)

Circle the independent clause. The conjunction is in bold to help you.

1. **As** we drove around Singapore, I noticed many temples.
2. I squealed with excitement **because** we went inside the temples.
3. **Even though** WaterWorld was next, I was very impatient.
4. **After** I took my pictures, we travelled to WaterWorld.
5. I should have taken my phone out of my pocket **before** I went down the waterslide.

Embedded clauses and commas

Another way to add a subordinate clause into a sentence is to drop it in the middle of a sentence. This is called an embedded clause. You then need two commas, one each side of the clause.

Example: Singapore, although it is hot and humid, is my favourite holiday destination. (embedded clause underlined)

We know it is an embedded clause because it is in the middle of the sentence, has a comma on each side and doesn't make sense by itself. The independent clause, Singapore is my favourite holiday destination, can stand on its own as a complete sentence.

Circle the embedded clause in these sentences.

6. My phone, although it was dripping with water, was given to the teacher.
7. My best friend, who had followed me down the slide, found my phone at the bottom of the pool.
8. My parents, after we had a heated conversation, understood it was an accident.
9. My teacher, who knew where to shop, helped me buy a cheaper replacement phone.
10. The relief on my face, after I bought the phone, was clear for all to see.

Put commas in these sentences. Remember, they go after a subordinate clause if it is at the start of a sentence and on either side of an embedded clause.

11. Before we flew home we visited Universal Studios.
12. The ride which was very expensive would test my level of bravery.
13. I was smart because I put my phone in my pocket.
14. The ice-cream which I ate right before the ride made me feel sick. Oops!
15. Mum and Dad who usually have a great sense of humour will laugh about this one day.

Score 2 points for each correct answer!

TARGETING ENGLISH HOMEWORK YEAR 6 © PASCAL PRESS ISBN 978 1 925726 63 3

AC9E6LY09

Suffixes to describe nationality

People from Singapore are called Singapor**ean** while people from Australia are called Austral**ian**. A suffix is added to the country name to form an adjective to describe the inhabitants and their nationality. There are eight major suffixes used for this purpose:

-ian (Italian, Norwegian)

-ean (Korean, Zimbabwean)

-an (American, Mexican)

-ese (Chinese, Japanese)

-er (Icelander, New Zealander)

-ic (Icelandic)

-ish (English, Irish)

-i (Pakistani, Kuwaiti)

However, some adjectives have a different spelling altogether from the original word. It seems that there is no reason for which suffix is used, but history plays a role in how they were chosen. The suffixes to go with country names were borrowed many years ago from Greek, Latin, French and even Arabic.

Complete the table with the adjective of each country. You may need to use a dictionary.

Country name	Nationality – adjective to describe those who live there
Israel	*Example:* Israeli
Portugal	(1)
Iraq	(2)
Chile	(3)
Malta	(4)
Peru	(5)
Finland	(6)
Denmark	(7)
Ukraine	(8)
Switzerland	(9)
Greenland	(10)

Greek base words

Your genealogy is your family tree – your family history. Your family tree may include some of the countries listed previously. The word genealogy comes from the Greek base word gene/gener 'meaning birth or origin'. Words can be built from that base word by adding a prefix and suffix. These affixes can change the meaning of the original base word.

The words in the list below are built from the Greek base word 'gene/ gener'. Complete the paragraph with the correct words. You may need to use a dictionary.

photogenic	genealogy	gender
generations	genuine	generic

My auntie researched our family tree or (11) ______________. She even added pictures to the names. I am afraid that my uncle is not very (12) ______________, so my auntie did not want to put his photo on the tree. She said that it would spoil it. My auntie had to research back many (13) ______________. Each (14) ______________ was colour coded, blue for males and red for females. My auntie used a basic or (15) ______________ template that she had downloaded, but it looks like a (16) ______________ snapshot of our history.

Score 2 points for each correct answer! SCORE /32

Reading & Comprehension

AC9E6LY04, AC9E6LY05, AC9E6LA06, AC9E6LA08

Imaginative text – Narrative

TERM 1

The Encounter

Tap, tap, tap, echoed off the paving stones of the old harbour as the figure loomed into sight. The yellow streetlights barely pushed back the blackness of the moonless night and fell weakly onto the approaching figure. The bulky form was bundled in a once-elegant red velvet coat that stopped at the knees, but grime and dirt made it look faded and worn. Their jet-black hair was tied into a stiff pigtail and topped with a black, triangular hat with a brim that curled in on itself. That is when I saw the eyes, glittering black and unblinking, and that is when they saw me. Fear swept through me like a searing wind.

A dirty finger with a black, broken nail pointed at me and indicated that I should come closer. It was the large pistol, also aimed towards me, that made me comply. As I cowered in front of my captor, I became angry at putting myself in danger. Everyone knew the ships were in port, and the captains were looking for new crew, willing or not. Why did I stay out so late and walk along the harbour road? As I looked up, I saw the face was set and expressionless, but there was a glow behind the eyes. Dirty lace was bunched around the throat and protruded at the ends of the sleeves. That is when my gaze fell to what was making the noise. One leg was missing from above the knee. In its place was a thin, wooden stump that tapped along the pavement at each step. With gut-wrenching clarity, I realised this was one of the captains from the ships. I was like a rat caught in a trap.

A whistle sounded in the distance and a shot echoed through the dark like a thunderclap. It awakened the night and stirred the captain to action. Close by, I could hear the shouts of police after their prey. They would protect their citizens against the threat of the captains. Their pounding footsteps approached closer to where we stood. With a vice-like grip, I was pulled to the side of the path, scarcely daring to breathe as a perilously pointed knife was lodged menacingly under my throat. Five dark figures were racing down the path to where we lay. I could not shout out for help. I could only hope for a miracle.

The sounds of thudding feet receded into the night as they passed us. Breathing was difficult, and my eyes were wide and black with horror as the face neared mine. She smiled, showing stained and blackened teeth. "You're mine now!" she snarled as she dragged me to the waiting ships in the harbour. I was slowly realising I was to be a part of her crew. Fear crawled at the pit of my stomach, but, somewhere, I also felt some thrill of excitement. I always wondered what it would be like to be a pirate, and now I would find out. With increasing alarm, I realised … be careful what you wish for.

TARGETING ENGLISH HOMEWORK YEAR 6 © PASCAL PRESS ISBN 978 1 925726 63 3

Reading & Comprehension

Write the answer or shade the bubble next to the correct answer.

The answers to these questions are in the text.

1. **Is the captain of a slim build or larger build?** ______________________

2. **How do you know? What clue is in the text?** ______________________

3. **What makes the tapping noise?** ______________________

____

Think about these questions and search for the answers in the text.

4. **The narrative builds a picture of the captain by describing her. Write three descriptions of the captain from the text.**

____

____

____

5. **A simile is figurative language which is an imaginative way of describing something by comparing it to something else using 'like' or 'as'. Example: She was as quiet as a mouse. Write three similes from the text.**

____

____

____

Use inferencing skills to answer these questions. The answers are not in the text. Think about what you know and what the author says.

Personification is figurative language where something non-human is given human qualities, such as in this passage from the text: The yellow streetlights barely pushed back the blackness of the moonless night and fell weakly onto the approaching figure.

6. **What human actions does the author give the streetlights?**

____

____

7. **Why would the captain have picked that particular night to 'look' for crew? Look at the description of the setting.**

____

____

8. **Using precise verbs improves descriptions. In the last paragraph, instead of 'said', the captain snarled the words, "You're mine now!"**
The word snarled is used to show:
   - ○ the captain likes dogs.
   - ○ the captain spoke in an angry, fierce way.
   - ○ the captain was going to treat the narrator like a dog.

Use your experience and opinions to answer these questions. The answers are not in the text.

9. **The text finishes with ... be careful what you wish for. What does this mean?**

____

____

____

10. **The captain is revealed as a she in the last paragraph. Why do you think the author waits until the end to reveal this information?**

____

____

____

Comprehension Reflections

Look at the top of the opposite page. This text is an I__________ text – N__________.

Write one thing you learned or found interesting:

____

Write one question you have or something you want to find more information about:

____

____

Rating   

Score 2 points for each correct answer! SCORE /20  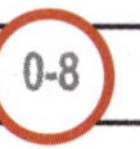 

TARGETING ENGLISH HOMEWORK YEAR 6 © PASCAL PRESS ISBN 978 1 925726 63 3

Grammar & Punctuation

AC9E6LA08

Figurative language – Similes and metaphors

Using figurative language helps you develop as a reader and writer. There are different types of figurative language.

Similes are used to compare two things that are not actually alike, using the words 'like' and 'as'. *Example:* I run **like** a cheetah. This means I share a similar characteristic, which in this case is 'speed'. Three similes were used in this unit's text.

Metaphors compare things without using 'like' or 'as'. Instead, metaphors can use words such as is, are or was/were. *Example:* The captain's eyes **were** glittering black diamonds.

Read these sentences and label each one as either a simile (S) or a metaphor (M).

1. The captain was like a ghost, prowling around the harbour. __________
2. Her heart was a lump of coal. __________
3. The narrator's hands were blocks of ice in the cold morning. __________
4. Her face was a mask of horror. __________
5. The police swarmed over the harbour like ants. __________
6. Their whistles were daggers, piercing the night. __________
7. The pirate ships disappeared like smoke on the water. __________

Alliteration

Alliteration is when beginning sounds in words are repeated.

Example: She held a **p**erilously **p**ointed knife. This is an alliteration due to the repetition of the 'p' sound.

Advertisers often use alliteration on their packaging or in their advertising.

Onomatopoeia

Onomatopoeia is when words sound like what they are describing. *Examples:* snap, crackle, pop

Advertisers also regularly use onomatopoeia in advertising.

Think of your own food item. Provide it with a creative name that is an alliteration and gives some idea as to what the product is. Write a sentence about your product using at least two onomatopoeia words.

8. Product: ______________________________
9. Name using alliteration: ______________________________
10. Sentence using onomatopoeia words: ______________________________

____

____

Personification

Personification is when something non-human is given human characteristics. *Example:* The pirate ships **marched** along the coast. There is also an example of personification in this unit's text.

Circle the object being personified and underline what it is doing that makes it a personification.

Example: The (pirate ships) <u>marched</u> along the coast.

11. The bullets cried out in the still night.
12. The streetlights stood to attention when the captain passed by.
13. The coat sat stiffly on the captain's shoulders as it was encrusted with years of dirt.
14. The captain's hat stared menacingly down at all who gazed upon it.
15. The night looked down with sadness at the kidnapping of a new sailor.

Score 2 points for each correct answer! SCORE /30 0-12 14-24 26-30

TARGETING ENGLISH HOMEWORK YEAR 6 © PASCAL PRESS ISBN 978 1 925726 63 3

Phonic & Word Knowledge

UNIT 7

AC9E6LY08, AC9E6LY09

TERM 1

Spelling generalisations

Many English words have been adopted from other languages and cultures, so they don't fit spelling 'rules'. Rather than call them 'rules', we say phonics/spelling generalisations because there are always exceptions to the rules. When you come across groups of these loan words that don't fit the generalisation, look for patterns in their spelling instead.

Words with silent 'e'

One phonics generalisation is that sometimes silent 'e' makes the long vowel sound.
Example: h**o**p (short vowel sound) + e = h**o**pe (long vowel sound with silent 'e')

However, the words have, love, give, and glove do not have long vowel sounds. They do have a similar pattern though. They all have a 'v' followed by a silent 'e'. Words in the English language typically don't end with 'v' but rather 've'.

① – ⑩
Sort the following words into long or short vowels.

WORDS

olive drove above drive
slave glove brave active
shave native

Long vowel sound	Short vowel sound

Words ending with 'ge' or 'dge'

In English, words do not end with the letter 'j'. However, they do end in a 'j' sound.

Example from the text: The knife was **lodged** menacingly under my throat. How did the author know whether to spell with 'ge' or 'dge'?

The spelling generalisation for words that end in a 'j' sound is:

- spell with -dge if there is a short vowel before the 'j' sound. *Examples:* lo**dge**, bri**dge**
- spell with -ge if there is a long vowel before the 'j' sound. *Examples:* hu**ge**, ca**ge**
- spell with -ge if there is a consonant or vowel team before the 'j' sound. *Examples:* reven**ge**, gou**ge**

Remember! There are always exceptions to the spelling generalisations.

Circle the correct spelling of the 'ge' or 'dge' words.

⑪	heritage	heritadge
⑫	language	languadge
⑬	porrige	porridge
⑭	lege	ledge
⑮	cringe	crindge
⑯	frige	fridge
⑰	knowlege	knowledge
⑱	cartrige	cartridge
⑲	hinge	hindge

Use five words from the previous activity to complete the following text.

As a pirate, I have to eat ⑳ ______________ every day. I hate it and ㉑ ______________ every time it is served.

I have to learn a whole new ㉒ ______________ such as 'scuttlebutt' and 'avast'.

But the ㉓ ______________ that I will be sailing the seven seas while my friends are doing homework makes me smile. I have sent a picture home for Mum to stick on the ㉔ ______________.

Score 2 points for each correct answer! SCORE /48

Informative text – Explanation

Gender Stereotypes

What are little boys made of?
Snips, snails and puppy-dogs' tails.
What are little girls made of?
Sugar and spice and everything nice.

These lines are part of a nursery rhyme that was written about 220 years ago about boys and girls. What does it say about how boys and girls were expected to behave 220 years ago?

"Girls love pink and wear it all the time while boys only like to wear blue as it is a masculine colour."

The nursery rhyme and the statement above are biased. That means they have an unfair belief about a group of people based on a stereotype. A stereotype can be a label or a very simple idea about how, in this case, boys and girls should behave. So how did some of these stereotypical ideas originate? Why is pink associated with girls and blue with boys?

What colours were babies wearing before pink and blue? In many countries and cultures, babies were generally dressed in white or the natural colour of the fabric that was available at the time. Up until the early 1900s, in many western countries, boys and girls wore dresses until about the age of six when they would also get their first haircuts. Young boys and girls were dressed to look very much the same.

Colour was not added to babies' clothing until about 170 years ago and the colours were not associated with gender. That is, not until 100 years ago when some department stores in the United States tried to assign colours to babies. They recommended pink for boys as red is associated with strength and boldness and is too harsh for girls. Blue was recommended for girls because it is soft and dainty and associated with the sky. Of course, the department stores did this to sell more clothing as one colour would not suit all babies. Not everyone took up this idea.

Assigning pink and blue occurred after World War II, over 80 years ago. It was more of a marketing idea than linking pink and blue with how boys and girls behaved. The manufacturers, who made the clothes, decided on the specific colours. They helped persuade people through advertising to choose pink for girls and blue for boys.

It is not always as simple an explanation as that. Gender stereotypes are complex. You learn how males and females behave from your family, friends, school, culture and religion. You can be exposed to many messages about how boys and girls should look, behave and play. You will often see gender stereotypes when online: playing online games, watching online videos and communicating with others through comments, photos and even avatars. Not everyone does, wants to or has to fit the stereotypes of how boys and girls should behave or look.

Are boys made of puppy-dogs' tails and snails? And are girls are made of sugar and spice and everything nice? Does this describe you?

TARGETING ENGLISH HOMEWORK YEAR 6 © PASCAL PRESS ISBN 978 1 925726 63 3

Reading & Comprehension

UNIT 8

TERM 1

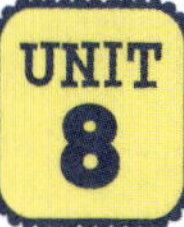

Write the answer or shade the bubble next to the correct answer.

The answers to these questions are in the text.

1. What does **biased** mean?

2. What is a **stereotype**?

3. Two hundred years ago, **very young boys** wore dresses.
   ○ True ○ False

4. What colour did babies wear before pink and blue came into fashion?

Think about these questions and search for the answers in the text.

5. What **group** decided that pink should be for girls and blue for boys?

6. How do children learn about the way females and males behave? Name three ways.

Use inferencing skills to answer these questions. The answers are not in the text. Think about what you know and what the author says.

7. What does the **nursery rhyme** say about how boys and girls were expected to behave 220 years ago if boys were compared to puppy-dogs' tails and girls compared to sugar and spice?

8. Why would the **department stores** want people to buy coloured clothing for their children?

Use your experience and opinions to answer these questions. The answers are not in the text.

9. Read the nursery rhyme at the start of the text again.
   What would you say boys and girls are made of today?

10. Think about all the ways you learn how boys and girls behave. What has had the biggest impact on you and why?
    Biggest impact: ____________
    Why? ____________

Comprehension Reflections

Look at the top of the opposite page. This text is an I__________ text – E__________.

Write one thing you learned or found interesting:

Write one question you have or something you want to find more information about:

Rating

Score 2 points for each correct answer! SCORE /20 0-8 10-14 16-20

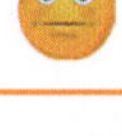

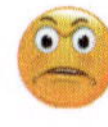

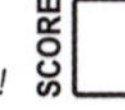

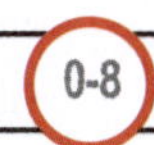

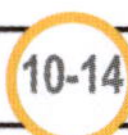

UNIT 8

Grammar & Punctuation

AC9E6LA05, AC9E6LA09

Embedded clauses

This unit's reading text contains a complex sentence with an embedded clause.

Example: The manufacturers, **who made the clothes**, decided on the specific colours.

The embedded clause in bold is subordinate and does not make sense on its own. An embedded clause has two commas, one either side it. If the embedded clause starts with who, that, which, whose, where and when, it is called an embedded relative clause.

Insert the commas either side of the embedded relative clause in these sentences. The relative pronouns are underlined to help you.

1. My great grandfather <u>who</u> lived to one hundred wore dresses as a very young boy.
2. He wore a dress <u>which</u> I think is really cool and leather shoes.
3. The photo of him <u>which</u> Mum keeps in a frame shows him with long, curly hair.
4. Great Grandfather did not get a short haircut <u>which</u> is evident in the picture until he started school.
5. My great grandfather <u>whose</u> picture we were discussing lived through two world wars.

Comparative and superlative adjectives

When comparing two or more things, we use comparative and superlative adjectives.

Example: I am **cuter than** my sister, but my great grandfather has to be **the cutest** of the whole family.

(comparative adjective: cuter than; superlative adjective: the cutest)

Here are some rules on how to form these adjectives for comparisons.

Syllables	Comparative adjective – compare 2 things	Superlative adjective – compare more than 2 things
One-syllable words – tall	tall**er** than	the tall**est**
Two-syllable words ending in: le, y, ow – narrow	narrow**er** than	the narrow**est**
Two-syllable words **not** ending in: le, y, ow – helpful	**more** helpful than	the **most** helpful
Three-syllable words – important	**more** important than	the **most** important

Write the correct comparative or superlative adjective in these sentences.

Example: I have the (long) **longest** hair of all my family.

6. Dad has the (short) ____________ hair of all my family. Actually, he has no hair at all!
7. My hair is (silky) ____________ than my brother's.
8. However, his is (tangled) ____________ than mine.
9. My mum's haircuts are the (expensive) ____________ of all the family.
10. My dad is bald, but he is probably (intelligent) ____________ out of all of us. Maybe being bald is not so bad.

Score 2 points for each correct answer! SCORE /20

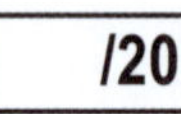

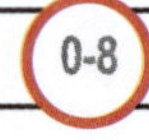

TARGETING ENGLISH HOMEWORK YEAR 6 © PASCAL PRESS ISBN 978 1 925726 63 3

AC9E6LY09

Syllables

A syllable is a word part that contains a vowel (a, e, i, o, u). Usually, a word has as many syllables as it has vowels.
Example: yes-ter-day (3 syllables and 3 vowels)
Some **rules for syllables**.

a	Divide between **two middle consonants** (not ch, wh, sh, ph, kn, wr, ck or qu).	lad-der whis-ker	VC/CV
b	If the **first vowel is long**, divide straight after it and before the consonant.	hu-mid pi-lot ho-tel ba-by	V/CV
c	If the **vowel is short**, divide after the consonant.	cab-in com-ic lem-on sev-en	VC/V
d	If **two vowels make separate sounds**, they need to be divided. Do not divide vowels if they make one sound *e.g.* 'ai'.	po-et di-et ne-on vi-o-lin	V/V
e	Divide **compound words**.	house-boat foot-ball	
f	Divide before **'consonant + le'**.	trou-ble	
g	Divide after 'k' in **'ckle' words**.	trick-le	
h	Divide between **prefixes and suffixes.**	un-paid thought-ful	

Open and closed syllables

Words that follow rule b, a long vowel sound that is spelled with a single vowel letter, are also called 'open' syllables.

Words that follow rule c, a short vowel sound followed by a consonant, are called 'closed' syllables.

Divide these words into syllables and write the letter of the rule used. Refer to the table to find the letter for each rule.

Word	Syllables	Rule
Example: buckle	bu-ckle	g
① jumbo		
② fluid		
③ music		
④ reread		
⑤ finish		
⑥ rainbow		
⑦ table		
⑧ nation		
⑨ beagle		
⑩ damage		

Test your knowledge! Using the rules (a to h), write the syllables of these very long words. Good luck!

⑪ conversational (5 syllables)

____

⑫ divisibility (6 syllables)

____

⑬ oversimplification (7 syllables)

____

⑭ biodegradability (8 syllables)

____

⑮ antidisestablishmentarianism (12 syllables)

____

Score 2 points for each correct answer! SCORE /30

Reading & Comprehension

Imaginative text – Narrative

The Tree

He could see the intruder making their way swiftly along the road towards him, towards his family. The wind pulled and tugged at the intruder's clothing, billowing it behind them like a menacing black cloud. Their speed and size were alarming. He stood poised for action. His black, beady eyes were fixed on his target, ready to strike when the intruder was closer. He could hear his family behind him, safe and huddled together, but the intruder was too close, far too close.

He braced for battle, muscles tensed like springs and his heart racing in his chest like a hammer. In a flurry of motion, he launched his attack, cutting through the air, a pirate of the sky. The intruder's screams and flailing arms were no defence against his swift and accurate attack, and they soon retreated, bruised and battered. He, however, settled back by his family, safe once again. He was ready for any other intruder who passed by too close.

****

Sarah always took the same route to school, through the park and under the large trees that spread their trunks like welcoming arms. Except for one spot, one spot where danger lurked and attack was imminent. It was early spring, and the wind was still fresh on her face as she made her way to school. The wind played with the edges of her parka, creating a sail behind her and a regret that she had not zipped it up before getting on her bike.

The tree, that one tree, was getting closer. Perhaps if she cycled really fast, it would not swoop her this time. Too late! The attack was swift, coming from above and aiming for her face. Sarah swung her arms around her head and tried to deflect the piercing beak and flapping wings. A little black-and-white tornado raged around her head until she made her way from under the tree and back into the safety of the open air and the treeless path.

****

Sarah loved to run most days when she had the time, especially in the park. She was running along the path, enjoying the cool air and the rhythmic movement of her body. However, the tree was up ahead. Over the last weeks, she had been attacked, but this time she had researched and formed a plan. As she approached the tree, she stopped running and continued to walk along the path, all the while searching until she located the problem with her eyes.

There he was, watching her, getting ready to attack, but this time she stared back. They locked eyes, each staring intently into the eyes of the other. She continued to walk, staring at him the whole time until she was 80 metres away from the tree. Relief flooded her body and she felt a sense of elation that she had safely passed the one element that made her afraid. She knew her former enemy had an excellent memory and would remember her tomorrow. Perhaps she may even get to think of him with fondness, but that would have to wait for tomorrow.

TARGETING ENGLISH HOMEWORK YEAR 6 © PASCAL PRESS ISBN 978 1 925726 63 3

Reading & Comprehension

TERM 1

Write the answer or shade the bubble next to the correct answer.

1. **Why was he ready to strike the intruder?**

   ____

2. **What season of the year did this take place?**

   ____

3. **Who was the intruder and what were they doing?**

   ____

4. **Who or what was he, the one doing the attacking? Why would 'he' attack?**

   ____

   ____

5. **How did the runner escape from being swooped?**

   ____

6. **What type of figurative language is this?**
   ... billowing it behind them like a menacing black cloud.
   - ◯ personification
   - ◯ alliteration
   - ◯ simile
   - ◯ metaphor

7. **What type of figurative language is this?**
   ... they soon retreated, bruised and battered.
   - ◯ personification
   - ◯ alliteration
   - ◯ simile
   - ◯ metaphor

8. **What type of figurative language is this?**
   The wind pulled and tugged at the intruder's clothing ...
   - ◯ personification
   - ◯ alliteration
   - ◯ simile
   - ◯ metaphor

9. **What type of figurative language is this?**
   ... he launched his attack, cutting through the air, a pirate of the sky.
   - ◯ personification
   - ◯ alliteration
   - ◯ simile
   - ◯ metaphor

10. **What would you do to stop yourself from being swooped, other than staring at him, if you had to pass by the tree in the text?**

    ____

    ____

    ____

    ____

    ____

    ____

Score 2 points for each correct answer! SCORE /20

TERM 1 REVIEW

Grammar & Punctuation

TERM 1

Complex sentences

Complex sentences have one independent clause and one or more subordinate clauses joined by a conjunction. The conjunction can be placed either in the middle of the sentence or at the start. A comma is used after a subordinate clause (the clause that does not make sense on its own) if the subordinate clause starts the sentence.

In these sentences, the conjunction is in bold. Add commas if needed and underline the independent clause (the clause that makes sense on its own).

Example: <u>She stared at him the whole time</u> **until** she was 80 metres away from the tree. (no commas)

1. **Although** he was wary he continued to stare her straight in the eyes.
2. She walked under the tree slowly **even though** she was in his territory.
3. **As** she walked further away from the tree Sarah started to feel rather pleased with herself.
4. **After** she arrived at school Sarah was determined to find a new route that avoided the tree.

Embedded clauses

An embedded clause has commas on each side of it.

Underline the embedded clause in each sentence and add in the commas.

Example: She loved to run most days, <u>when she had the time</u>, especially in the park.

5. The students although they were warned decided to play under the tree.
6. Sam who didn't listen to the warning strode under the tree.
7. The tree although it was the shortest in the park was easily about 10 metres tall.
8. Sam even though she felt nervous climbed quickly and sturdily.
9. A flurry of feathers and a pecking beak which would one day give her nightmares sent Sam crashing to the ground.
10. Sam's friends who had been laughing ran from the fierce attack they were under.

Comparative and superlative adjectives

Remember! Use er, est, more or most with adjectives when comparing two or more things.

11 – 15

Correct Sam's work by circling the mistakes and writing the correct adjective underneath. You need to correct five mistakes.

It was the most easiest climb I have done, and I nearly reached the top. That's when the

most biggest creature I have ever seen attacked me. I was bigger and intelligenter than

it, so I just stayed where I was. It was the most terriblest looking thing, but I told it off

and made it back away. I don't want to brag, but I thought I was the braver of all my

friends. That's my story.

Score 2 points for each correct answer! SCORE /30   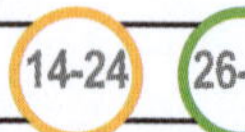

TARGETING ENGLISH HOMEWORK YEAR 6 © PASCAL PRESS ISBN 978 1 925726 63 3

Phonic & Word Knowledge

TERM 1

Crossword

Use these 17 words from the units this term to fill in the crossword.

- Words with a schwa sound: hideous, neighbour
- Precise vocabulary: manoeuvre, hurled, annihilate, flabbergasted, nimble
- Word with silent 'p': pneumonia
- Greek 'aero' word: aeroplane
- Words ending in 'ge' and 'dge': cringe, knowledge
- Consonant alternation: resign, resignation, muscular, designate
- Loan words from Asia: verandah, pyjamas

Down

1. to bend in fear
3. to destroy
4. to quit or to accept
5. to select someone or something
8. lung inflammation
12. person living next door

Across

2. garments for sleeping in
6. threw with force
7. ugly or disgusting to look at
9. roofed platform on the outside of a house
10. powered flying vehicle
11. relating to muscles
13. facts and information gained
14. quick in movement
15. the act of giving up
16. a series of moves
17. greatly surprised

Score 2 points for each correct answer! SCORE /34

AC9E6LY04, AC9E6LY05, AC9S6U02

Persuasive text – Exposition

TERM 2

Straighten the Earth Campaign Flyer

Is winter too cold for you? Do you want to escape the heat or humidity? Do you suffer from allergies at certain times of the year? If you have answered 'yes' to any of these questions, then the seasons are not for you. Join our campaign to put an end to seasons on Earth.

Seasons are regular changes of the weather at different times of the year based on temperature and rainfall. They usually last for three to four months for those living in the mid-latitudes. However, seasons can be up to half a year in the tropics and polar regions. What if there were no seasons and you could live somewhere that has the same temperature or weather all year round?

We all know that the Earth takes 365¼ days to make one lap or revolution around the Sun. In that time, we experience different seasons on Earth, but what causes them? The problem is that the Earth is tilted. If we drew an imaginary line passing from the North Pole to the South Pole, we would see that the line does not stand straight but is tilted. This tilt is called the Earth's axis.

The Earth's tilted axis causes the seasons. Throughout the year, different parts of Earth receive the Sun's most direct rays. When the North Pole tilts towards the Sun, it's summer in the Northern Hemisphere, and it's winter (or cooler) in Australia and the Southern Hemisphere. When the South Pole tilts towards the Sun, it's summer in the Southern Hemisphere and winter in the Northern Hemisphere. Because of this annoying tilt, you must adjust constantly to changing conditions. This means that you need a wardrobe full of clothes to suit the seasons – winter clothes in winter and summer clothes in summer. You also have to tolerate the seasons that you don't like to finally enjoy the ones you do.

What if scientists could straighten the Earth on its axis? This means there would be no seasons, and you would experience the same temperature all year round. Tropical regions would constantly be hot and humid, and as you moved further from the equator, the temperatures would get colder. The polar regions would always be freezing cold. If we rid the Earth of seasons, you could choose to live in a place that has your ideal weather all the time. What's not to like?

Some scientists believe that humans and life as we know it would be negatively affected if the seasons disappeared. They say that the life cycles of many plants and animals are linked to the different seasons and many species wouldn't survive. However, there is no proof of this, and these negative people only want to cause drama. We should ignore those who stand in the way of progress.

Join our campaign today for a better, straighter Earth, one where you know what the temperature will be all year round. You can be one of the first to choose where you want to live based on the temperatures you enjoy the most. All you need to do is donate to the cause. We need to back the scientists who can straighten the Earth. No tilt is wanted or needed. Remember our slogan: **Give seasons the flick, straighten the Earth real quick!**

TARGETING ENGLISH HOMEWORK YEAR 6 © PASCAL PRESS ISBN 978 1 925726 63 3

Reading & Comprehension

Write your answers on the lines provided.

The answers to these questions are in the text.

1. How many days does it take the Earth to revolve around the Sun?

2. What causes the seasons?

3. What season is it in Australia when the **North Pole** is tilted towards the Sun?

Think about these questions and search for the answers in the text.

4. Write **two** sentences to explain why a tilted axis causes seasons on Earth.

5. If scientists were able to straighten the Earth's axis, what would be one positive and one negative consequence?

   Positive consequence:

   Negative consequence:

6. What is the author's opinion of the Earth's tilt?

7. Name **two** things the author wants you to do.

Use inferencing skills to answer these questions. The answers are not in the text. Think about what you know and what the author says.

8. **These negative people only want to cause drama. We should ignore those who stand in the way of progress.** Do we need to hear the other side of the argument?

   Write a sentence explaining why it is important to hear both points of view.

9. Why would the author call those with the opposite view **negative people**?

Use your experience and opinions to answer this question. The answer is not in the text.

10. Would you want Earth to have a straight or tilted axis?

    Write a sentence to explain your answer.

TERM 2

Comprehension Reflections

Look at the top of the opposite page. This text is a P__________ text – E__________.

Write one thing you learned or found interesting:

Write one question you have or something you want to find more information about:

Rating   

Score 2 points for each correct answer! SCORE /20 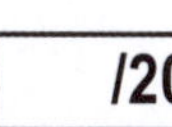   

Grammar & Punctuation

AC9E6LA08

Persuasive devices – Rhetorical questions

Persuasive devices are used to sway the reader to a particular point of view. Several of these devices have been used in this unit's text.

Rhetorical questions are used to engage the reader. These questions are not meant to be answered but are included to get the reader's attention. *Example:* What's not to like?

TERM 2

Write two rhetorical questions from the text.

① ______________________________

② ______________________________

Emotive language

Emotive language is used to make the reader feel certain emotions to persuade them to do something or think a certain way.

Read these sentences from the text. Underline the words that are used to evoke an emotional response from the reader.

Example: Do you **suffer** from allergies?

③ Ignore those who stand in the way of progress.

④ Join our campaign today for a better, straighter Earth.

⑤ You have to tolerate the seasons.

⑥ Negative people only want to cause drama.

Modality

Modality is how certain you are about something. High modality words are often used in persuasive texts to convince the reader of a particular point of view.

Examples from the text:

- You **must** adjust constantly to changing conditions.
- You **need** a wardrobe full of clothes to suit the seasons.
- You **have to** tolerate the seasons that you don't like.

High modality words: must, shall, will, always, essential, vital, clearly, have to

Low modality words: may, might, possibly, sometimes, could, maybe, perhaps

Change the modality of the following sentences from high to low or low to high using the list of modality words above. Use different modality words for each sentence.

⑦ I must do my homework every night. ______________________________

⑧ You could help around the house by doing the dishes. ______________________________

⑨ I might not watch TV while doing homework. ______________________________

⑩ My teacher has to give me more homework. ______________________________

⑪ – ㉒ Circle the emotive language in the passage and underline the words showing high or low modality. Find 12 examples in total.

Poor, suffering teachers have to take on the heavy task of marking homework. Students could possibly help by selflessly volunteering to leave homework for a week. Students believe it is essential to do homework every night. However, hardworking teachers struggle to keep up with the onerous marking required.

Score 2 points for each correct answer! SCORE

TARGETING ENGLISH HOMEWORK YEAR 6 © PASCAL PRESS ISBN 978 1 925726 63 3

Phonic & Word Knowledge

UNIT 9

AC9E6LY08, AC9E6LY09

Spelling pattern – 'y' = short 'i' sound

In English, the short 'i' sound is often represented by the letter 'i'. However, sometimes the letter 'y' is used to spell the short 'i' sound instead. The 'y' spelling is common in words of Greek origin. *Examples:* rhythm, crystal

Unjumble the words in the table by using the definitions. Each word has a 'y' that makes a short 'i' sound. The beginning letter is provided.

	Jumbled words	Definitions	Correctly spelt words
1	yonexg	The Earth's atmosphere is one-fifth of this gas.	o__________
2	yssshtniee	Combine elements or ideas to form something new.	s__________
3	mpomtsy	Something that is experienced by a patient and is associated with a particular disease	s__________
4	plytaic	Something that is normal or standard	t__________
5	srlicy	The words in a song	l__________
6	marydip	A massive monument with a square base and four triangular sides found in Egypt	p__________

TERM 2

Unpredictable digraphs

Unpredictable digraphs (vowel teams), also known as ambiguous vowels, are a pair of vowels that make different sounds in different words. *Examples:* 'ea' and 'ou'

7 **Practise reading this passage that is packed with unpredictable digraphs 'ea' and 'ou'. How many times did you need to read it before you made no mistakes? Do your final read in front of an adult.**

Students may have trouble and stumble on unpredictable words. If they are not very thorough in the reading of this text, they can tear up and want to tear it up. They see it as a great threat and become precious about their previous efforts. Students queue up to read to me, and once read, I give them a score. I feel wounded when their mouths are not rounded enough and every minute I remind them of the minute differences in sound. When reading rhymes, rhythm is important. Although it may seem tough, it is not a great threat, so give it a go!

How many times did you read it before you were error free?__________

Diphthongs

A digraph is made of two letters that make one sound. Diphthongs are a different type of digraph, and they are found in many words. In a diphthong, there is one sound, but it is a 'sliding' sound. The first vowel is usually longer and stronger than the second one and your mouth changes shape when saying it.
Examples of diphthongs: oil, boy, cow, cloud

8 – 21 **Read this passage in which 14 diphthong sounds are underlined. Cover it and have someone read it to you as a dictation. Write the dictation on the lines below. Score a point for every underlined diphthong you spell correctly.**

A prowler was spotted around the council fountain. The appointed guard, Troy, had his mouth full of his dinner, a chocolate brownie. When Troy finally shouted out, the prowler did not cower like a coward but avoided Troy and sped away.

____

____

____

____

____

Score 2 points for each correct answer! SCORE /42 0-18 20-36 38-42

AC9E6LY04, AC9E6LY05, AC9E6LA02, AC9HP6P09, AC9HP6P10

Persuasive text – Discussion

Should Fast-food Advertising be Banned?

Good afternoon boys and girls.

The topic of my discussion is whether fast-food advertisements should be on any social media platform before 8 pm, which is prime viewing time for primary school students. This topic has been debated over several years mainly due to health concerns around fast food and its effects on growing children. However, the fast-food industry is also an important manufacturing industry that contributes to Australia's economy.

I define advertising as being an industry that calls our attention to a product or service. The purpose of advertising is to persuade you to do something, buy something or think a certain way. It is important to understand advertising so that you know how to make up your own mind without being easily persuaded.

On the one hand, I love my pizza, burgers and chips, but the concern is that we are eating too much of what is considered fast food. Advertising on social media platforms has an influence on our food choices, and children have influence or power in the household. This 'pester power' is a nagging technique used by children the world over to persuade the adults in their household to do or buy what they want. If we are constantly exposed to fast-food advertisements on social media before dinnertime, we are more likely to be persuaded to use our pester power to influence what we snack on or what we eat at mealtimes.

Over-consumption of fast food has been linked to obesity, heart disease, diabetes and poor dental health. These conditions affect children as well as adults, which is a real concern. There are other effects, such as anxiety and migraines, that are long term and are becoming apparent as children grow to adulthood. Habits are often formed during childhood, so it is important to make sure that we eat a healthy diet to become healthy adults.

On the other hand, fast-food outlets have developed many more healthy choices, such as high-protein meals and salad bowls. Having fast food does not always mean unhealthy food choices. As with everything, moderation is key. Let's face it, there are times when we need a quick, hot meal. Fast food can fill that gap, especially when it is delivered to our home. Advertising lets us know what choices there are and encourages us to be adventurous in our choices.

We may have pester power, but the adults are in charge and ultimately have the purchasing power. Advertising is persuasive – it's meant to be – and we are bombarded with advertisements for toys and other goods, not just fast food. We have to learn that we can't have everything. Banning fast-food advertisements on social media platforms will not teach us that. The responsible adults at home need to teach us restraint. The fast-food industry is a very important industry for our economy, and advertising just lets us know what is available. In fact, many of us will probably end up working part-time in a fast-food outlet while growing up.

In conclusion, I still like my pizza, but how persuaded am I by advertising? Do the advertisements make me hungry? Do I use 'pester power' to sometimes get fast food and how often does it happen? Should advertising fast food on social media be banned before 8 pm? My opinion is ...

TARGETING ENGLISH HOMEWORK YEAR 6 © PASCAL PRESS ISBN 978 1 925726 63 3

Reading & Comprehension

Write the answer or shade the bubble where required.

The answers to these questions are in the text.

① **What is the definition of advertising?**

____

____

② **What is the purpose of advertising?**

____

____

③ **Why is it important to understand advertising?**

____

____

Think about these questions and search for the answers in the text.

④ **What are some of the problems associated with eating too much fast food? Name three, including one long-term effect.**

____

____

____

____

____

⑤ **What is pester power?**

____

____

⑥ **How is pester power used to increase the amount of fast food a family may eat?**

____

____

____

⑦ **According to the text, what is the role of responsible adults in a household?**

____

____

____

____

____

Use inferencing skills to answer this question. The answer is not in the text. Think about what you know and what the author says.

⑧ **Do you believe children have pester power in the household?**

◯ Yes ◯ No

Write one sentence to explain your answer.

____

____

Use your experience and opinions to answer these questions. The answers are not in the text.

⑨ **We have to learn that we can't have everything. Why do we have to learn that? Write one sentence to explain your thinking.**

____

____

⑩ **Do you think fast-food advertising should be banned on social media platforms before 8 pm?**

◯ Yes ◯ No

Give one reason for your answer.

____

____

Comprehension Reflections

Look at the top of the opposite page. This text is a P__________ text – D__________.

Write one thing you learned or found interesting:

____

Write one question you have or something you want to find more information about:

____

____

Rating   

Score 2 points for each correct answer! SCORE /20    

0-8 10-14 16-20

TERM 2

Persuasive techniques and devices – Discussion

The text for this unit is a discussion where two points of view are presented. One side of the discussion is introduced with, 'On the one hand' and the other point of view is introduced with, 'On the other hand'.

It's your turn to get dinner ready for the people you live with. Everyone wants fast food. Think of a reason why you would order fast food using this sentence beginning.

1. On the one hand, ____.

Now think of a reason why you would not order fast food using this sentence beginning.

2. On the other hand, ____.

Personal pronouns

Personal pronouns can also be used as a persuasive device to help sway the reader of a text.

Example from the text: It is important to understand advertising so that **you** can make up **your** own mind.

The author involves the reader by using the pronoun 'you'.

Rewrite your answers to questions 1 and 2 using the pronoun 'you' to speak directly to the audience.

3. On the one hand, ____.
4. On the other hand, ____.

Imperatives

An imperative command or instructional/bossy language can be used in persuasive writing to tell the reader what to do or how to think. Imperative verbs are used to make the command.

Examples: **Eat** only fresh food.

Enjoy our stunning menu.

Don't miss out on …

5 – 9 Read this passage and underline all the imperative verbs.

Get on board and join us in the campaign to ban fast-food advertising to children. Improve the eating habits of your family and make better decisions on what to eat. Act now!

10 – 15 Read this passage and underline all the imperative verbs.

Demand the best by placing your fast-food orders with us. Order over the phone, or text and have your food in minutes. Revitalise family meals with our delicious take-away menu. Act now!

Hyperbole

Hyperbole (pronounced hai-per-buh-lee) is where exaggeration is used for dramatic effect and to emphasise a point. What is said in a hyperbole is usually impossible or not true but can make something sound more dramatic than it really is.

Example: My family will eat anything.

Your family would not eat anything, but it stretches the truth and shows that they are easy to please.

Example: Eating fast food will kill you.

Fast food won't kill you, but it may harm your health if it is eaten too often.

Rewrite your answers to questions 1 and 2 at the top of this page using hyperbole to exaggerate your point.

16. On the one hand, ____.
17. On the other hand, ____.

Score 2 points for each correct answer! SCORE /34   

TARGETING ENGLISH HOMEWORK YEAR 6 © PASCAL PRESS ISBN 978 1 925726 63 3

Phonic & Word Knowledge

AC9E6LY08, AC9E6LY09

Latin-based words with 'duct'

This unit's text uses the word product. The base word 'duct' or 'duce' is Latin, meaning to 'lead or produce'. In the table below are the prefixes that can be added to this base word.

Fill in the missing information.

Prefixes	Base words	New words
Example: pro	duct	product
de	(1)	deduct
(2)	duct	induct
aque	duct	(3)
(4)	(5)	introduce
(6)	(7)	deduce
re	duce	(8)

Select a word from the table and write it next to its meaning below.

(9) to remove or take away ________________

(10) a constructed water course or channel ________________

(11) to infer or to work out ________________

(12) to admit someone to an organisation ________________

(13) to decrease ________________

Choose words from the table to insert in the passage below.

If you work at a fast-food outlet, they will need to (14) ________________ you or train you so that you know what to do. You cannot just expect people to (15) ________________ what to do. You need to train them. The (16) ________________ that you sell will be a convenience food. Be careful not to make mistakes or they may (17) ________________ money from your wages to cover the cost. This will (18) ________________ your wages at the end of the week.

Latin suffix 'ence/ance'

The Latin suffix 'ence/ance' means 'a state or condition'. *Examples:* confidence, importance

But how do you know which one to use?

Spelling generalisations

Suffixes	Generalisations	Examples
ance	when the base word ends in 'ant'	defiant = defiance
	when the verb ends in 'ure', 'ear' or 'y' **change 'y' to an 'i'**	assure = assurance appear = appearance defy = defiance
ence	when the base word ends in 'ere' or 'ent'	adhere = adherence violent = violence

Using the information in the table, write these words with the correct suffix 'ence/ance'.

(19) interfere ________________

(20) revere ________________

(21) persistent ________________

(22) clear ________________

(23) insure ________________

(24) significant ________________

(25) dominant ________________

(26) rely ________________

(27) **Look up the word belligerent (adjective). Write a sentence to explain why you are not that.**

I am not belligerent because ________________
____
________________.

Score 2 points for each correct answer! SCORE /54  0-24  26-48  50-54 

Reading & Comprehension

AC9E6LY04, AC9E6LY05, AC9E6LA02, AC9E6LA08, AC9HS6K08

Persuasive text – Argument

SIC – We know where you are!

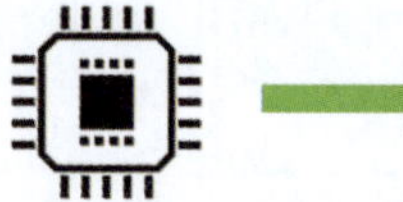

Hi Chris,

I'm sending this email to show you some advertising ideas for your new product SIC: Student Identification Chips. It's a great idea! Kids eat food with the microchip inside, and the microchip lodges in their stomachs for 12 months before it dissolves. Teachers will know who is in class, the school will know where students are located during school hours, and parents and caregivers will be able to track their child's whereabouts at any time of the day. I understand that we have password protection, so schools can only access this chip during school time, and parents and caregivers can access it 24 hours per day. No-one can hack the chip and track kids without permission. What an invention!

Now, kids may not like being tracked all the time, so we must persuade them and the adults to think that they need it and want it. Have a look below at some ideas using persuasive devices.

Persuasive devices	Examples
Rhetorical questions	Do you know where your children are right now? Does panic set in when you can't reach your child/parent by phone? Do you worry about safety? Do you worry about stranger danger?
Repetition – Rule of three	nibble, swallow, follow watched, protected, loved easy to administer, easy to follow, ease of mind
Emotive language	lost, vulnerable, missing, helpless, innocent, secure, protected, safe danger, menace, threat, jeopardy
High modality	must, should, have to, invaluable
Exaggeration – Hyperbole	It will save your life! SIC – Gives you confidence. SIC – It does not get better than this. It's so easy to manage, anyone could do it!
Imperative language – Commands	You must get one now before stocks run out! Protection the family cannot do without! Don't be the odd one out – everyone will have one.
Conditionals	**Unless** you act now … **If** you have felt afraid walking home …
Figurative language	SIC is 'nacho' common chip. (pun, play on words) It's as necessary as oxygen. (simile)
Humour	Get rid of the chip on your shoulder. Swallow it instead! Act like a seagull. Eat the chip!

We must persuade adults and kids that they need SIC. Unfortunately, they may be smart consumers and try the following strategies before they buy: finding more information; comparing prices; saving for the future; and questioning if they really need it before buying. However, I think humour may be the way to go by using a pun. They'll forget all those things I mentioned and buy it because they like the advertisement.

TARGETING ENGLISH HOMEWORK YEAR 6 © PASCAL PRESS ISBN 978 1 925726 63 3

Reading & Comprehension

Write the answer or shade the bubble where required.

The answers to these questions are in the text.

① What does SIC stand for?

______

② What type of text has been sent to Chris?

○ report ○ letter
○ email ○ narrative

③ What strategies do **smart consumers** try before they buy?

______

④ What is a pun? ______

Think about these questions and search for the answers in the text.

⑤ Once students eat the microchip, how is it used?

______

⑥ How is the chip protected? Who can access it?

______

⑦ You have been asked to write an advertisement for SIC using one of the **persuasive devices** in the table. Which one would you choose? Write a sentence to explain your choice.

I would choose ______.

I chose this because ______.

Use inferencing skills to answer this question. The answer is not in the text. Think about what you know and what the author says.

⑧ Do you think the advertisement at the end of the text would be **effective** in persuading people to buy SIC?

○ Yes ○ No

Write a sentence to explain your answer.

______

Use your experience and opinions to answer these questions. The answers are not in the text.

⑨ Do you think using SIC is a good idea?

○ Yes ○ No

Write a sentence to explain your answer.

______

⑩ How else could an edible locating microchip be used?

______

TERM 2

Comprehension Reflections

Look at the top of the opposite page. This text is a P______ text – A______.

Write one thing you learned or found interesting:

______

Write one question you have or something you want to find more information about:

______

Rating   

Score 2 points for each correct answer! SCORE /20  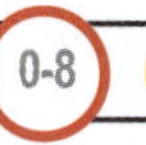 

Grammar & Punctuation

Present tenses for persuasion

Do you want to be more persuasive? Use present tense. Present verbs are used in advertising because they inspire action, and they can be more persuasive than past verbs.

Which sentence below is more persuasive?

a I **was** happy when I used SIC. (past tense)

b I **will definitely use** SIC a lot. (future tense)

c I **love** using SIC. (present tense)

Sentence (c) is present tense and is more persuasive because it is talking about what is happening right now.

This table explains the four types of present tense:

Present simple	Present continuous	Present perfect	Present perfect continuous
base form of the verb	auxiliary verb (am, is, are) + verb + ing	auxiliary verb (have, has) + verb + ed (or irregular spelling of past verb)	auxiliary verb (have, has) + been + verb + ing
We **use** the chip.	We **are using** the chip.	We **have used** the chip.	We **have been using** the chip.

Create some sentences that could be part of an advertising campaign for or against SIC using these sentence starters.

Use any form of the present tense listed in the table with the following verbs, or think of your own: hate, track, find, monitor, feel.

Hint: Some verbs, such as love, hate, like, know, want, cannot be used in continuous tenses.
Example: I **am loving** the chip. (incorrect)

Example: The microchip **is working** really well. (correct)

1 Students ______________________________
______________________________.

2 Parents ______________________________
______________________________.

3 Teachers ______________________________
______________________________.

4 My school ______________________________
______________________________.

5 I ______________________________
______________________________.

Fill in the spaces of this conversation with the best present form of the verb in brackets. Use the table to help you.

Example: "I believe you (use) **are using** the chip," said the teacher to a parent.

"Oh yes, I (use) 6 __________ __________ it all term. It's great!" he replied. "In fact, my child, Sam, (use) 7 __________ __________ __________ the chip to keep track of the dog as it always jumps the fence."
"Really?" answered the teacher. "So Sam fed the cookie to the dog?"
"Oh yes, Sam (feed) 8 __________ __________ __________ the dog all the cookies from the students who did not want to be tracked. I suppose parents (wonder) 9 __________ __________ why their child keeps wandering around the block all the time. That's how Sam walks the dog."

Sam's dog

Advertising often uses present simple tense for effect. Rewrite these statements to make them more persuasive by changing them to present simple tense.

Example:
Parents **had wanted** to use SIC.
Parents **want** to use SIC.

10 Schools **had used** SIC. ______________________________
____

11 Students **were feeling** safer while using SIC.
____
____

12 Sam's dog **loved** the cookies. ______________________________
____

Score 2 points for each correct answer! SCORE /24 0-10 12-18 20-24

TARGETING ENGLISH HOMEWORK YEAR 6 © PASCAL PRESS ISBN 978 1 925726 63 3

Phonic & Word Knowledge

AC9E6LY09

Play on words – Eponyms

Where do our words come from besides Latin and Greek? Some words come from people's names. If an invention, place or discovery is named after a person, it is called an eponym.

Choose the correct person that the item is named after. You may need to do some research.

(1) The cardigan is named after:

a the 7th Earl of Cardigan who had his troops wear the garment into battle.

b Sarah Cardigan who knitted the first cardigan which soon became popular.

c Fred Cardigan who owned a woollen mill and invented the garment to use excess wool.

(2) The sandwich is named after:

a a popular take-away food chain manager who invented it when they ran out of burger buns.

b Fred Sandwich who showed it on a TikTok video and it went viral.

c The Earl of Sandwich who, 250 years ago, did not want to leave his game of cards and asked for meat placed between two pieces of bread to be brought to him so he could eat with his hands.

(3) America is named after:

a Italian map maker, Amerigo Vespucci.

b viking explorer, Lief America, who started a settlement in North America 1000 years ago.

c Americo, the son of the explorer, Christopher Columbus.

Portmanteau

A portmanteau is when parts of words are combined to create a new word.
Example: breakfast + lunch = brunch

Complete these portmanteaus.

(4) friend + enemy = ______________

(5) motor + hotel = ______________

(6) smoke + fog = ______________

(7) iPod + broadcast = ______________

(8) labrador + poodle = ______________

(9) fourteen + night = ______________

(10) information + commercial = ______________

(11) interconnected + network = ______________

(12) spoon + fork = ______________

(13) electronic + mail = ______________

(14) twist + whirl = ______________

(15) screen + snapshot = ______________

Create your own portmanteaus by combining two words to create a new word. Write the meaning of your new word.

Example: sandwiches + soggy = sandoggies
Meaning: Sandwiches that have become soggy in your lunchbox.

(16) ______________ + ______________ = ______________

Meaning: ______________

(17) ______________ + ______________ = ______________

Meaning: ______________

Neologisms

A neologism is a newly created word that is not part of our official language.
Examples: app, spam

It can also be an existing word that has gained a new meaning.
Examples: sick, wicked

You can make up your own new words by adding the suffix 'esque', meaning 'like or resembling', to a variety of nouns. This would form an adjective to describe someone or something.
Example: word + esque = wordesque

Meaning: someone good at spelling

Create your own 'esque' words and their meanings.

(18) ______________ + esque = ______________

Meaning: ______________

(19) ______________ + esque = ______________

Meaning: ______________

Score 2 points for each correct answer!

SCORE /38 0-16 18-32 34-38

TERM 2

AC9E6LY04, AC9E6LY05, AC9S6U03

Informative text – Explanation

Energy

Claps of thunder echoed around the cold, grey, stone house and rain lashed at its windows. At the very top of the house was a small, cramped laboratory where a young scientist waited to harness and redirect the electrical energy from the storm. Lightning rods protruded from the roof and connected to the lifeless body below, a body deformed and stitched together to look more like a monster than a human being. Victor Frankenstein was about to create his monster, according to the author Mary Shelley in her book, *Frankenstein*.

Over 200 years ago, scientists had a limited understanding of electrical energy, and they conducted many different experiments. In her book, Shelley used the current thinking around energy for that time, which is why her scientist gave life to his monster using electrical energy from lightning.

We know a lot more about energy now, but what is it? Energy is the ability to do work. It is not a 'thing' because you cannot pick it up or weigh it. The universe is made of matter which has weight and occupies space, but energy is something different. It isn't matter.

There are many different types of energy that can be grouped into two forms: kinetic and potential. Kinetic energy is an energy of movement, such as with moving objects. There is also potential energy, which is stored energy. This table lists the types of energy under these two forms.

Kinetic – movement energy	Potential – stored energy
Sound – caused by objects vibrating; moves through the air	**Elastic** – as in a coiled spring or stretched rubber band
Heat – caused by the vibration of atoms and molecules; can also be called thermal energy	**Gravitational** – when an object is in a high position and can fall, like a rollercoaster
Light – travels in waves and is produced when an object's atoms heat up	**Chemical** – found in food, oil, gas etc.
Electrical – the movement of tiny parts of atoms called electrons	

Albert Einstein, a famous scientist who died over 70 years ago, developed a law of physics that is still used today. He said that energy cannot be created or destroyed. It can, however, transform or change from one type of energy to another. For example, power stations do not create energy. They transform different types of energy into electrical energy.

Energy can be transferred, which means it can be moved from one place to another. For example, electrical energy moves from a wall plug to an appliance that is plugged in. Electricity is the flow of electrons through a conductor, usually in the form of a wire. This flow is called an electric current. A lightning strike or bolt is a massive flow of electric current from the cloud to the ground.

In Mary Shelley's book, Victor Frankenstein manages to transfer and transform the electric current from the lightning to bring life to his monster. Thank goodness that is not possible, but what a great story!

TERM 2

TARGETING ENGLISH HOMEWORK YEAR 6 © PASCAL PRESS ISBN 978 1 925726 63 3

Write the answer or shade the bubble next to the correct answer.

The answers to these questions are in the text.

① **What is energy?** ____________

② **What does the text say energy is not?** ____________

③ **What is kinetic energy?** ____________

④ **What is potential energy?** ____________

⑤ **Energy is created in power stations.**

◯ True ◯ False

Think about these questions and search for the answers in the text.

⑥ **Why did Mary Shelley write about using electrical energy from lightning to give the monster life?** ____________

⑦ **What is the difference between transferred and transformed when describing electricity?** ____________

⑧ **What law in physics did Einstein develop?** ____________

Use inferencing skills to answer this question. The answer is not in the text. Think about what you know and what the author says.

⑨ **Using the table in the text, what types of energy do the following situations use?**

Digesting your meal ____________

Using a slippery dip ____________

Using a rubber band and a ruler to flick paper ____________

Turning on the TV ____________

A baby crying ____________

The warmth from the sun ____________

Use your experience and opinions to answer this question. The answer is not in the text.

⑩ **The text states, Victor Frankenstein manages to transfer and transform the electric current from the lightning to bring life to his monster. Thank goodness that is not possible. Why do you think the author wrote that last sentence?** ____________

Comprehension Reflections

Look at the top of the opposite page. This text is an I__________ text – E__________.

Write one thing you learned or found interesting: ____________

Write one question you have or something you want to find more information about: ____________

Rating  

Score 2 points for each correct answer!

TERM 2

Grammar & Punctuation

AC9E6LA06, AC9E6LA08

Precise verbs

The choice of verbs is very important in creating interesting, descriptive sentences.

Example from the text: Claps of thunder **echoed** around the cold, grey, stone house and rain **lashed** at its windows.

This is better than: Claps of thunder **were heard** around the cold, grey, stone house and rain **fell** on its windows.

The words **echoed** and **lashed** are precise verbs and give an indication of the storm's strength.

Rewrite these sentences by replacing the verbs in bold with one of the precise verbs listed in brackets. Choose precise verbs to show your meaning. Add or delete words to create interesting, descriptive sentences.

1. I **walked** slowly up the hill. (trudged, crawled, sauntered, strolled, meandered)

____

____

2. Instinctively, I **bent** down when I saw a dingo. (crouched, stooped, squatted, ducked, bowed)

____

____

3. The animal **ran** towards me. (sprinted, darted, scurried, scampered, lunged)

____

____

4. It **held** onto my jacket with its teeth. (grasped, clung, clutched, gripped, seized)

____

____

5. I **fell** down the hill, jacketless. (dropped, plummeted, plunged, tumbled, crashed)

____

____

6. I **cried** at the base of the hill. (wept, sobbed, whimpered, howled, snivelled)

____

____

Figurative language – Hyperbole

Hyperbole is an exaggerated statement or claim that is not meant to be taken literally. For example, if someone says you are a monster, they do not mean you were created by Frankenstein; however, your behaviour may be questionable.

Write the literal or real meaning of these hyperbolic sentences.

Hyperbole	Literal or real meaning
I could eat a horse.	*Example:* I am very hungry.
I have a ton of homework.	7
My leg is falling off.	8
He never stops talking.	9
I was dying of laughter.	10
They live on the other side of the universe.	11

Be creative and write your own hyperbolic sentences on the following topics.

Example: I have told you many times before.

I have repeatedly told you 24/7.

12. I waited for a long time.

____

____

13. It was very expensive.

____

____

14. When Mum finds out, you will be in trouble.

____

____

Score 2 points for each correct answer! SCORE /28

TARGETING ENGLISH HOMEWORK YEAR 6 © PASCAL PRESS ISBN 978 1 925726 63 3

Phonic & Word Knowledge

AC9E6LY08, AC9E6LY09

Verbing – Adding suffixes 'ate', 'ise', 'ify'

Verbing is when you take a noun or adjective and turn it into a verb or doing word by adding a suffix, such as -ate, -ise, -ify.

Examples:
oxygen (noun) + **ate** = oxygen**ate** (verb)

To turn a noun or adjective into a verb, use spelling generalisations:

- change 'y' to 'i' *e.g.* glory = glori**fy**
- if the word ends in 'e', remove the 'e' when the suffix begins with a vowel *e.g.* captive = captiv**ate**.

Change the following nouns and adjectives into verbs. Write them in the table.

popular, false, computer, regular, intense, active, motive, equal, simple, pressure, valid, liquid

-ate	-ise	-ify
①	*Example:* **popularise**	⑧
②	⑤	⑨
③	⑥	⑩
④	⑦	⑪

Choose words from the table to complete this passage. Use context clues, like similes, to help you.

Frankenstein had to ⑫ ______________ the monster and start its heart by using electricity. He had to ⑬ ______________ and strengthen the amount of electricity by using the lightning from the storm. If he used too much electricity, he might ⑭ ______________ the monster into a soggy mass.

Bringing the monster to life would ⑮ ______________ or support all his research. It would ⑯ ______________ or promote his research and make him famous. They would glorify and praise his name in history forever, or so he thought. Frankenstein's drawings were very complex. He did not ⑰ ______________ them. Lightning hit the building and travelled to the monster, it ...

Unpredictable digraphs

In Unit 9, we looked at unpredictable digraphs. One example of this is the many ways to spell the 'or' sound. It can be spelt with different letter combinations, such as 'aw', 'au', 'al'.

Underline the vowels that make the 'or' sound in these words.

Example: <u>Au</u>gust

⑱ alright	㉒ autumn
⑲ awesome	㉓ altogether
⑳ always	㉔ walk
㉑ cautious	㉕ draw

Help Frankenstein by completing the passage with the 'or' sounding words from the previous question.

Oh Monster, you are ㉖ __________. When I first started to ㉗ __________ you at the start of ㉘ __________, I knew I would ㉙ __________ succeed in creating you. People will be very ㉚ __________ around you but ㉛ __________ with your head high. You are ㉜ __________ a complex character. In fact, you are many people put together. I will make things ㉝ __________ for you so do not worry. You are my monster.

Score 2 points for each correct answer! SCORE /66   

0-30 32-60 62-66

TARGETING ENGLISH HOMEWORK YEAR 6 © PASCAL PRESS ISBN 978 1 925726 63 3

AC9E6LY04, AC9E6LY05, AC9S6U03

Informative – Explanation

Teacher Feedback on Electrical Circuits Test

Sam, I am giving you feedback on the science test that you did last week. I am offering you the chance to resubmit the test next week as I think you are more capable than you demonstrated in the test. I will explain some of the areas where you need to improve.

In your test, you show some misconceptions or misunderstandings. Where did you get the idea that electricity was the march of very fast-moving invisible ants along wires? You go on to explain that they are eaten up when they arrive at the object that they are supplying power to. This is not correct. There are no ants in electrical circuits.

Everything we touch is made up of tiny particles called atoms. These atoms have smaller parts inside them called protons, neutrons and electrons. Protons carry a positive charge, whereas electrons carry a negative charge. The electricity we use for lights and appliances comes from electrons moving around in a circuit.

A circuit must have several things, and one of them is a power source like a battery or power outlet. Batteries have negative and positive charges. When connected to a circuit, electrons are repelled by the negative side and move through wires to reach the positive side of the battery. This is called a current of electricity, powering anything that is part of the circuit. When trying to draw a circuit, think of it as a circle. The paths may split off here and there, but they always form a line from negative to positive, like a circle. Unfortunately, in your test, you drew a straight line for a circuit. You did include a switch, which is good. When they are turned off, switches break the circuit, causing the electrons to stop moving. But the electrons do not disappear or get used up. A circuit also needs a conductor to let the electrons move and usually this is metal wiring.

When asked in the test to describe electricity in nature, you mentioned solar panels and the solar lights in your garden. That is not what I meant. The question meant 'forms of energy' in nature such as lightning, static electricity and bioelectricity, which are all forms of naturally occurring electricity. One example of bioelectricity includes electric eels as they have an electrical current that they generate to use for protection and hunting. Another example is the electricity that makes the muscles in our heart contract. This in turn causes the heart to pump blood around our bodies. One last example of bioelectricity is also in the human body. It is in the nerves that carry small electrical currents which send messages to different parts of our bodies.

I'm sure you will do better in the next test, but to make sure, I have assigned some reading for your homework. Don't worry, I have let your parents know, and they are more than willing to make sure you read up on electrical circuits over the weekend.

Ms W

TARGETING ENGLISH HOMEWORK YEAR 6 © PASCAL PRESS ISBN 978 1 925726 63 3

Reading & Comprehension

UNIT 13

Write the answer or shade the bubble next to the correct answer.

The answers to these questions are in the text.

① Electricity is the march of very fast-moving invisible ants along wires.

◯ True ◯ False

② Where are electrons found? ______

③ Where does the electricity we use for lights and appliances come from?

④ What does a **conductor** do in a circuit?

Think about these questions and search for the answers in the text.

⑤ Give three examples of **bioelectricity**.

⑥ Which diagram best illustrates a circuit and how the electrons move in a circuit?

◯ 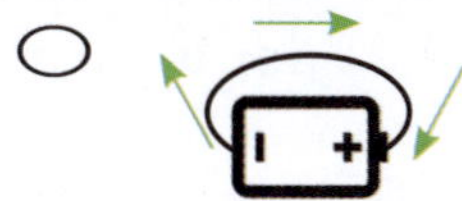

◯ 

◯ 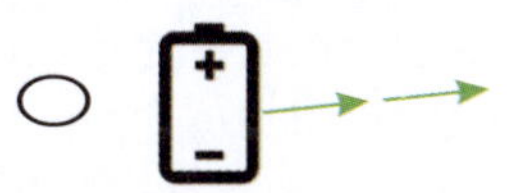

◯ 

⑦ What happens to electrons when a switch in a circuit is turned off?

Use inferencing skills to answer these questions. The answers are not in the text. Think about what you know and what the author says.

⑧ Why do you think the **negative side** of a battery repels electrons?

⑨ People who suffer a heart attack are often given aid using a defibrillator. Defibrillators are devices that apply an electric charge or current to the heart. Why do you think an **electric charge** would be given to the heart?

Use your experience and opinions to answer this question. The answer is not in the text.

⑩ Electricity costs are going up. How could you use an electric eel to help your household with their energy bill? Be creative and think of two ways.

Comprehension Reflections

Look at the top of the opposite page. This text is an I______ text – E______.

Write one thing you learned or found interesting:

Write one question you have or something you want to find more information about:

Rating   

Score 2 points for each correct answer! SCORE /20 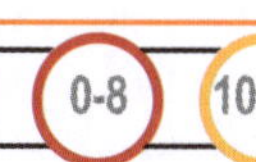 

TERM 2

TARGETING ENGLISH HOMEWORK YEAR 6 © PASCAL PRESS ISBN 978 1 925726 63 3

Grammar & Punctuation

AC9E6LA09

Punctuation to create meaning

Punctuation is important to create meaning in sentences. This includes the use of capital letters, full stops, question marks, commas and quotation marks.

Read the two texts and draw what each one is explaining. The difference in punctuation makes a difference to the meaning!

1 The ants were climbing on the wall in the kitchen, over by the stove. Mum jumped with joy. The exterminator had arrived in a van. On a bike, our neighbour rode up to say hello. He had ants earlier that year. The ants had taken over the grassed area at the back. Thankfully, it was now an ant-colony-free zone!	2 The ants were climbing on the wall. In the kitchen, over by the stove, Mum jumped. With Joy, the exterminator had arrived. In a van, on a bike, our neighbour rode up to say hello. He had ants. Earlier that year, the ants had taken over. The grassed area at the back, thankfully, it was now an ant colony. Free zone!

Punctuation in complex sentences

Punctuation is important, especially in complex sentences. Complex sentences use commas to separate dependent and independent clauses when the dependent clause is first in the sentence.

Example:

Sam believed ants were in an electrical circuit because he misunderstood electricity and circuits. (no comma)

Because he misunderstood electricity and circuits, Sam believed ants were in an electrical circuit. (comma is used)

Rearrange the following sentences to start with the conjunction and dependent clause. You will need to add a comma.

3 Electrons flow (or move) from the negative side of the battery when a battery is connected to a circuit.

4 Sam started reading about electricity after he got home.

Punctuation in direct speech

Punctuation is also very important in direct speech. Quotation marks go around the exact words a character says. There is always a punctuation mark before a quotation mark unless it is at the start of a sentence. A capital letter is used when someone starts speaking.

Example:

Sam called out, “I'm home. Anybody there?”

“Hi, Sam. How was your day?” Sam's mum asked, looking directly at him.

Punctuate the rest of the conversation.

5 Oh, it was okay said Sam, trying to act relaxed

6 Dad walked in and said I have read a message from your teacher, something about a test

7 Sam swallowed hard really I wonder what that could be about

8 Dad looked at Sam and asked so you know nothing about it

9 Sam replied I think the teacher sent a message telling you how fantastic I was today

10 Sam's mum looked away, rather amused, and said I think we have ants in the kitchen

Score 2 points for each correct answer! SCORE /20 0-8 10-14 16-20

TERM 2

TARGETING ENGLISH HOMEWORK YEAR 6 © PASCAL PRESS ISBN 978 1 925726 63 3

Phonic & Word Knowledge

AC9E6LY09

Prefix 'mis'

Remember! A prefix goes at the beginning of a word and changes the meaning of that word. Sam had a **mis**conception or **mis**understanding around electric circuits. The prefix 'mis' is from Latin and means 'bad or wrongly', so Sam had some wrong ideas about electrical circuits.

Add the prefix 'mis' to these words.

1. take ______________________
2. treated ______________________
3. calculation ______________________
4. trusted ______________________
5. construed ______________________
6. management ______________________

Choose the best 'mis' word from the previous activity for each space in the passage.

Sam's parents thought the ant problem was easy to fix. They (7) ________________ the size of the problem. It was a (8) ________________ to think the ants would go away by themselves. Sam's parents decided to use talcum powder as a deterrent. However, due to a (9) ________________ on how much powder was needed, the ants simply marched on. Due to their (10) ________________ of the situation, the ants increased in numbers and invaded the cupboards. Sam's parents (11) ________________ poisonous substances as they felt it (12) ________________ the environment. The ants were winning!

Prefix 'bio'

Sometimes if you don't know the meaning of a word, you can figure it out if you know what part/s of the word mean. The word **bio**electricity is used in the text. The prefix 'bio' comes from Greek, meaning 'life'. Therefore, bioelectricity is electricity produced by or occurring within living organisms.

Write the 'bio' words in the list next to the correct definitions.

biohazard, biofuel, biogas, biochemist, biology, biosphere, bioelectric, biopic, biodegradable

(13)		something that can be decomposed by bacteria or other organisms
(14)		an expert in science who looks at chemical reactions in living organisms
(15)		fuel obtained from living matter
(16)		areas of the atmosphere or planet that are suitable for life
(17)		gas produced by fermenting living things
(18)		a movie that shows the life of a person
(19)		relating to electricity made in a living organism
(20)		a branch of science that looks at living organisms; an environmental science
(21)		a biological substance that is dangerous to people or the environment

(22) – (36) Find the 15 'mis' and 'bio' words listed on this page in the Word Find. The words are horizontal and vertical, and one word is diagonal.

n c s f q e o x e v l g b b l h t e l b u h n i x d i o t d
z m z q p a u p r r q m w v o i p a y d b i o c h e m i s t
j j y e h b r e i i a i h r p z b h j b d j v t e k g r h j
k x x f p h a h q b m i y u b i o s p h e r e t f r e l q u
j f a l j f l v j v m z o r m t f o k r r q g e j b m q l c
h j p r e f c z f o t t m f e y h z h w r a n y c n t m g q
z y m r r i g m i l n g b t h l l f x x r p q g o m x e f n
h s k i b t t n v m h q m i s m a n a g e m e n t w i m u J
b s w r h z m o b i m u j s k x s q m w x m b d l v f y v w
b q b m v l z m q s o h h m g l n v z q p h d w t x s e z q
i v p i n o z u u t z y s i r r x v o l u m p v z m y k h q
o w s s m x e f q r d d m s h g c w g l o b g c k s o h p y
h t k c h a p d u u c a f c z s b q r y m t j x c b i g g k
a t c a d d q n l s n n s o u t z s j z e i v i k y o t b a
z z f l s a e u q t k c z n t p k q q d o y s h p n h s i o
a n d c y i q u y e o y k s s r g w p h l e t t a a w n o d
r g a u e s p x e d n l c t y w t n n q d k a v r a z i p f
d f x l a j r a h d h d i r b e x e f u h t h f v e v b i b
o f v a b i m r j k b n o u i e w m e a x n u v d k a t c n
n k b t h b x b q s q p e e o n h e a e h d o e a d j t p s
y g k i e z u x b j t f a d d b i o g a s g m b b p c v e z
r e n o h e q c m z f e d h e o y b h j p o i h y r w r n d
t y s n b i o l o g y c q f g y r r u t z l s h f s x e s x
s l d a f z l t q y j c r j r t r g s f x m t r p p l g m j
n f h b i o e l e c t r i c a i n b h h r q a s y s a n h i
q f u k a l q u w d m f z n d c o b w m l z k j r r e k d m
y l y y w t i b p d r s a x a c b m d b f e e u s l f d s k
c v l f j z a c s k e o v j b l x b s y m l d o d p q y m u
m r i y n l v s x j o j e o l p y z a k w d b h z d t x k w
b x m o b i o f u e l n t h e r t i o k k p e d w h b c m m

Score 2 points for each correct answer!

SCORE /72   

TERM 2

Reading & Comprehension

AC9E6LY04, AC9E6LY05, AC9HS6K01

Imaginative text – Description

Letter Home, November 1900

My dear sister, Margaret,

I hope you are well, back in the mother country. Things are quite tight here in the colonies at the moment. The papers call it a depression. Well, I can tell you that I am depressed! It's hard to get food on the table every day, and with eight children it is a struggle. Christmas will be very lean this year. Oh, I do miss the snow and snuggling up to a fire.

The papers are full of Federation talk. It's been going on ever since that politician Henry Parkes made a speech in Tenterfield. That's nearly 12 years ago. I must say, he had a glorious head of hair and was still a striking man when he died three years ago at the age of 80. It seems like he will have his way as all the colonies will soon join and form a country. Just think, Margaret, I will not be called a colonist but an Australian!

Oh, I am sick of all the debates in the paper, but some good points have been made. You know my Fred is now a salesman for a tannery that makes leather shoes. He must travel to other colonies to make sales, and he says that all the different taxes and laws for each colony make it hard to do business. He also says that travelling is difficult because each colony has different rail gauges. He hops on and off trains all the time and pays taxes each time! What a cheek!

My neighbour, Mr Sam, says Federation will protect us. I tell you, Margaret, I feared what he would tell me next. He said that each colony has a little army, but with Federation we could join forces and have a bigger one to protect us from invasion. He tells us that we are vulnerable to attack from other nations with larger populations and military forces. My dear Margaret, I found that news very disturbing. I could hardly sleep that night.

Mr Sam went on to say that if we Federated, there could be laws passed to keep out people we don't want in Australia. "Keep it British," he said. You know the gold rush really brought many different people here. In fact, there are times when I do not hear English being spoken at all. To tell you the truth, I find that quite exciting, but I would never tell Fred that. Another exciting thing is that some of my friends have talked about the right to vote for women. Now that is exciting if Federation brings that about for all of us. If I were allowed to vote, I would've voted for Parkes.

The big problem, according to the newspapers, is that the colonies do not agree on many things. Some of the larger and more populous colonies feel they will lose power, and the smaller colonies feel they will not be listened to if Federation goes ahead.

Anyway, I believe Federation will occur very soon. You know, Margaret, I really see myself becoming less attached to the mother country. The longer I live here, the more I start to see myself as belonging here. I suppose I am saying, don't expect me to come home. Actually, I am home, here in Australia.

Your loving sister, Rose

TERM 2

TARGETING ENGLISH HOMEWORK YEAR 6 © PASCAL PRESS ISBN 978 1 925726 63 3

Reading & Comprehension

Write the answer or shade the bubble next to the correct answer.

The answers to these questions are in the text.

1. What country was the **mother country**?

____

2. The politician, Henry Parkes, was against Federation.

◯ True ◯ False

3. What item could a **tannery** make? _______________

4. What made it hard for Fred to do business with the other colonies?

____

5. What was the big problem with Federation?

____

Think about these questions and search for the answers in the text.

6. Why was the author of the letter not allowed to vote?

____

7. Why did the author feel that she would not visit the mother country?

____

Use inferencing skills to answer these questions. The answers are not in the text. Think about what you know and what the author says.

8. Why do you think the term **mother country** was used?

____

9. Mr Sam explained that each colony had a small army, and this would change with Federation. Why did the author find this information from Mr Sam disturbing?

____

Use your experience and opinions to answer this question. The answer is not in the text.

10. Some of the larger colonies felt they would lose power with Federation. Which of the colonies (states) do you think were powerful?

____

Why do you think that? _______________

Comprehension Reflections

Look at the top of the opposite page. This text is an I__________ text – D__________.

Write one thing you learned or found interesting:

____

Write one question you have or something you want to find more information about:

____

Rating   

Score 2 points for each correct answer! SCORE /20   

TERM 2

Grammar & Punctuation

AC9E6LA09

Punctuation in direct speech

As seen in the last unit, punctuation is important to create meaning, especially in a conversation. To punctuate a conversation, there are some rules to be aware of:

- Enclose the spoken words in quotation marks and use dialogue tags to show who is speaking and how they are saying their words. *Examples:* he explained; she demanded with a smile
- If the dialogue tag comes after the dialogue, use a comma inside the quotation marks. The dialogue tag begins with a lowercase letter (except in the case of proper nouns). *Examples:*
  - "I don't know what you mean," the student said.
  - "I think you do," Mr Wilson replied.

TERM 2

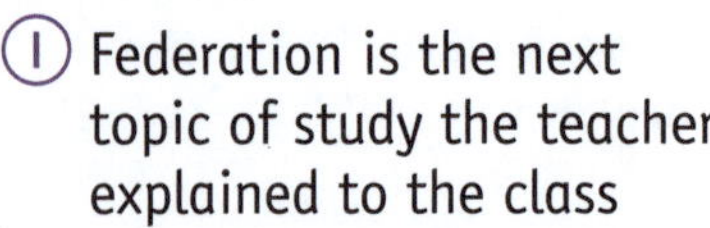

Punctuate the following conversation.

1. Federation is the next topic of study the teacher explained to the class
2. Sorry, but I already know all about this stated Sam to the teacher
3. I'm sorry, Sam, but I don't think you do the teacher persisted
4. Oh, I do, so I don't need to stay in class for these lessons Sam said very confidently

- If the dialogue ends with a question mark or exclamation mark in the quotation marks, begin the dialogue tag with a lowercase letter. *Example:*
  - "Tell me, how did you learn about Federation?" the teacher inquired.

Punctuate the following conversation.

5. Oh, I just watch YouTube. Don't you asked Sam
6. Please, tell us what you know exclaimed the teacher with a smile
7. Oh, how long before recess asked Sam, darting a look at the clock on the wall

- If the dialogue tag precedes the dialogue, the comma goes before the opening quotation marks. The first word of the dialogue inside the quotes is capitalised. *Example:*
  - Sam drew a large breath and explained, "It's about becoming one country."

Punctuate the following conversation.

8. The teacher beamed and said fantastic Sam, please go on
9. Sam started to look confused and asked you mean there's more
10. With an encouraging smile, the teacher asked why did people want Federation

- If the dialogue tag is mid-sentence, put one comma before the tag and another comma after the tag. Then open the quotation marks with a lowercase letter (unless it is a proper noun). *Example:*
  - "Listen, Sam," said Mr Wilson patiently, "how would Federation protect Australia?"

Punctuate the following conversation.

11. Well started Sam there was not a combined army or navy to fight against invaders
12. What other reasons asked Mr Wilson smiling were there for Federation

- If the dialogue tag separates two complete sentences, put a full stop after the dialogue tag and start the next sentence with open quotes and a capital letter. *Example:*
  - "It was to help businesses," Sam said hopefully. "They had so many taxes and different trains you had to catch between colonies!"

Punctuate the following conversation.

13. That's right exclaimed Mr Wilson. However, some people did not want Federation
14. Some powerful people were worried explained Sam. They thought they would lose money and power to the smaller states
15. I am most impressed, Sam said Mr Wilson. I know you'd love to continue after recess

Score 2 points for each correct answer! SCORE /30   

0-12 | 14-24 | 26-30

TARGETING ENGLISH HOMEWORK YEAR 6 © PASCAL PRESS ISBN 978 1 925726 63 3

Phonic & Word Knowledge

UNIT 14

AC9E6LY09

Suffix 'ion'

This unit is about Federation. The word federation is a noun and comes from the verb 'federate'. The suffix 'ion' turns verbs (action words) into nouns (naming words). It comes from Latin and means 'an action or condition'. There are various spelling generalisations for adding the suffix 'ion' as shown in the table below.

Complete the Practice section in the table. The first one has been done for you.

	Generalisations	Examples	Practice	
1	words ending in 'ate' drop the 'e' and add 'ion'	federate – federation	*e.g.* **translate – translation** vibrate – ____________ decorate – ____________	donate – ____________ populate – ____________
2	words ending in 'ss' add 'ion'	discuss – discussion	confess – ____________ impress – ____________	repress – ____________ express – ____________
3	words ending in 'mit' drop the 't' add 'ssion'	permit – permission	omit – ____________ admit – ____________	commit – ____________ remit – ____________
4	other words ending in 'e' take off the 'e' and add 'ation'	prepare – preparation	admire – ____________ examine – ____________	determine – ____________ observe – ____________

Homophones

The process to federate the six Australian colonies into the Commonwealth of Australia took over 50 years from its beginnings in the 1840s to the official proclamation on 1 January 1901. If you were fighting for Federation, you needed a lot of patience, or is it patients?

The words patience and patients are homophones. This means that they have different spellings and meanings but the same pronunciation. Patience means 'tolerance' while patients means 'people receiving medical treatment'. How well do you know your homophones?

Choose the correct homophones in the sentences below by circling the answer. You may need a dictionary to help you. Can you score full marks?

5. I _____ that the Federation of Australia was a complex topic.
new / knew

6. I did not have a lot of _____ into the topic.
insight / incite

7. The local _____ has a list of people who lived in my area during that time.
counsel / council

8. I would like to _____ this information.
elicit / illicit

9. If it is _____ many pages to read, I may let an adult look at it for me.
too / two / to

10. I bet the information will be on special paper or _____.
stationary / stationery

11. Even though it was a long _____ ago, I am interested in the topic.
thyme / time

12. Federation occurred during the _____ of Queen Victoria.
reign / rain

13. I wonder if I should _____ to that in my research report?
elude / allude

14. I am going to draw a _____ bolt over Queen Victoria's head to show she was thinking of Federation.
lightening / lightning

15. I am _____ committed to getting a good grade for this assignment.
wholly / holy

Score 2 points for each correct answer! SCORE /30 0-12 14-24 26-30

TERM 2

Reading & Comprehension

AC9E6LY04, AC9E6LY05, AC9S6U02

Imaginative text – Narrative

TERM 2

Superpowers and Gravity

Pat put down the comic he had been reading and switched off the bedside lamp. The comic book fluttered to the floor as he started to doze, falling open at the picture of Dr G, a scientist who could mentally control gravity. Thoughts of the doctor floated in Pat's mind like confetti at a wedding, forcing their way into his dreams and wonderings. As the night marched on, an eerie glow emanated from the comic by the bed, forming a small globe of light that seeped into Pat's sleeping form.

Pat sat upright in bed, fully aware that something had happened. As he thought about his dreams, the comic book lifted from the floor into his hand. That's when Pat knew he was a mini version of Dr G, the controller of gravity. Wonderful ideas sprung into Pat's mind, such as lifting the school and moving it elsewhere so he could watch the teachers' faces when they arrived to find an empty space. Or lifting his family's house to a location where it would be a permanent vacation for his family. Or better still, feeling weightlessness like the astronauts. That would be fun. Pat considered turning off Earth's gravity for a second. Surely it couldn't cause any harm. Or maybe he could aim for something bigger like turning off the Sun's gravity. Little did Pat know that that would have a massive effect on nearly everything because so many things are designed around the current state of gravity.

Gravity is an invisible force that pulls objects towards each other. Earth's gravity is what keeps you and many other things on the ground. It also keeps the moon in Earth's orbit. The Sun has the greatest gravitational pull in our solar system. It is at the centre of our solar system, and its huge size means its gravitational pull is strong enough to hold the planets in orbit around itself. If the Sun suddenly lost its gravitational pull, then the planets in our solar system, including us, would fly off in straight lines away from the Sun to drift in space. We would join the predicted 200 billion other planets that are currently floating free in our galaxy, the Milky Way. We would be alone together with other wandering planets.

Pat concentrated and squeezed his eyes shut. Suddenly, there was no force of gravity on planet Earth to hold things down. Things like people, chairs, tables and the comic book began to rise up. In fact, everything that was not stuck in place suddenly started floating. However, it wasn't just the small things that started to float. The water from rivers and oceans started to rise upwards. Without gravity, even the air in the atmosphere began to float into space. No-one would last long if the planet did not have gravity.

Pat's eyes grew large with fear as house and car alarms sounded throughout the neighbourhood, and in the blink of an eye, gravity was restored. A shaken but relieved Pat sat on the edge of his bed, wondering what the morning news reports would make of it. Then a slow smile spread across his face, like an uncurling worm. At least one headline would question the whereabouts of an entire school building. Pat had a plan.

TARGETING ENGLISH HOMEWORK YEAR 6 © PASCAL PRESS ISBN 978 1 925726 63 3

Reading & Comprehension

Write the answer or shade the bubble next to the correct answer.

The answers to these questions are in the text.

1. **Use context clues to work out the meaning of emanated in the first paragraph.**
   - ◯ poured
   - ◯ stemmed
   - ◯ flowed
   - ◯ radiated
   - ◯ all of the above
   - ◯ none of the above

2. **What is gravity?**

____

____

3. **What would happen if the sun lost its gravitational pull on Earth?**

____

____

____

____

Think about these questions and search for the answers in the text.

4. **How did Pat become a mini version of Dr G?**

____

____

____

____

5. **Why would no-one last long if Earth had no gravity?**

____

____

____

____

6. **At the end of the text it says, Pat had a plan. What could Pat's plan be?**

____

____

____

____

Use inferencing skills to answer these questions. The answers are not in the text. Think about what you know and what the author says.

7. **Why would Pat want to watch the teachers' faces when they arrived to find an empty space instead of the school?**

____

____

____

8. **Why did Pat restore the Earth's gravity?**

____

____

____

Use your experience and opinions to answer these questions. The answers are not in the text.

9. **If Earth joined the predicted 200 billion planets floating in the Milky Way, what would be one negative and one positive point?**

Positive: ______________________________

____

Negative: ______________________________

____

10. **If you had control over gravity, what are two things you would like to use your powers for? Be creative.**

____

____

Comprehension Reflections

Look at the top of the opposite page. This text is an I__________ text – N__________.

Write one thing you learned or found interesting:

____

Write one question you have or something you want to find more information about:

____

____

Rating   

Score 2 points for each correct answer! SCORE /20 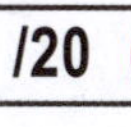  

TERM 2

Grammar & Punctuation

AC9E6LA08

TERM 2

Figurative language – Similes and personification

This unit's text uses figurative language, such as similes and personification, to improve descriptions.

A simile is when a comparison is made using the words 'like' or 'as'.

Examples: Thoughts of the doctor floated in Pat's mind **like** confetti at a wedding.

Then a slow smile spread across his face, **like** an uncurling worm.

Personification is when a thing/object is given human emotions and behaviours.

Example: As the night marched on … (The night cannot march.)

Write two similes to describe how the school moved away. Use the sentence starters provided.

1. The school took off like ______________________________.
2. The school was as ______________________________.

Write two sentences with personification to describe how the school moved away. Give the school human-like behaviour.

3. ______________________________
4. ______________________________

Oxymorons

An oxymoron is a combination of words that are the opposite of each other. *Examples:* a small crowd; seriously funny

Oxymorons can be used to add drama to a feeling or event. *Example from the text:* We would be **alone together** with other wandering planets. (dramatises the plight of the Earth if it drifted into space)

Circle the oxymoron in the following sentences.

5. Pat's idea of making the school disappear went over like a lead balloon.
6. The police arrived at Pat's house like uninvited guests.
7. When Pat was asked about the disappearance of the school, there was a deafening silence in the room.
8. Pat's only choice was to confess, or was it?

Create oxymorons by adding an opposite word to each of the following.

9. ______________ smile
10. ______________ scream
11. ______________ secret
12. ______________ whisper

Write one sentence to explain each oxymoron.

13. Pat took a working vacation at home for the rest of the term.
____
14. Pat's brother felt sorry for him and gave him the larger half of his pizza.
____
15. Pat's brother gave his unbiased opinion about what Pat did with the school.
____

Score 2 points for each correct answer!

SCORE 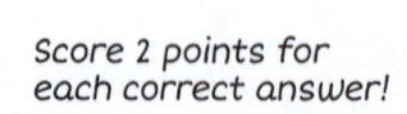

TARGETING ENGLISH HOMEWORK YEAR 6 © PASCAL PRESS ISBN 978 1 925726 63 3

Phonic & Word Knowledge

AC9E6LY08, AC9E6LY09

Spelling generalisations with 'ie'

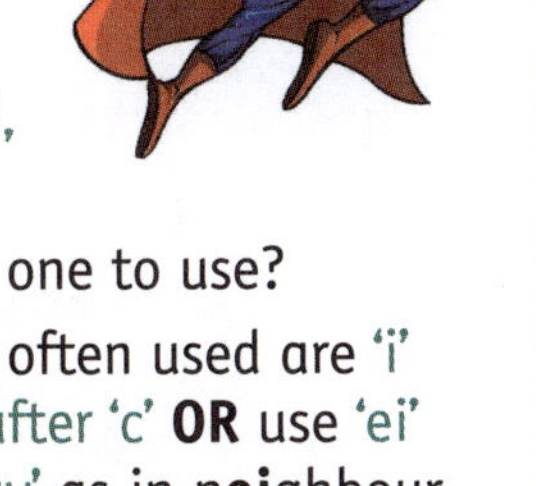

The text contains words with the 'ie' or 'ei' letter patterns. *Examples:* n**ei**ghbourhood, rel**ie**ved, w**ei**ghtlessness

How do you know which one to use?

Generalisations that are often used are 'i' comes before 'e' except after 'c' **OR** use 'ei' when the sound is like 'ay' as in n**ei**ghbour and w**ei**gh. Of course, there are exceptions to these generalisations.

① – ⑱ Use the **generalisations** to place the following list words in the appropriate row of the table. The first few have been done for you.

> ceiling, achieve, receipt, beige, brief, conceit, sleigh, vein, patience, receive, weight, pierce, freight, neighbour, deceit, feint, hygiene, deceive, priest, perceive, friend

Generalisations	Examples
'i' before 'e'	achieve
except after 'c'	ceiling
or when sounding like 'ay'	beige

Some common **exceptions to the generalisations** are listed below. Match each list word with its **definition** by writing it on the lines provided.

> seize, leisure, either, weird, caffeine, forfeit, neither, counterfeit, their, height, foreign

e.g. **either** one or the other

⑲ ____________________: not the one nor the other

⑳ ____________________: a stimulant found in tea and coffee

㉑ ____________________: a fake or forgery

㉒ ____________________: strange or unfamiliar; outside your country

㉓ ____________________: to lose or give up something as a consequence of something that you have done

㉔ ____________________: free time or relaxation

㉕ ____________________: measurement of someone from head to foot

㉖ ____________________: belonging to or connected to someone

㉗ ____________________: very strange and unusual

㉘ ____________________: to take something quickly and keep hold of it

㉙ – ㊱ Pat wrote a story for homework. Help Pat edit his work by correcting his **spelling mistakes** and giving him a score. Cross out the incorrect spelling and write the correct spelling on the line below. The eight errors are in **'ie' and 'ei' words.**

It was my turn to seeze the day. I held the power

____

to defy gravity and niether teachers nor

____

students could stop me. My plan was to have

____

all teachers on the ceeling by recess. However,

____

Mr Wilson is bigger than most teachers because

____

of his hieght and wieght. I had to forfit Mr

____

Wilson to acheeve my goal. For a breef time,

____

I was unstoppable. I was **Super Pat!**

Score 2 points for each correct answer! SCORE /72  0-34  36-66  68-72

TERM 2

AC9E6LY04, AC9E6LY05, AC9HS6K06

Informative text – Explanation

Passing the Bill - No Homework for Sam

Hi Mr W,

I'm submitting my homework for you to mark. I think it's pretty good, and I hope you think so too. I presume good marks will be coming my way?

You asked us to show our understanding of what you have taught us about Parliament and the passing of laws or bills, so I used my family to form a parliament. Of course, it was based on the Westminster System with two different houses. This is how I organised my parliament:

The Lower House consists of my sister, Kim, and me as Members of Parliament or MPs. We occupy the lounge room because we have green chairs in this room. The Lower House in the national parliament in Canberra, called the House of Representatives, and our state parliaments, called the House of Assembly, have green as the main colour of the room. We are the house that introduces a bill, which is a proposal of a new law. I want to create a new law, so I will start with a proposal or bill. My proposal is: Children who live in the house at 22 Jenkins Street (our house) do not do homework. I, of course, had to speak to my proposal. The main reason for my proposal is that we spend six hours at school every school day and need downtime to relax and be with family members. Homework takes away that downtime. My sister and I voted on the bill, and it was passed. Unfortunately, it is not a law yet.

This bill was taken to the Upper House, which is symbolised by the colour red, so we used the kitchen. The kitchen has red table mats and Mum was cooking in there at the time. The Upper House is called the Senate in the national parliament in Canberra, and in our state, it is called the Legislative Council. The bill was hotly debated in the Upper House by the senators (Mum and Dad) who suggested amendments as well as a committee to be formed to gather further information. The amendments were: No homework on Friday nights and weekends, and the committee (Mum) rang up the school to talk to my teacher to find out the school's homework policy. The amended bill was taken back to the Lower House for rewriting and voting.

A law cannot be passed unless both houses agree. Reluctantly, I rewrote the bill. It now reads: Children who live in the house at 22 Jenkins Street (our house) do not do homework on Friday nights or weekends, or any other night if they are up to date with the work required. This was again submitted to the Upper House to be discussed.

I am happy to announce that the senators agreed, and the bill was then sent to the King's representative for signing. This is called the Royal Assent. When a bill is passed in the national capital, it goes to the Governor General for signing. When a bill is passed in the state parliament, it goes to the Governor. We asked Mr Simmons, who lives next door and was born in England, to sign it in place of the King. He was very impressed to be asked, and we even took pictures of the signing. We now hang the new law in a picture frame in the lounge room – I mean the Lower House. I did ask Mum if MPs get paid, but unfortunately, she said not in Jenkins Street Parliament. I feel I have a new bill to propose.

TARGETING ENGLISH HOMEWORK YEAR 6 © PASCAL PRESS ISBN 978 1 925726 63 3

Reading & Comprehension

Write the answer or shade the bubble next to the correct answer.

The answers to these questions are in the text.

1. **What does MP stand for?**

____

2. **What is the main colour of the Lower House of Parliament?**

____

3. **What is the Lower House called in the national parliament in Canberra?**

____

4. **What is a bill?**

____

5. **What colour symbolises the Upper House?**

____

6. **What is the Upper House called in the national parliament in Canberra?**

____

Think about these questions and search for the answers in the text.

7. **When a bill or new law is passed in the green or Lower House, it becomes law.**

◯ True ◯ False

8. **Outline the steps taken to pass the bill about homework by filling in the missing words. The first letter has been given to you.**

The bill was first introduced in the L__________ __________.

It was voted on and passed and then the bill was sent to the U__________ __________.

A c__________ was formed to find out more information.

The bill was changed. It was a__________.

The bill was rewritten and voted on in the L__________ __________.

The bill was again submitted to the U__________ __________ to discuss.

Once it was passed in both houses, the bill went to a representative of the K__________ to sign and make it law.

Use inferencing skills to answer this question. The answer is not in the text. Think about what you know and what the author says.

9. **At the end of the text, Sam says he has a new bill to propose. What would that bill be?**

____

Use your experience and opinions to answer this question. The answer is not in the text.

10. **If you had a parliament at your house, what bill would you like to pass? Why?**

Bill

____

Why?

____

Comprehension Reflections

Look at the top of the opposite page. This text is an I__________ text – E__________.

Write one thing you learned or found interesting:

____

Write one question you have or something you want to find more information about:

____

Rating

Score 2 points for each correct answer! SCORE /20 0-8 10-14 16-20

TERM 2

Grammar & Punctuation

AC9E6LA09

Apostrophes for possession

Apostrophe-itis has been infecting school students throughout Australia! Take care not to catch it! **Do not** add an apostrophe on a plural noun just because it ends in 's'. *Example:* I have two dog**s**. (no apostrophe on dogs)

However, if one dog owns or possesses something, then you add an apostrophe + 's'. *Example:* This is the dog**'s** bowl. (One dog owns the bowl.)

Work through these exercises to help cure yourself of the condition! Does someone own something? Then add an apostrophe.

1. The Kings signature is needed. (The King owns the signature.)
2. The Senates colour is red. (The Senate owns the colour.)
3. The bills could not be passed. (Plural noun. There is no possession.)
4. Sams bill was passed. (Sam owns the bill.)

Plural nouns ending in 's'

What if there are two or more dogs who own bowls? Now, dogs is a plural noun ending in 's'. If two or more dogs own bowls, then we add an apostrophe after the 's' to show possession. *Example:* The dogs' bowls need a wash. (two or more dogs)

Add an apostrophe where needed.

5. In the street, other families children wanted the same bill. (Family is plural and shows possession.)
6. The Senators love their red chairs. (Senators is plural but doesn't show possession.)
7. Many kings signatures have been added to many bills in the past.
8. All the teachers discussions were about Sam's bill.

Plural nouns not ending in 's'

Some nouns do not end in 's' when they are plural. *Examples:* child – children, woman – women

When these plural nouns show possession, add an apostrophe + 's'. *Example:* The children**'s** recess was cut short.

Add an apostrophe to the plural nouns to show possession.

9. The mens fashion was at the back of the shop.
10. The womens fashion was at the front of the shop.
11. The peoples vote was counted.
12. The sheeps wool was used to make clothes. (many sheep)

Singular nouns ending in 's'

When a singular noun ends in 's' like bus or class, add an apostrophe + 's' to show possession.

Examples: the bus**'s** timetable (one bus)

the class**'s** discussion (one class)

With names ending in 's', add an apostrophe + 's'. This is more common in Australia.
Example: Thomas**'s** job

Or you can just add an apostrophe at the end of the name. *Example:* Thomas' job

This is not as common in Australia.

Add an apostrophe after the names.

13. It was James idea to pass a bill about homework.
14. Lois family thought the bill was a great idea.

15 – 22 If you pass the next test, you are cured from Apostrophe-itis! Make 8 corrections to the following text to pass.

Sams bill caused a lot of discussion. Many families furniture was examined for green and red so that they too could have their own Upper and Lower Houses. All the teachers discussions in the staffroom revolved around the bill, and the schools homework policy was reviewed. Initially, it had been Jamess idea, but Sams family passed the bill. In the district, many schools discussions and many classes discussions were about homework.

Score 2 points for each correct answer! SCORE /44

TARGETING ENGLISH HOMEWORK YEAR 6 © PASCAL PRESS ISBN 978 1 925726 63 3

Phonic & Word Knowledge

AC9E6LY08, AC9E6LY09

Verbs to nouns using suffixes 'er' and 'or'

The suffixes 'er' and 'or' turn verbs into nouns. These nouns usually refer to people's roles or jobs, such as teacher and governor (which is from the text). How do we know whether to use 'er' or 'or'? Nouns with the suffix 'er' are more common. The table below outlines some generalisations.

① – ⑫ Write the **'er' and 'or' nouns in bold** in the correct section in the table.

watch – **watcher**, read – **reader**, visit – **visitor**, contract – **contractor**, travel – **traveller**, educate – **educator**, organise – **organiser**, credit – **creditor**, jump – **jumper**, generate – **generator**, write – **writer**, instruct – **instructor**

Generalisations for 'or'	Examples	Generalisations for 'er'	Examples
verbs with more than one syllable ending in 'it'	edit – editor	verbs ending in silent 'e'	bake – baker
verbs with more than one syllable ending in 'ate'	narrate – narrator	verbs ending with a single consonant (sometimes double last consonant)	bat – batter
Verbs ending in 'ct'	act – actor	verbs ending with two or more consonants	dust – duster

⑬ – ㉜ You have been invited to a Game Show to represent your class. You need to complete the tasks below by working out which **noun** from the completed table above is being described.

Guess the noun!

Clue 1 – a speaker

Clue 2 – a reporter

Clue 3 – a teller of tales

Clue 4 – a person who delivers commentary in a book or film

The word is ________________. If correct, collect **1 point.**

Clue 1 – a tourist

Clue 2 – a holidaymaker

Clue 3 – someone who is making a journey

The word is ________________. If correct, collect **3 points.**

Clue 1 – a person who works for themselves and is their own boss

Clue 2 – a person who has their own business and sells their services to others

The word is ________________. If correct, collect **6 points.**

Clue 1 – a person who observes

The word is ________________. If correct, collect **10 points.**

Score 2 points for each correct answer! SCORE /64

Imaginative text – Narrative

The Entry Fee

The sky frowned down upon the three friends as they started their walk home from school. The wind played with the ends of their jackets and tugged at their collars. It enticed them to run for shelter because rain was coming. All three looked upwards when the first few drops of rain became heavier and more consistent. They decided to run before the sky unleashed its anger. They had just walked out of the school gate, and the only shelter available was an abandoned movie theatre on the next corner. Its windows were locked, but for some reason its door was open, inviting them inside. Without hesitation, all three ran out of the storm and into the gloom of the theatre. A heavy darkness was within.

The main foyer was lined with dusty posters of the movies that had been shown over the years. Some posters looked more recent than others. A ticket booth blocked their way into the main part of the theatre, but the three friends ignored the barriers and signs, and proceeded to the auditorium which was the main seating area. As they passed through, a sign fluttered to the ground and settled in the dust. Large, printed words were barely visible on the faded yellow paper. It called for an admission to be paid upon entry.

The three friends ran along the aisles and played some games of chasey around the rows of threadbare seats that sat stiffly facing the front of the theatre. Eddies of dust stirred under their feet and quickly settled back onto the old, wooden floor that sloped upwards from the screen at the front of the theatre. That's where they noticed the first flicker of light. It started at the corner of the screen and soon spread to create a dull glow. The friends were mesmerised and soon sat quietly in a row of seats with their eyes glued to the screen. At first it was faint, but music was coming from the speakers as if a movie was about to start. The smell of popcorn drifted into the theatre, and the sound of hushed conversation from an audience emanated round the auditorium, creating a sense of excitement about what was about to come.

The light in the theatre dimmed, and the three friends were astonished to see their own images projected on the screen in front of them. It was a recording of their entry into the theatre and their passage past the ticket booth. A sign was seen fluttering from the booth, and the mystical camera caught its dance as it moved with the air currents to settle on the floor. The magnified sign with its faded words was clearly displayed on the large screen.

******

"I keep telling you, Ben. We need to fix this door properly or someone will wander in and hurt themselves," grumbled Alex as both men tugged at the old theatre door. "Luckily, it looks like no-one has been in here at all."

"Well," replied Ben, "we won't have to worry for long. The owners have finally decided to pull it down next week. This is valuable property, you know."

As the men pulled the door shut, a poster slowly peeled off the wall and fluttered to the floor. It showed three school children in the theatre with the movie heading, *PAID IN FULL*.

TARGETING ENGLISH HOMEWORK YEAR 6 © PASCAL PRESS ISBN 978 1 925726 63 3

Reading & Comprehension

Write the answer or shade the bubble next to the correct answer.

1. Why did the three friends enter the movie theatre?

2. What did the friends fail to notice as they entered the **auditorium**?

3. Once in the auditorium, what did the three friends see on the screen that **astonished** them?

4. What was going to happen to the theatre?

5. After reading the story, what clues did you see in the text that made you feel that something bad was about to happen? Write three clues.

6. What does **mesmerised** in the third paragraph mean? Use context clues to choose the best meaning.
   - ◯ Their memory was wiped.
   - ◯ They were fascinated.
   - ◯ They were drugged.
   - ◯ They were bored.

7. What do you think the author meant by **a heavy darkness was within**?

8. Why was the floor of the theatre sloped?

9. What happened to the three friends?

10. What happened to the three friends next? Write three sentences to finish the story using your own ideas.

TERM 2

Score 2 points for each correct answer! SCORE /20 0-8 10-14 16-20

Grammar & Punctuation

Figurative language

The wind played with the ends of their jackets … This is a personification from the text where the wind is given the human properties of playing with the jackets of the three friends.

Find three more examples of personification in the text and write them on the lines below.

1. ____________________
2. ____________________
3. ____________________

Punctuation in direct speech

The text, *The Free Entry*, includes a short conversation between Ben and Alex. Add the necessary punctuation to the following conversation.

4. Have you finished marking the maths tests yet asked Mr Wilson, the class teacher.
5. Are you kidding replied Ms Smith, the maths specialist I have four classes to mark.
6. Sorry replied Mr Wilson it's just that I'm worried about three of my students.
7. Oh I know who you mean she answered with a frown they have been missing for a week now, haven't they
8. Mr Wilson shifted uneasily on his feet and added it's just that the street has become so busy since they started knocking down that old theatre that I fear for all students' safety.
9. Ms Smith looked out the window and replied yes I know what you mean.

At that moment a crash was heard as one of the theatre walls was knocked in.

Persuasive techniques and devices

You are a resident on the street where the old theatre is located, but you have no idea about the students that are trapped inside. Write two points about the demolition of the old theatre.

On the one hand, give a reason why an old building should be saved in the neighbourhood.

On the other hand, give a reason why the building should be demolished.

10. On the one hand, ____________________.
11. On the other hand, ____________________.

Emotive language and personal pronouns

You are now one of the students trapped in the theatre. How would you plead your case and persuade the powers that have you trapped to let you go? Use emotive language and personal pronouns, such as you, we and I in your argument.

12. Write at least two reasons why you should be freed. Will you plead for your friends as well or just yourself?

____

Score 2 points for each correct answer! SCORE /24

TARGETING ENGLISH HOMEWORK YEAR 6 © PASCAL PRESS ISBN 978 1 925726 63 3

Phonic & Word Knowledge

Eponyms

When a thing or place is named after somebody, it is called an eponym.

Write a sentence to explain who each eponym is named after. You may need to do some research.

1. caesar salad ____________________
2. diesel ____________________
3. Fahrenheit ____________________
4. Disneyland ____________________
5. Barbie™ ____________________

Spelling generalisations with 'ie'

In Unit 15, generalisations of the 'ie' and 'ei' spelling pattern were outlined.

Circle the correct spelling of the missing 'ie' or 'ei' word in each sentence.

6. The three students argued over who was a better _____. **friend / freind**
7. If one gave up the others for freedom, would that _____ on their mind? **wiegh / weigh**
8. The police were still searching for them in the _____ that they were still in the _____. **beleif / belief** **nieghbourhood / neighbourhood**
9. Police wondered why their parents had not _____ any ransom notes. **received / recieved**
10. The police did not have _____ evidence to start looking elsewhere. **sufficeint / sufficient** (Be careful! Not all words follow the generalisations.)
11. One of the parents had a _____ dream about movies and movie posters. **weird / wierd**
12. They felt it was _____ that the dream meant something. **inconcievable / inconceivable**
13. Meanwhile, the three students felt as if a _____ had been put in front of their eyes. **veil / viel**
14. They heard the crash as the _____ of the wall opposite them fell to the ground. **weight / wieght**
15. They had to _____ they could escape somehow. **believe / beleive**

Unpredictable digraphs

Unpredictable digraphs include the different ways to spell the 'or' sound. This sound can be spelt using 'aw', 'au', 'al'.

Unscramble the words with unpredictable digraphs you used in Unit 12.

16. eeoamsw (aw) – Starts with aw__________
17. ward (aw) – Starts with d__________
18. scuuitsoa (au) – Starts with ca__________
19. ttghleeaor (al) – Starts with al__________
20. uunmta (au) – Starts with au__________

Score 2 points for each correct answer! SCORE /40

TARGETING ENGLISH HOMEWORK YEAR 6 © PASCAL PRESS ISBN 978 1 925726 63 3

AC9E6LY04, AC9E6LY05, AC9E6LE01

Imaginative text – Narrative

The Real Hero

The TV blared with the sound of explosions while superpowered heroes flitted across the screen. Chris and Jess watched, transfixed, as the heroes saved humanity from evil once again. Neither one of them noticed the smoke, coiling like a ghostly snake under the door and climbing swiftly and lightly up the wall. It slid silently along the ceiling, becoming thicker until a layer of smoke filled the room.

Jess stiffened as she smelt the smoke and saw it enveloping the room. Grabbing Chris by the hand, Jess darted for the door, but the smoke had become so thick it choked their lungs and stung their eyes. They remembered the family's fire plan and fell to the floor where the smoke was not as thick. They felt along the wall for the door. Fear gripped them as they fought the panic that bubbled underneath and threatened to paralyse them.

Suddenly, a window smashed and hands grabbed and guided both children out of the house before the flames took hold. Jess gasped for air as she lay on the lawn looking into the face of her hero. The heroes that Chris and Jess had been watching a few moments ago had no resemblance to the hero sitting on the lawn with them. There was no cape, no superpowers or rippling muscles, just a concerned look on his face, a face that was very familiar to both children.

"Mr Quibb," Jess stammered, "did you just save us?"

Mr Quibb gave a little nod of his bald head and quicky moved aside when the children's parents and the attending ambulance officers arrived. Mr Quibb was the family's neighbour, a person who shuffled more than walked and who rarely was seen outside of his house. He was different to the other neighbours and was the butt of many jokes and pranks from the neighbourhood children, Chris and Jess included. However, he had risked his own life to save them, a fact that Chris and Jess felt very keenly.

The news vans arrived quickly on the scene and started filming the fire-damaged house. As Jess was loaded into the back of an ambulance to be taken to the hospital, she noticed a reporter standing nearby, ready to make a live report to the news desk.

"Wait!" cried Jess. "I want to say something."

The reporter moved towards her and the camera operator swung the camera towards them.

"I want to say thank you to a local hero who saved us," Jess declared into the microphone.

"I want to say thank you to Mr Quibb. He doesn't look like a hero, and he has no superpowers, but he is a hero to Chris and me. I just never realised I lived next door to one."

As the reporter left, Jess caught sight of Mr Quibb who, with a little smile, went back to his house. Jess thought to herself that heroes could be anyone who makes a difference to others through their words or actions, just like Mr Quibb.

TARGETING ENGLISH HOMEWORK YEAR 6 © PASCAL PRESS ISBN 978 1 925726 63 3

Reading & Comprehension

UNIT 17

Write your answers on the lines provided.

The answers to these questions are in the text.

① Reread the last two sentences of paragraph one.
The author **compares** the smoke to ______________________.

② What was the family's **fire plan**?

③ Who smashed the window? ______________________

④ How did Mr Quibb look different to the heroes on TV?

Think about this question and search for the answer in the text.

⑤ Why was Mr Quibb the butt of many jokes and pranks from the neighbourhood children?

Use inferencing skills to answer these questions. The answers are not in the text. Think about what you know and what the author says.

⑥ After being rescued, why did Jess think that heroes could be anyone?

⑦ Why do you think Jess wanted to talk to the reporter about Mr Quibb?

⑧ How do you think Jess will treat Mr Quibb after the rescue?

Use your experience and opinions to answer these questions. The answers are not in the text.

If you take Jess's definition of a hero, **'anyone who makes a difference to others through their words or actions,'** who would you consider a hero in your life? Explain your thinking in two sentences.

⑨ Who? ______________________

⑩ Why? ______________________

TERM 3

Comprehension Reflections

Look at the top of the opposite page. This text is an I__________ text – N__________.

Write one thing you learned or found interesting:

Write one question you have or something you want to find more information about:

Rating   

Score 2 points for each correct answer!

SCORE 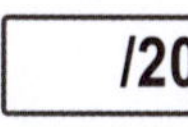   

Grammar & Punctuation

AC9E6LA05

Complex sentences – Conjunctions

The text contains this complex sentence: The TV blared with the sound of explosions while superpowered heroes flitted across the screen. The main or independent clause is at the beginning and the subordinating conjunction joins it to the subordinate or dependent clause. Dependent clauses add more detail in complex sentences.

The sentence can be rewritten as: While superpowered heroes flitted across the screen, the TV blared with the sound of explosions. (notice the use of a comma)

Find two more complex sentences in the first two paragraphs and write them on the lines below. Circle the subordinating conjunction and underline the independent clause.

1. ______________________________

2. ______________________________

Rewrite the sentences by changing the positions of the clauses. Circle the subordinating conjunction and underline the independent clause.

3. ______________________________

4. ______________________________

Different types of subordinating conjunctions

There are different types of subordinating conjunctions. The most common ones are shown in the following table:

Time-related	Cause and effect	Place and location
connect an action or any event to a point in time	show the relationship where one clause or phrase is the **cause** of the other	introduce clauses related to a specific location or place
Examples: after, once, while, during, when, before	Examples: because, since, as, due to, consequently, therefore	Examples: where, wherever, everywhere, anywhere

Join the two sentences below with a cause-and-effect subordinating conjunction. It can go at the beginning or middle of the sentence. You may need to leave out words or add words so that your sentence makes sense.

5. Mr Quibb was not considered a hero. Mr Quibb did not look like a superhero.

____

Join these two sentences with a time-related subordinating conjunction.

6. Mr Quibb saved the two children from the fire. He was considered a hero.

____

Underline the subordinating conjunction in each sentence and write what type of subordinating conjunction it is.

7. Wherever heroic deeds are done, heroes are to be found. ______________

8. Because Mr Quibb acted quickly, the children are now safe. ______________

9. The children were taken to hospital after Mr Quibb pulled them out of the burning house. ______________

10. Since the family had a fire plan, the two children knew what to do in the fire. ______________

Score 2 points for each correct answer! SCORE /20   

TERM 3

TARGETING ENGLISH HOMEWORK YEAR 6 © PASCAL PRESS ISBN 978 1 925726 63 3

Phonic & Word Knowledge

AC9E6LY09

Silent letters in words

Silent letters are very common in English words. They can help differentiate homophones (words that sound the same but have different spellings). *Examples:* be, be**e**

Some silent letters give information about the origin of a word. Many words that we have borrowed from French have silent letters. *Examples:* de**b**t, forei**g**n

This sentence from the text has words with silent letters. *Example:* … the smoke, coiling like a g**h**ostly snake under the door and clim**b**ing swiftly and lightly up the wall.

① – ⑱ Almost every letter in the alphabet is silent in at least one word. In the white boxes, write one new word that has not already been mentioned. The yellow boxes have already been done for you.

a	b	c	d	e
f – not ever silent	g	h	i	j
k	l	m – only words like mnemonic	n	o
p	q – only word is lacquer	r – February	s	t
u	v – not ever silent	w	x – French-borrowed words such as faux	y
z – French-borrowed words such as rendezvous				

⑲ Which letters are not ever silent in English?

____

⑳ Circle the word that has a silent 'a'. (can't be used in the table) magic / avian / basically

㉑ Circle which language's loan words have a silent 'z'. French / Italian / German

㉒ What is the silent letter in bustle, hustle and rustle? (can't be used in the table)

____

Mnemonic strategies

A mnemonic (pronounced neh-mon-ik) strategy or technique can help you to remember information. *Example:* To remember how to spell friend, you can say, I **fri** the **end** of my **friend**.

Use the French word rendezvous.

㉓ Write its meaning. ______________________

____

____

㉔ How would you remember to spell 'rendezvous'? Use the example of friend.

____

____

Chunking

Chunking is also a strategy that can help you to remember information more easily. If you needed to learn the number 47895328463, you could chunk it into smaller pieces. *Example:* 4789 532 8463

㉕ **Learn the number above in its chunked form.**

Come back after 5 minutes, cover the page and write what you remember.

____

Score 2 points for each correct answer! SCORE /50   

TERM 3

Reading & Comprehension

AC9E6LY04, AC9E6LY05, AC9E6LA02

Informative text – Report

Reporting and Reviewing

When reading and writing, it is important to know the difference between subjective and objective language. Subjective language tends to reflect a person's opinions and emotions. It can also be biased, which means it can favour one side over another. Objective language tends to be based more on fact, observation and logical argument. Neither is better than the other, but it is important to know where and how they can be used.

What would it look like if an incident was reported subjectively and then objectively?

Eyewitness report:

I work in a local corner shop, and we sell food and drinks to the local customers. Baked beans are our specialty. On this particular day, a tall, skinny school kid wearing a hoodie came into the shop. I didn't see their face, but I'm sure they had sneaky-looking eyes. Two other people were in the shop, but they were adults. All of a sudden, my wonderful display of baked beans cans tipped over, and some of the cans spilled their contents all over the floor. I had spent a long time stacking all those cans of beans. It was the kid who did this, a vandal. Anyway, everyone left the shop as soon as the cans fell.

Police report:

On Tuesday 6 August, three people were in Betty's Baked Beans store when an incident occured involving 30 cans of baked beans that fell to the ground. Two adults and a youth were in the shop at the time. There was no camera or direct line of view for the witness to identify how the stack of baked beans came to fall to the floor. After the cans fell, all three people left the store. The matter is under further investigation.

Which is more useful when making an incident report, subjective or objective language?

What would it look like if a film review was written subjectively and objectively?

The film is riveting from start to finish. You will not be bored in this action-packed film. The special effects are worth seeing on the big screen, and, although rated G, it has scenes where you are on the edge of your seat. It is filmed in Australia and is about a group of primary school students who find a time portal that can take them to events throughout history. There are some very humorous scenes and enough action to keep you entertained. It's certainly worth a visit to the theatre to watch, especially for primary-aged children.

The film is 90 minutes long and has a cast of more than 60 actors. It was filmed in Australia at various locations and was released two months ago. It cost $15 million to make and has made that amount in takings over the first week of its release. It is showing in theatres across Australia. It deals with the theme of time travel.

Which is more useful when writing a film or book review, subjective or objective language?

Understanding subjective and objective language and their differences can help when you are reading and writing. It can also help you to make good judgements about the information you hear and read to work out what is fact and what is opinion.

TARGETING ENGLISH HOMEWORK YEAR 6 © PASCAL PRESS ISBN 978 1 925726 63 3

Reading & Comprehension

Write the answer or shade the bubble next to the correct answer.

The answers to these questions are in the text.

1. What is **subjective** language?

____

____

2. What is **objective** language?

____

____

3. Which one is better than the other?

◯ subjective language
◯ objective language
◯ Neither is better than the other.

Think about these questions and search for the answers in the text.

4. When the shop owner says, **"I'm sure they had sneaky-looking eyes,"** is this subjective or objective language?

____

5. Which form of language do you think is more useful when making a police report?

◯ subjective language
◯ objective language

Why? ______________________________

____

____

____

6. Which form of language do you think is more useful when writing a film or book review?

◯ subjective language
◯ objective language

Why? ______________________________

____

____

____

Use inferencing skills to answer these questions. The answers are not in the text. Think about what you know and what the author says.

7. The shop owner was **biased**. Who **were** they biased against and **why** do you think that may be the case?

____

____

8. What other occasions would you need to use **objective language** rather than subjective language? Name two occasions.

____

____

Use your experience and opinions to answer these questions. The answers are not in the text.

Write a very brief report on a movie you have watched. Write a brief sentence to explain the **main idea** of the movie and then write two sentences containing **subjective language on your opinion** of the movie and **who you recommend it to.**

9. Main idea ______________________________

____

____

10. Opinion ______________________________

____

____

____

____

Comprehension Reflections

Look at the top of the opposite page. This text is an I__________ text – R__________.

Write one thing you learned or found interesting:

____

Write one question you have or something you want to find more information about:

____

____

Rating   

Score 2 points for each correct answer! SCORE /20   

TERM 3

Present and past tenses

When writing reports and narratives, we can use present or past tenses. There are four present and four past tenses to choose from.

Past tense is often used when writing a report like a police report or when writing a story or narrative. *Example:* ... all three people **left** the store. (simple past tense)

Present tense is often used when writing an information report such as about an animal.

The most commonly used tenses are simple past and present perfect.

Simple Present Tense Routine actions – do every day verb in the base form I **go** to school every day. I **play** cricket.	Simple Past Tense Actions completed in the past verb + ed / verb in the past tense Nathan **met** me at the park. I **talked** to him.
Present Continuous Tense (Progressive) Activities happening now auxiliary verb (am/is/are) + main verb+ing Sam **is watching** a movie.	Past Continuous Tense (Progressive) auxiliary verb (was/were) + main verb+ing I **was talking** to my teacher.
Present Perfect Tense Action started in the past and continues into the present auxiliary verb (have/has) + past participle of the verb Chris **has left** the hall. I **have reached** home.	Past Perfect Tense auxiliary verb (had) + past participle of the verb Alex **had eaten** his dinner before we reached the venue.
Present Perfect Continuous Tense have/has + been + verb+ing They **have been waiting** for you. Archana **has been checking** her phone.	Past Perfect Continuous Tense had + been + verb+ing Toby **had been practising** the guitar when the teacher called for him.

Narratives are usually written in past tense. Switch between the verb tenses in bold. Use the table and change the past tense to the corresponding present tense. The first one has been done for you. You may need to leave out or change some words in the sentences so that they make sense.

Example: Sally **entered** the shop and **was wearing** a hoodie.

Sally **enters** the shop and **is wearing** a hoodie.

1. Sally **had brought** money to buy a birthday present for her brother.

____

2. However, it **had been raining** that day, so Sally **had worn** the hoodie to stay dry.

____

3. She **slid** on the shop floor due to the puddle and **crashed** into the baked beans display.

____

4. She **froze**, horrified at what she **had done**. She **fled** the scene in embarrassment.

____

Sally has written an information report about beans. Information reports are usually written in present tense. Help Sally change the past tense verbs in the following sentences to the corresponding present tense so that they make more sense.

5. Baked beans **were** a dish that **contained** white common beans.

____

6. According to scientists, baked beans **provided** fibre that **supported** our health.

____

7. However, baked beans **proved** to be a dish that **had** high levels of sugar and salt.

____

Score 2 points for each correct answer! SCORE /14 0-4 6-10 12-14

TERM 3

TARGETING ENGLISH HOMEWORK YEAR 6 © PASCAL PRESS ISBN 978 1 925726 63 3

Phonic & Word Knowledge

AC9E6LY09

Alternations

Alternations are the sound changes that occur in words that are related to spelling and meaning.
Example: The silent consonant 'c' in **muscle** is sounded when a suffix is added to form the word **muscular**.
Unit 2 looked at some of these words. Let's now expand your list.

Sort the list words under the correct headings in the table below. Write which silent letter is now sounded.

assignation, debit, crumble, assign, condemnation, solemn, debt, columnist, solemnity, condemn, column, crumb

	Original word	Word with suffix added	Silent consonant now sounded
	Example: solemn	solemnity (soh-lem-nuh-tee)	n
①			
②			
③			
④			
⑤			

⑥ **Haste is a tricky word!**

Which consonant is silent when a suffix is added to form hasten?________________

Some of the words from the table have been used in the text below. Unscramble the words and write them on the lines provided.

The police officer had an ⑦ (snniiaagtso) ______________ with the shop owner to investigate the baked beans incident. The shop owner had a very ⑧ (lemons) ______________ face as she was in ⑨ (tbde) ______________ to the baked beans factory and the cans were on loan. The police officer did not want the newspaper ⑩ (usolimtnc) ______________, who had come to report on the story, to get in the way. The vandalism had already drawn ⑪ (nnnooieadmct) ______________ from the baked beans factory's owner. The officer proceeded with the investigation, looking for any ⑫ (mbcur) ___________of evidence.

Decide which silent consonants are missing from the 20 words in the word list. Write the consonants in the blanks. Then find and circle each word in the word search puzzle.
Words are hidden vertically, horizontally and diagonally.

⑬ autum__ ⑳ cas__le ㉗ de__t
⑭ __onest ㉑ i__land ㉘ __nee
⑮ __nife ㉒ mus__le ㉙ lis__en
⑯ of__en ㉓ solem__ ㉚ whis__le
⑰ __rite ㉔ __rong ㉛ desi__n
⑱ assi__n ㉕ ta__k ㉜ hast__
⑲ g__at ㉖ Chris__mas

l	h	r	a	a	u	d	e	b	t	h	m	d	g	s	s	o	w
h	q	i	t	u	c	a	s	t	l	e	o	x	j	w	h	o	h
h	o	e	s	a	t	q	a	w	y	a	s	s	i	g	n	b	i
n	g	n	e	l	l	u	u	s	f	i	q	m	a	e	w	s	s
z	k	o	e	m	a	k	m	c	h	r	i	s	t	m	a	s	t
a	x	n	f	s	f	n	v	n	l	h	a	s	t	e	g	l	l
r	a	d	i	t	t	v	d	k	m	u	s	c	l	e	w	s	e
r	u	k	z	f	e	k	n	e	e	l	w	x	l	l	r	y	o
z	m	g	a	z	e	n	x	i	l	i	s	t	e	n	i	f	l
v	b	s	o	l	e	m	n	c	n	z	o	k	v	q	t	h	e
d	e	z	e	s	c	v	u	g	n	a	t	p	q	h	e	q	q
w	w	r	o	n	g	v	p	d	d	e	s	i	g	n	j	e	u

Score 2 points for each correct answer!

SCORE /64   

TARGETING ENGLISH HOMEWORK YEAR 6 © PASCAL PRESS ISBN 978 1 925726 63 3

AC9E6LY04, AC9E6LY05, AC9E6LE01, AC9E6LE04

Imaginative text – Poetry

Our Hero

Anna was playing in the sun with her brother Adam when she sensed that they were not alone. Carefully, so as not to frighten him, Anna signalled to her brother to come to her side. That way, she could grab him if they needed to make a run for it. Their parents were out working, and the two young ones had decided to play outside. However, they had strayed far from home into an area they were unfamiliar with.

A great shadow fell onto their faces as danger towered over them. Large, unblinking eyes stared down at them, and Anna knew she had to think quickly.

While pushing her brother behind her, she said in the most confident tone she could muster, "Please, sir, if you are hungry, we can get you some food. Only please do not harm us!"

With a dangerous smile, the stranger replied, "Food, you say? I'll tell you what you can do. Lead me to your home and I will let you go."

Home was not just home to her immediate family, it was home to a large extended family of aunts, uncles and many cousins. Home was one place that she could not lead him to.

Anna pretended to agree and led the stranger in the opposite direction from home, hoping to find a place where they could dash away to safety. The stranger was fast, faster than they would be, but they had their size as an advantage. They were small and nimble.

While they scurried ahead, the stranger bent from side to side as his legs pushed his ample body forward, his gaze never wavering from the two young ones in front of him. In desperation, Anna decided to lead him towards a narrow opening between two rocks. As soon as Adam was through, she planted two legs into the rocky soil and, with her other four legs, she gathered up a large rock and threw it with all her might into the predator's eye. He screamed and lashed his tail while Adam and Anna ran to safety.

Due to her bravery, the family created a ballad that is recited to all the young ones to show that heroes come in all shapes and sizes.

A ballad is a type of poem that tells a story. Each verse has four lines, and the poem can have as many verses as necessary to tell the story. A ballad will often have a refrain. This is a line that keeps recurring throughout the poem. This ballad has an ABCB rhyme scheme. This means the 2nd and 4th lines rhyme. Can you work out the number of syllables in each line?

Old Lizard wanted ants for lunch,
He chirped and lips did smack
For lizards chirp when hunger strikes,
But ants are aware and act.

Old Lizard beaten by an ant,
Not fair, he then would rant,
Two against one, I had no chance,
'Cos ants are aware and act.

Anna did beat him at his game,
A rock thrown, that's a fact,
It blinded Old Lizard's left eye,
'Cos ants are aware and act.

Anna gives a lesson to all,
Courage, she did not lack,
Heroes need not be big and tall,
'Cos ants are aware and act.

TERM 3

TARGETING ENGLISH HOMEWORK YEAR 6 © PASCAL PRESS ISBN 978 1 925726 63 3

Reading & Comprehension

Write your answers on the lines provided.

The answers to these questions are in the text.

1. What creatures are Adam and Anna? ______

2. What does a ballad do? ______

3. What is a refrain? ______

4. What is the **refrain** in this ballad? ______

Think about these questions and search for the answers in the text.

5. How many legs does Anna have? Why does she have this number of legs? ______

6. Why is the ballad **recited** to all the young ones? ______

Use inferencing skills to answer these questions. The answers are not in the text. Think about what you know and what the author says.

7. Why does the author write that Old Lizard has a dangerous smile? ______

8. Why does Old Lizard want Adam and Anna to lead him to their home? ______

9. Why would being **small and nimble** be an advantage for the young ones? ______

10. Why is Anna able to throw a large rock into Old Lizard's eye? ______

Use your experience and opinions to answer this question. The answer is not in the text.

11. Using the rhyming scheme ABCB, write one verse of a ballad. Count the number of syllables in each line of the ballad in the text. Remember what a ballad is about. ______

Comprehension Reflections

Look at the top of the opposite page. This text is an I__________ text – P__________.

Write one thing you learned or found interesting: ______

Write one question you have or something you want to find more information about: ______

Rating

Score 2 points for each correct answer! SCORE /22 0-8 10-16 18-22

TERM 3

Grammar & Punctuation

AC9E6LA06

Noun-verb agreement – Present simple tense

The text explains that: A **ballad tells** a story. 'Ballad' is a singular noun followed by the singular verb 'tells'. To make this sentence with a plural subject and plural verb, it would read: **Ballads tell** a story.

To write a correct sentence in present simple tense, you need to be aware of noun–verb agreement, which was introduced in Unit 5.

Subject	Verb in Present Simple Tense
He, She, It and singular nouns	plays (singular) add 's' or 'es'
You, We, They and plural nouns	play (plural) no 's'

Practise singular and plural subjects. Circle the correct present simple verb to go with the subject in these sentences.

1. Anna is a hero. She **shows / show** the ability to think on her feet.
2. Old Lizard **does / do** not want to mess with her again.
3. The ant **works / work** all day to collect food.
4. They **believes / believe** Anna deserves the ballad written for her.

Plural subjects – Present simple tense

When two nouns that are joined by 'and' are the subject of a sentence, they are considered to be a plural subject.

Examples: Anna **and** Adam **are** lucky to be alive. (Use 'are' not 'is'.)

The ant **and** lizard **enjoy** eating their food. (There is no 's' or 'es' on the verb.)

Practise singular and plural subjects. Circle the correct present simple verb to go with the subject in these sentences.

5. Adam and Anna **gathers / gather** food with the adults during the day.
6. Spiders and lizards **patrols / patrol** the area looking for ants to eat.
7. Old Lizard and Anna **is / are** wary of each other.
8. They **avoids / avoid** each other where possible.
9. Adam **avoids / avoid** fighting with Anna.

Singular pronouns

Singular (indefinite) pronouns, such as anybody, anyone, each, every, everyone, no-one, someone, something take on a singular verb.

Example: Everybody **supports** the teacher.

Circle the correct verb to go with the subject in these sentences.

10. No-one **is / are** ready to fight the lizards.
11. Usually someone **takes / take** charge of the anti-lizard training.

Plural pronouns

Plural (indefinite) pronouns such as many, several and few take the plural form of the verb. *Example:* Both **have** finished their work.

Circle the correct verb to go with the subject in these sentences.

12. Both **has / have** shown bravery.
13. Several **is / are** looking to prove their bravery.
14. Many **trains / train** regularly at the ant gym.

Use your imagination to complete sentences about the exercises the ants do at the ant gym. Circle the correct verb in the sentence.

15. Everyone **feels / feel** safer now that ______________________.
16. No-one **supplies / supply** their own ______________________.
17. Many **uses / use** the gym to ______________________.
18. Several **trains / train** with ______________________.

Score 2 points for each correct answer! SCORE /36

TERM 3

TARGETING ENGLISH HOMEWORK YEAR 6 © PASCAL PRESS ISBN 978 1 925726 63 3

Phonic & Word Knowledge

AC9E6LY09

Ants have a preference for turning left when exploring new spaces. However, they seem to use both sides of their mandible, which is on the outside of their face, for cutting and carrying. So it seems that ants are ambidextrous – able to use their left and right sides equally well. However, a vast majority of humans favour their right hand, and fewer than one person in 100 is ambidextrous.

Affix – 'ambi'

Ambi is a Latin prefix that means 'both or twofold'. Dexterous means 'skilful in hand and body'. Ambidextrous means able to use the right and left hands equally well.

Match the 'ambi' words with their meanings by joining them with lines. You may need a dictionary to help you.

1	ambidextrous	uncertain if you like something or what you should do about something
2	ambiguous	able to use the right and left hands equally well
3	ambience	a strong desire to achieve something
4	ambivalent	the atmosphere or mood of a place
5	ambition	not clear or decided

6 **Are you ambidextrous? Try out the alphabet test.**

Write the alphabet as one word with your left hand and then again with your right hand. Measure the time it takes for each hand. If the time is very similar for both hands and your writing looks equally good, the chances are that you are ambidextrous.

Left hand ______________________

____

____

____

Right hand ______________________

____

____

____

Your results

Time for left hand ______________

Time for right hand ______________

Neatness score for left hand /10

Neatness score for right hand /10

Do you consider yourself ambidextrous?

____

Explain why in one sentence.

____

____

Affix – 'astro'

Astro is a Greek word that means 'pertaining to space'. It is not a whole word and needs to be added onto. Therefore, it acts as a root word and it can be a prefix as well.

Examples of 'astro' words: astronomy, astrology, astronaut, astrobiology, astrophysics, astrodome

Find the mystery word!
Replace the third letter of each word below with a new letter to create a different word. When read vertically, the new letters will reveal the mystery word, which is in the list above.
One letter has already been done for you.

	Word	New word
7	nest	ne_t
8	part	pa_t
9	side	si_e
10	tile	ti_e
11	step	st_p
12	lime	li_e
13	boot	bo_t
14	spin	sp_n
15	sins	sits

16 The mystery word is ______________.

Score 2 points for each correct answer! SCORE /32  0-14  16-26  28-32 

TERM 3

Imaginative text – Narrative

Protesters and Grandma

Mum says I have to be more understanding and thoughtful, but I find it very difficult. Grandma has come to live with us because she is not able to cope at home on her own. She has what Mum calls, 'the beginning of dementia'. All I know is that Grandma gets in my way and asks me the same questions after I have just told her the answers. I must make sure that she doesn't turn the stove on and walk away from it or leave the fridge door wide open. Mum says to talk to her to find out more about her, but she's old, and I don't think there's anything I want to know from Grandma.

One day, it became so difficult that I escaped to the old shed in the back garden. A lot of the space in there was occupied by Grandma's belongings from her home, and Mum had asked me if I could at least tidy it up for her. As I reluctantly moved boxes into an orderly stack, an old shoe box fell over and tipped its contents over the floor. There, staring up at me from the floor, were old newspaper clippings about protest marches and a picture of a young woman smiling at the camera, holding a sign or placard. I looked closely at the picture because the face was familiar. Then it dawned on me. It was Grandma. I could never picture Grandma as young, but there she was. She was staring up at me from the floor, a young and vibrant woman with short hair and, I must admit, a short skirt. She was holding up a sign saying, 'Equal pay for equal work'. I had to find out more, so I went to ask Mum.

It seems that Grandma was involved in protest rallies in the 1970s. According to Mum, women had campaigned from the early 1900s to be paid the same as men for the same work. Men were paid more because they were men. It was not until 1972 that women were granted equal pay with men. I thought women had always had the same rights as men, but Mum said they hadn't. They had to protest to get them.

I took the clippings and photo to Grandma, and her face lit up. She started talking about how she felt when she was doing the same work as a male colleague and getting less pay because she was a woman. She told me about the rallies or protest marches and how excited they all were when the policy changed. She said it was also a landmark decision when the government in 1984 passed the Sex Discrimination Act. It seems this act was passed to protect people from unfair treatment.

Grandma then told me about her grandmother who was a suffragette before Federation in 1901. A suffragette, Grandma told me, is a woman seeking the right to vote through organised protests. Wow, even back then women in my family were involved in protests and the fight for equality. The suffragette movement fought for the right of women to vote, and they succeeded in Australia in 1902. It seems that the newly formed Federal Government of Australia passed an act which granted most men and women the right to vote in, and to stand for, federal elections. Australia was one of the first countries to do so.

It's not so bad having Grandma in our house. In fact, I have grown to like it. We have great conversations, and if I have to answer the same questions, I don't mind.

TARGETING ENGLISH HOMEWORK YEAR 6 © PASCAL PRESS ISBN 978 1 925726 63 3

Reading & Comprehension

Write the answer or shade the bubble next to the correct answer.

The answers to these questions are in the text.

1. **Why did the author's grandmother come to live with them?**

   ____

   ____

2. **What is a suffragette?**

   ____

   ____

3. **Women have always had equal pay with men.**

   ◯ True ◯ False

Think about these questions and search for the answers in the text.

4. **Complete this timeline of Australia's history.**

   Early 1900s ____

   ____

   1901 ____

   ____

   1902 ____

   ____

   1972 ____

   ____

   1984 ____

   ____

5. **How has the author's opinion of Grandma changed and why?**

   How changed? ____

   ____

   Why? ____

   ____

Use inferencing skills to answer these questions. The answers are not in the text. Think about what you know and what the author says.

6. **I looked closely at the picture because the face was familiar. Then it dawned on me. It was Grandma.**

   Using context clues, what does the word dawned mean?

   ◯ registered ◯ fell
   ◯ ended ◯ The sun rose.

7. **Why did Grandma's face light up after reading the clippings?**

   ____

   ____

8. **It is not stated in the text, but what gender (male/female) do you think the author is?**

   ◯ male ◯ female

   Why do you think that? ____

   ____

Use your experience and opinions to answer these questions. The answers are not in the text.

9. **When have you felt so strongly about something that you wanted people to hear your opinion about it?**

   ____

   ____

10. **Why did you feel this way?** ____

    ____

    ____

    ____

Comprehension Reflections

Look at the top of the opposite page. This text is an I__________ text – N__________.

Write one thing you learned or found interesting:

____

Write one question you have or something you want to find more information about:

____

____

Rating

Score 2 points for each correct answer! SCORE /20 0-8 10-14 16-20

TERM 3

Grammar & Punctuation

AC9E6LA09

Apostrophes

It seems that Grandma was involved in protest rallies in the 1970s. Many students are tempted to put an apostrophe before the 's' in 1970s, but this is not necessary. So, when do we use apostrophes?

Apostrophes for possession

Unit 16 looked at using apostrophes for possession. Now, let's look a bit deeper. What if two people possess or own the same item? For example, if Kate and George own a house together, the sentence would be Kate and George**'s** house is near the city. In this case, only add apostrophe + 's' to the second name.

If Kate and George each owns a house, the sentence would be Kate**'s** and George**'s** houses are near the city. In this case, add apostrophe + 's' to both names.

Never use an apostrophe with possessive pronouns: his, hers, its, theirs, ours, yours, whose. They already show possession. It's means 'it is', which is a contraction.

Rewrite the sentences below and add apostrophe + 's' to the nouns where needed.

1. Kate and George mum was in hospital.

____

____

2. Kate and George offices are in different buildings.

____

____

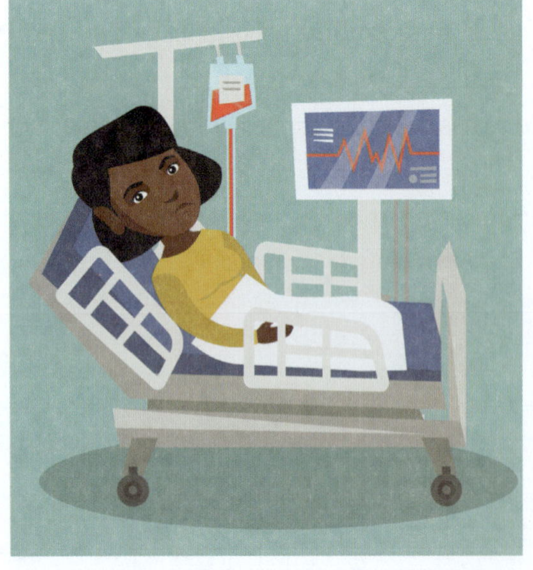

Apostrophes for omissions

In contractions, one or more letters (or numbers) have been omitted. An apostrophe shows where the missing letters or numbers would have been.

Examples:

don't = do not   the '70s = the 1970s

Circle the correct word/s to complete each sentence.

3. **Your / You're** right! Chocolate is better than vanilla.

4. **Its / It's** not very often that **there / they're / their** home this early.

5 – 16 Add any apostrophes for possession, missing 's' and apostrophes for contractions/ omissions where needed. Can you find 12?

Grandma pictures from the 70s were starting to fade. I offered to frame them and hang some in Mum and Grandma bedrooms. However, the pictures werent large enough to be seen properly. It wasnt ideal. I realised that it was important to enlarge the pictures as Grandma eyesight was not the best. I borrowed Kate and George printer to make larger prints. I value Mum and Grandma opinions about the presentation of the pictures. I would award myself several A, but that just my opinion.

Score 2 points for each correct answer!

TARGETING ENGLISH HOMEWORK YEAR 6 © PASCAL PRESS ISBN 978 1 925726 63 3

AC9E6LY09

French loan words

Many English words have come from different languages. These are called loan words. In the text, there are two loan words from the French language. The word suffrage comes from the Latin word 'suffragium', meaning 'the right to vote' but the 'ette' suffix comes from French. The other French word is colleague (ko-leeg). It means 'a person you work with within your profession or business'.

Circle the 17 French loan words in the text below. You may need to use a dictionary.

① – ⑰ In the modern world, sport has become very important. Some sports are considered an art form such as ballet. However, it can cost a lot of money to join a sports team, and it can require a lot of energy. Many children are opting out of sport and turning to restaurants and cafes to learn how to cook. Simple omelette or soup recipes are easy to follow and could be added to any menu. Making a soufflé or rich cake, called a gateau, would be a much more difficult task and require a magnificent occasion like a party on the terrace. So many children are saying bon voyage to their sporting clubs and picking up kitchen utensils instead.

English loan words to French

The English language has also influenced the French language. Due to the rise in technology and internet, there are many English words that the French have adopted.

Examples: sandwich, burger, steak, cookie, parking, shopping, cool, internet, weekend, T-shirt, smartphone, trailer (movies), spoiler, cliffhanger, teaser

⑱ **How many words (4 letters or more) can you make using the letters in the grid? Write your words in the table.**

Your total __________

30 + Brilliant

25–30 Excellent

20–25 Very good

15–20 Pretty good effort

10–15 Keep persisting

c	e	l
g	a	n
l	e	h

Six-letter words	Five-letter words	Four-letter words

⑲ **Find the nine-letter word** __________

Score 2 points for each correct answer!

SCORE

/38

TERM 3

Informative text – Explanation

Chemical Reactions

A magical little man appeared suddenly before the miller's daughter. The daughter's task was to spin a room full of straw into gold for the king. She had to complete the task before morning or lose her life. She sobbed in terror and despair at such an impossible task. However, the strange little man came to her aid and converted the straw into gold, but for a heavy price. His name was Rumpelstiltskin.

This story has been told in many languages for thousands of years but was written down only two hundred years ago.

Many have dreamed of being able to turn straw into gold like the fabled Rumpelstiltskin. For over 4000 years, people called alchemists believed a base metal such as lead could be turned into gold. Alchemists believed that lead was just a lower form of gold that hadn't fully matured, meaning that all lead had the ability to eventually become gold.

The idea of alchemy, or turning base metals into gold, disappeared 300 years ago when modern chemistry showed that no number of chemical reactions or changes could ever create gold. Alchemists believed everything was made of four basic elements: air, earth, fire and water. They thought that changing the proportions of these four elements would turn a substance into something new.

Primary school students now learn how everything in the universe is made of atoms. In chemical reactions or changes, atoms are rearranged to form one or more new substances. Gold, however, is an element and cannot be made through ordinary chemical reactions.

If we sent the alchemists back to primary school today, they would need to learn the difference between physical and chemical changes. The distinction or difference between physical and chemical change is not clear-cut as at times one can lead to the other. However, some of the differences are shown in the table below.

Physical changes	Chemical changes
melting, boiling, freezing, dissolving, evaporating	rusting, digesting, cooking, burning
The appearance of the matter changes but the kind of matter in the substance does not. **No new substance is formed.** e.g. A melted ice cube changes appearance, but the substance is still water and can be refrozen to make an ice cube again.	The kind of matter changes, and at least **one new substance** with new properties is **formed.** e.g. When wood is burned in a fire, it is no longer wood and becomes ash. Ash cannot be made into wood again.
The **particles** (parts inside atoms) of which it is made, and the number of particles **remain unchanged**.	The new substances are different from the original, the **particles are different**, and the number of particles can change.
Can be reversed but this can be difficult. Cutting paper into tiny pieces or crushing a rock are physical changes but to restore the original piece of paper or rock is difficult.	It is irreversible.

Although alchemy is long gone, and alchemists never achieved their goal of turning lead into gold, they did practise what would one day become modern chemistry.

TERM 3

TARGETING ENGLISH HOMEWORK YEAR 6 © PASCAL PRESS ISBN 978 1 925726 63 3

Reading & Comprehension

Write the answer or shade the bubble next to the correct answer.

The answers to these questions are in the text.

① What did **alchemists** believe could be done?

______

______

② What type of change has occurred if the pipe outside my window has **rusted**?

______

Is this reversible?

◯ Yes ◯ No

③ Which change forms at least one new substance?

______

Think about these questions and search for the answers in the text.

④ Why was it not possible for alchemists to turn lead and other metals into gold?

______

______

______

⑤ If I crush a rock, it looks different, and I can't put it back to the way it was. What has not changed?

______

______

______

Use inferencing skills to answer these questions. The answers are not in the text. Think about what you know and what the author says.

⑥ Is lead today considered a lower form of gold?

◯ Yes ◯ No

Write a sentence to explain your answer.

______

______

______

______

⑦ Write one sentence to explain how modern chemistry and alchemy are similar.

______

______

______

______

⑧ Write one sentence to explain how modern chemistry and alchemy are different.

______

______

______

______

Use your experience and opinions to answer these questions. The answers are not in the text.

⑨ Name two occupations that could involve making chemical changes.

______

______

______

______

⑩ Name two occupations that could involve making physical changes.

______

______

______

______

TERM 3

Comprehension Reflections

Look at the top of the opposite page. This text is an I__________ text – E__________.

Write one thing you learned or found interesting:

______

Write one question you have or something you want to find more information about:

______

______

Rating

Score 2 points for each correct answer! SCORE /20 0-8 10-14 16-20

UNIT 21

Grammar & Punctuation

AC9E6LA09

Punctuation – Commas

Commas have an important role in creating meaning in written language. If they are misplaced, they can change the meaning of a sentence. *Example:* "Let's eat, Grandma!" has a very different meaning to "Let's eat Grandma!"

In previous units, you have used commas in complex sentences after a dependent clause, around an embedded clause and in dialogue (conversation).

Commas are also used:

- in compound sentences to separate independent clauses when they are joined by any of these five coordinating conjunctions: and, but, or, so, yet. *Example:* I love vanilla ice-cream**, but** Sam prefers chocolate.
- after introductory phrases or clauses. *Example:* **After much debate,** I had vanilla ice-cream.
- after interruptions and introductory words. *Examples:* **Hey,** that's my book! **Wow,** that's amazing!
- around words or phrases that explain something. *Example:* Mr Wilson**, my teacher,** is a very tall man.
- in lists to separate three or more items. *Example:* There were a few ice-cream flavours such as vanilla, chocolate, strawberry and coconut.

① – ⑮ Punctuate the following text with commas. There are 15 in total!

Sam a student at school is hoping to turn collected pencil shavings into gold.

Mr Wilson our teacher explained "Sam, you will not be able to turn the contents of your sharpener into gold." Mr Wilson went on "Gold which is a precious metal was created in the explosion of stars and not changed from something else."

(8 commas so far; another 7 to go!)

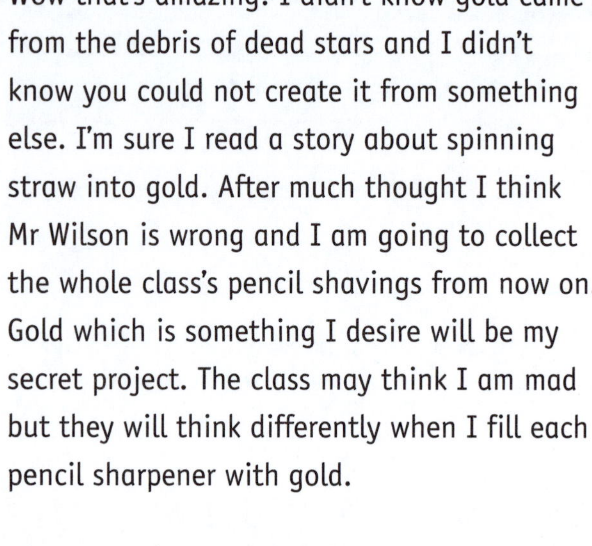
Wow that's amazing! I didn't know gold came from the debris of dead stars and I didn't know you could not create it from something else. I'm sure I read a story about spinning straw into gold. After much thought I think Mr Wilson is wrong and I am going to collect the whole class's pencil shavings from now on. Gold which is something I desire will be my secret project. The class may think I am mad but they will think differently when I fill each pencil sharpener with gold.

Mnemonic strategies – Acronyms

One mnemonic strategy to remember things is to make an acronym. You take the first letter of each item you want to remember and make a word. *Example:* To remember the rainbow colours, you can use the acronym **ROY G BIV**.

It reads as a name, but each letter stands for a colour in the right order: **R**ed, **O**range, **Y**ellow, **G**reen, **B**lue, **I**ndigo and **V**iolet.

An acronym can also be used to remember these co-ordinating conjunctions: **f**or, **a**nd, **n**or, **b**ut, **o**r, **y**et, **s**o. The beginning letters can form the acronym **FAN BOYS**.

Form two acronyms to help you remember when to use commas. The places to use commas are listed at the start of this page. Take the first letter of each word: Compound sentences, Complex sentences, Embedded clauses, Dialogue (conversation), Introductory phrases, Interruptions, Explanations and Lists.

Use the letters: C C E D I I E L.

⑯ ______________________

____

⑰ ______________________

____

Score 2 points for each correct answer! SCORE /34  0-14  16-28  30-34

TERM 3

TARGETING ENGLISH HOMEWORK YEAR 6 © PASCAL PRESS ISBN 978 1 925726 63 3

AC9E6LY09

Greek and Latin prefixes for size

Greek and Latin prefixes are used to create words to measure size. Mega is Greek for 'great'. *Example:* If Sam could transform pencil shavings to gold, he would become **mega** rich.

The Greek prefix 'hypo' is also a Greek root word, meaning 'beneath or below'. 'Hypo' is often confused with 'hyper'. A mnemonic strategy to remember whether to use 'hypo' or 'hyper' is to associate hypo with a **hypo**dermic needle that goes **beneath/below** the skin.

① – ⑭ Sort the following 14 words with size prefixes into the table under the correct headings.

hypercritical, microwave, supermarket, megaphone, hyperactive, megalopolis, superhero, hyperventilate, hyperbole, megadose, microcosm, superego, microbe, hypersensitive

Greek micro = small	Greek mega = great	Latin super = over or above	Greek hyper = over or above

⑮ – ㉖ Use 12 words from the first activity to complete the crossword.

Down

① a large amount of medicine
② very active
③ a type of high-frequency radio wave often used to heat food in an oven
④ very sensitive and very allergic to things
⑤ when a person is very critical of things
⑥ a smaller version of a much larger place or activity
⑦ the part of your mind which makes you aware of what is right and wrong
⑧ an extremely large city
⑨ another word for exaggeration

Across

⑧ a cone-shaped device used to increase the loudness of your voice
⑩ to breathe at a rapid rate
⑪ a tiny living organism

1 2 3 4 5 6 7 8 9 10 11

Score 2 points for each correct answer! SCORE /52 0-24 26-46 48-52

TERM 3

AC9E6LY04, AC9E6LY05, AC9HS6K03

Informative text – Report

Interviews - Ties to Home

Welcome to your local radio station AU1. Today we have several guests in the studio to tell us their stories of how they came to be in Australia. We asked each person to bring along something that represents their journey. First up is Brian.

Hi everyone, I brought along an old picture of a surfboard. I'll tell you why soon. My family was part of the Ten Pound Pom scheme after World War 2 (WW2) which ended in 1945. It seems that Australia became very nervous after the war as we were nearly invaded by the Japanese. The government wanted to bring more people into the country but only white British people. This was due to the White Australia policy at the time. Thank goodness we now have a policy of multiculturalism because Australia is so much richer for it. Anyway, things were tough in Britain after the war, and my mum saw lots of advertisements of sunny Australia and the beaches. She gave me this picture of a surfboard and said that in Australia, everyone surfs. I treasured that picture and dreamt of surfing. So, Mum and Dad decided to move here. They paid ten pounds each, and my brother and I were free. What a deal! We travelled on a passenger ship and arrived in Australia after a few months. Mum and Dad decided to live inland and not on the coast, so I've never been surfing or lived by the beach. I'm so glad we came to Australia though, and I still have that same picture!

Thank you, Brian. Next, we have Maria.

My name is Maria, and my family came to Australia from Italy in the 1950s. At that time, the Australian government had a policy called 'Populate or Perish'. I have since learnt that Australia felt unprotected during WW2 and the government decided they needed more people to live here. They preferred British people, but they also allowed migrants from European countries. After the war, things were very bad where we lived in Italy. My parents wanted a better life, so they migrated to Australia. We went to Melbourne, Victoria, which now has the largest Italian community in Australia. I have my mother's cooking pot that she brought from Italy because she cooked all the dishes from her homeland in that one pot. It represents the flavours that are my heritage, and I still use it to cook food for my family here in Australia.

Thank you, Maria. Next, we have Vi.

Hello, my name is Vi. Many Vietnamese people arrived as refugees after the end of the Vietnam war in 1975. After 1975 the Communists came to South Vietnam where my family lived, and because my relatives fought in the war against them, we had to leave. My father was scared as the Communist government had already put some of his friends in jail. We left in a small fishing boat and had to sneak away in the night until we reached international waters. We made it to Thailand and stayed in a refugee camp for two years before being accepted to live in Australia. I brought along a suitcase today as it held the only things that we were able to bring with us. Space on the boat was limited and that suitcase held our hopes and dreams. My family became Australian citizens, and our certificates are now kept in this suitcase.

What wonderful stories you have told. We thank you for your honesty and for sharing such personal information. That is all from me today on radio station AU1.

TARGETING ENGLISH HOMEWORK YEAR 6 © PASCAL PRESS ISBN 978 1 925726 63 3

Write your answers on the lines provided.

The answers to these questions are in the text.

① Why did the Australian government want to bring more people into Australia after WW2?

___

② Where is the **largest Italian community** in Australia?

___

③ Why did Vi have to leave Vietnam?

___

④ What did families have to pay to be part of the **Ten Pound Pom scheme**?

___

Think about this question and search for the answer in the text.

⑤ Why did Maria bring a **cooking pot** to represent how she came to be in Australia? ___

Use inferencing skills to answer these questions. The answers are not in the text. Think about what you know and what the author says.

⑥ Why would Brian keep the picture of the surfboard if he has never been surfing?

___

⑦ Write one sentence to explain what all three stories have in common.

___

⑧ Write one sentence to explain how the three stories are different.

___

Use your experience and opinions to answer these questions. The answers are not in the text.

Vi's family left with only one suitcase. If you were told you were going to live in another country but could only take **one small suitcase**, what would you put in it and why?

⑨ What would you take? ___

⑩ Why would you take these things? ___

Comprehension Reflections

Look at the top of the opposite page. This text is an I__________ text – R__________.

Write one thing you learned or found interesting:

___

Write one question you have or something you want to find more information about:

___

Rating   

Score 2 points for each correct answer! SCORE /20  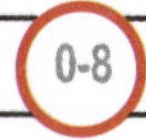  
0-8 10-14 16-20

TERM 3

UNIT 22

Grammar & Punctuation

AC9E6LA09

Playing with tenses – Past participles

Unit 18 looked at changing between present and past tense. This requires knowing present and past tense verbs and past participles.

Simple past tense verbs do not need helpers, while past participles need auxiliary verbs like 'had' or 'has'.

Examples: I **ate** a hotdog yesterday. (simple past tense – main verb)

I **have eaten** my breakfast. (present perfect tense – auxiliary verb 'have' + past participle)

Regular verbs form their simple past and past participle by adding the suffix 'ed'.
Example: walk – walk**ed** – walk**ed**

Irregular verbs do not form their simple past and past participles with 'ed'. They often look very different to the infinitive form of the verb.

Examples: fly – flew – flown take – took – taken

Write the missing past participle of the irregular verb in brackets.

Example: I **have** not (spoke) **spoken** about this in a long while.

1. No-one could **have** (know) ______________ how terrible the sea journey would be.
2. None of us had (think) ______________ about preparing for such a long and dangerous journey on a small boat.
3. We should have (see) ______________ it coming.
4. We could not have (predict) ______________ what happened next.
5. It was as if lightning had (strike) ______________. They found us!
6. I should have (do) ______________ something to make sure we were not discovered.
7. I should have (find) ______________ a less obvious way to the boat.
8. At first, I was (shook) ______________ when they found us, but then I recognised who they were.
9. I had not (give) ______________ any thought to telling my cousins of my family's escape plan from Vietnam.
10. We had (drive) ______________ from our village to the coast to catch a boat to freedom.
11. We should have (swing) ______________ by my uncle's house to tell him of our plan.
12. I have since (write) ______________ to my uncle to let him know we made it safely.
13. I could have (bring) ______________ more photos of my family, but we could only bring one small suitcase.

Complete the table with main verbs, past tense verbs and past participles.

	Infinitive verb	Past tense	Past participle
14	forbid	forbade	
15		forgot	forgotten
16	begin		begun
17	hide	hid	
18	sing	sang	
19	shrink		shrunk
20			stunk

Score 2 points for each correct answer!

SCORE /40   

TERM 3

TARGETING ENGLISH HOMEWORK YEAR 6 © PASCAL PRESS ISBN 978 1 925726 63 3

Phonic & Word Knowledge

UNIT 22

AC9E6LY09

Latin and Greek prefixes for numbers

The table below lists the Greek and Latin prefixes for numbers.

Number	Latin	Greek	Number	Latin	Greek
half	semi or demi	hemi	eight	octo	octo
one	uni	mono	nine	nona	ennea
two	bi	di	ten	decem	deca
three	tri	tri	eleven	undeca	hendeca
four	quadri	tetra	twelve	duodeci	dodeca
five	quinque	penta	twenty	viginti	icos
six	sexi	hexa	hundred	centi	hecto
seven	septi	hepta	thousand	milli	chili

Use the information in the table to fill in the missing numbers.

1. hexagon – a shape that has _____ sides
2. triannual – once every _____ years OR _____ times a year
3. century – a period of _____ years
4. nonet – a group of _____ people, especially musicians
5. octave – a stretch of _____ notes in music OR _____ lines in poetry
6. quadrilateral – a shape with _____ sides
7. millipede – an insect that is said to have _____ feet
8. bicycle – a vehicle with _____ wheels
9. pentameter – a poetry rhythm that uses _____ metrical feet
10. September – originally the _____ month of the Roman calendar
11. monarchy – a government with _____ ruler
12. bicentennial – an anniversary marking _____ years
13. dodecahedron – a shape with _____ sides

Match the numbers in the table with their Latin/Greek prefix. How long does it take you to correctly complete the activity?

9	5	100	11	10
4	6	7	1000	2
20	12	1	3	8

14. deca __________
15. octo __________
16. milli __________
17. viginti __________
18. penta __________
19. centi __________
20. septi __________
21. tetra __________
22. dodeca __________
23. uni __________
24. hexa __________
25. nona __________
26. tri __________
27. undeca __________
28. di __________

Record your time here: __________

TERM 3

Score 2 points for each correct answer! SCORE /56 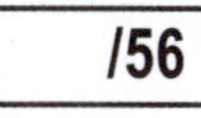   

AC9E6LY04, AC9E6LY05, AC9HS6K07

Informative text – Explanation

No Homework, Please - Head Honcho

Dear Prime Minister,

I am writing to you as I have a very significant problem. I thought I should go to the 'Head Honcho' or the person in charge, and there is no-one higher than you. I have recently learned that a country in Europe, Poland, has banned homework for Years 1–3 and made it optional for other primary year levels. Other than moving to Poland, I don't know how else to rid my life of homework. We need a similar policy here in Australia.

I know there are different arguments for and against homework. Some students and teachers believe it helps to practise what you have learnt at school during the day. I can see that for some students but not for me. I have a great memory. I feel homework takes time away from what I do on my iPad. If you passed a similar bill and it became law, then homework could be optional. Those who like doing it can continue and those who don't like doing it don't have to. It is a win-win policy, I say.

I'm looking forward to seeing this new bill in the news.

Yours faithfully,

Pat Wilson

Dear Pat,

Thank you for your interesting letter. I understand why you wanted to go to the 'Head Honcho', which is me. I think I need to explain to you, however, that there are different levels of government. I'm afraid that I am not the level that can help you with your homework issue.

There are three levels of government. Each level of government has its own responsibilities although, in some cases, these responsibilities are shared. I will put some information in a table to make it easier to read. I have not included all areas of law making.

Federal Parliament	Makes laws for the whole of Australia	Laws concerning defence, foreign policy, citizenship, taxation, Medicare, immigration etc.
6 State and 2 Mainland Territory Parliaments	Make laws for their states or territories	Laws concerning schools, hospitals, roads and railways, public transport, electricity and water supply, police, ambulance services etc.
Over 500 Local Councils	Make local laws for their region or district	Laws concerning local roads, footpaths, cycle ways, rubbish collection, parking, recreational facilities, sewerage, pet control etc.

As you can see, education falls into the state and territory's responsibility, but at this stage, homework policies are developed by the schools. Each school sets what they consider is a reasonable amount of homework for a student at each year level. In Australia, there is no homework policy set by Federal or State Parliaments. Perhaps this is an issue you need to discuss with your principal as they are your 'Head Honcho' on this matter.

Yours faithfully,

The Prime Minister

TARGETING ENGLISH HOMEWORK YEAR 6 © PASCAL PRESS ISBN 978 1 925726 63 3

Write the answer or shade the bubble where required.

The answers to these questions are in the text.

1. What is **Poland's policy** on homework?

2. Why does Pat feel that practising what was learnt at school is an unnecessary task for her?

Think about these questions and search for the answers in the text.

3. Why can't the Prime Minister help Pat with the homework bill?

4. Who does the Prime Minister recommend Pat see on the issue of homework?

5. Which level of government would you approach if you wanted **safer cycle paths** to your school?

Use inferencing skills to answer this question. The answer is not in the text. Think about what you know and what the author says.

6. What does Pat mean by a **win–win policy**?

Use your experience and opinions to answer these questions. The answers are not in the text.

7. Should Australia follow Poland's lead in homework policy?

   ◯ Yes   ◯ No

   Why do you think that?

8. If you had the chance to change something in your neighbourhood, state or in Australia, what would you change?

9. Why would you want this change?

10. Which **level of government** would you need to approach about this change?

Comprehension Reflections

Look at the top of the opposite page. This text is an I__________ text – E__________.

Write one thing you learned or found interesting:

Write one question you have or something you want to find more information about:

Rating   

Score 2 points for each correct answer! SCORE /20  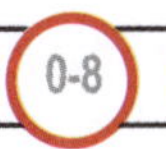 
0-8 10-14 16-20

TERM 3

Grammar & Punctuation

AC9E6LA01, AC9E6LA06

Formal and informal English

In the text, Pat writes to the Prime Minister and uses the term, 'Head Honcho'. 'Honcho' comes from a Japanese word for 'group leader'. It is an informal word which means it is the kind of language we would use with friends and relatives. When writing for school or to people in authority, we use formal English.

In the text below, Pat has used informal language, which is in brackets. The school will put Pat's text into their newsletter, so it needs to be formal. To help Pat, select the formal language from the box and write it in the appropriate space.

however, ascertain, numerous, as soon as possible, in conclusion, additionally, contact, consider, commence, children, oppose

I want the Prime Minister to (think about)
① ______________ my proposal
for homework as it affects (heaps of)
② ______________ (kids)
③ ______________ from all over
Australia. Homework has its place; (but)
④ ______________, I have an
idea to make it better for everyone. (Also)
⑤ ______________, I like the
idea that I can (get in touch with)
⑥ ______________ the leader of
our country. How wonderful is that?
It is not that I (go against)
⑦ ______________ homework,
I just think we need to (find out)
⑧ ______________ what
other countries are doing. (To sum up)
⑨ ______________, I would
like my bill to be law and (start)
⑩ ______________ (ASAP)
⑪ ______________.

Precise verbs

To improve your writing, you need to pay attention to the verbs you use. Precise verbs give the reader an idea of how the action occurred.

Example: I **ate** it all. OR I **scoffed** it all. (You ate it quickly and greedily.)

Precise verbs give the reader a clearer image of what is happening.

⑫ – ⑱ Pat wrote about going to meet the Prime Minister. Help Pat by using 7 precise verbs from the word list below to replace the words in bold. Rewrite the whole text on the lines provided. You will need to change some words so that the sentences make sense.

glared, frowned, scoffed, giggled, snickered, gripping, gobbled, bolted, wolfed, wandered, chomped, scowled, dashed, struggled, wrestled, grappled, clutching, fought, sank, clasping, slouched, clenching, slumped

I **ate** my lunch **quickly** as I was going to meet the head. Oops, I mean the Prime Minister.

My little brother **laughed** at me, so I **looked angrily** at him and **walked quickly** out to the waiting car. I found the seatbelt **hard to put on**, and then I **sat** back into the seat, **holding tightly onto** my speech.

____
____
____
____
____
____
____
____
____
____
____

Score 2 points for each correct answer! SCORE /36

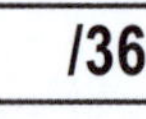

TERM 3

TARGETING ENGLISH HOMEWORK YEAR 6 © PASCAL PRESS ISBN 978 1 925726 63 3

Alternation of vowels

In Unit 2 we learnt about alternations. One example of vowel alternation is when vowels change from long to short in the same word when we add a suffix. *Example:* sublime – subliminal (long 'i' to short 'i')

There are three types of vowel alternations:

long vowel sound to short vowel sound *e.g.* cave – cavity

long vowel sound to schwa (an 'uh' sound) *e.g.* migrate – migratory

short vowel sound to schwa *e.g.* contribute – contribution

1 – 17 Complete the crossword with more vowel alternations! The bold words in the clues have a suffix added. Write the original word. Clue 1 Down has been done for you.

Down

1. Comes from **definition: define**
2. Comes from **distribution:** ______________
5. Comes from **declaration:** ______________
8. Comes from **combination:** ______________
11. Comes from **habitual:** ______________
12. Comes from **society:** ______________
13. Comes from **resident:** ______________
15. Comes from **inclination:** ______________
17. Comes from **narration:** ______________

Across

3. Comes from **contribution:** ______________
4. Comes from **migratory:** ______________
5. Comes from **deprivation:** ______________
6. Comes from **organisation:** ______________
7. Comes from **competition:** ______________
9. Comes from **prohibition:** ______________
10. Comes from **mobility:** ______________
11. Comes from **hesitation:** ______________
14. Comes from **president:** ______________
16. Comes from **ignorant:** ______________
18. Comes from **relation:** ______________

Score 2 points for each correct answer! SCORE /34   

0-14 16-28 30-34

TERM 3

AC9E6LY04, AC9E6LY05, AC9S6U04

Informative text – Explanation

Edible Science

I couldn't believe it! I just wanted to learn how to cook, and the sign said *Science in the Kitchen*. Why is schoolwork in the kitchen? Schoolwork stays in the classroom, or at least it should and not spoil my holidays. Dad said I need to know how to cook as it is part of basic survival. I think when I am older and move out of home, I'll go to Mum for basic survival and get home-cooked meals. I hope Mum does not read this!

I entered the holiday program with some reluctance, but I hoped I could at least eat my way through the two days of instruction. On arrival, we were told that cooking food is an irreversible chemical change. During cooking, the molecules that are present in food change to form new substances. Also, cooked food cannot be reversed back to its raw state.

The instructor said that we can tell that a chemical change has happened by looking for certain clues. One clue is gas, which is produced during a chemical change. This was the part I liked as we had to demonstrate this by baking a cake and making pancakes. We had to look for the bubbles in both the cake and pancakes because inside each bubble there was a little bit of gas. This gas is made when the ingredients change each other. The bubbles help make the baked food fluffy. We had to cut into our cake to spot the spaces where there had been bubbles of gas. After eating up my third slice of cake, I decided I should look for where the bubbles had been. There they were – little spaces where the gas had been! Thanks to them, my cake was fluffy and delicious. We also had to spot the bubbles when flipping the pancakes. I ended up taking cold pancakes home, but unfortunately the cake did not survive the trip home. I just managed to squeeze the last piece into my mouth before entering the front door. Sorry family.

I was looking forward to the second day. Perhaps schoolwork can be in the kitchen as long as I can eat it. We were told that we were looking at physical changes this time. We were looking for where there is a change in the state of matter. This is a reversible change. I did not quite understand this until the instructor said that there are three main states of matter: solid, liquid and gas. When you freeze fruit juice to make an ice block, it is a change in state. The juice changes from a liquid to a solid. Ice-cream melting on a hot day is also a change in state. The ice-cream changes from a solid to a liquid. The juice and ice-cream are still juice and ice-cream even when they change from one state of matter to another. I was so hoping we would change the state of matter with chocolate. Melted chocolate is the best, especially if you dip marshmallows or strawberries into it.

I must admit, I did enjoy learning about science even though it was during the holidays. I even devised a little test for my family. I asked Mum to get me some ingredients and I baked a cake, cut up strawberries, and melted some chocolate in the microwave. I also took some marshmallows and toasted them (not just heated them up) in the oven until they were golden brown. If my family members got the questions correct, they could join in the feast. If not, it was all mine. The task was to say which actions were physical changes and which were chemical changes AND they had to explain why. The actions were: baking a cake, melting chocolate, cutting up strawberries, mashing the strawberries and toasting marshmallows. Would you know the answers?

TERM 3

TARGETING ENGLISH HOMEWORK YEAR 6 © PASCAL PRESS ISBN 978 1 925726 63 3

Reading & Comprehension

Write your answers on the lines or spaces provided.

The answer to this question is in the text.

① **How many days was the *Science in the Kitchen* course?** ____________________

Think about this question and search for the answer in the text.

② **When is gas produced in cooking and why is it produced?**

____

Use inferencing skills to answer these questions. The answers are not in the text. Think about what you know and what the author says.

The text challenges you to decide which actions (listed below) were physical changes and which were chemical changes and explain why. Write your answers in the table.

The actions are baking a cake, melting chocolate, cutting up strawberries, mashing the strawberries and toasting marshmallows.

Chemical change	Physical change	Explain why this answer
③		
④		
⑤		
⑥		
⑦		

TERM 3

Use your experience and opinions to answer this question. The answer is not in the text.

⑧ **Create a new dish with four ingredients. However, the only changes allowed are physical changes. Write your recipe below.**

Ingredients: ____________________

____

Method: ____________________

____

____

____

____

____

Comprehension Reflections

Look at the top of the opposite page. This text is an I__________ text – E__________.

Write one thing you learned or found interesting:

____

Write one question you have or something you want to find more information about:

____

____

Rating   

Score 2 points for each correct answer! SCORE  /16 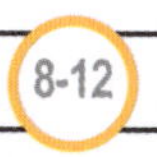 
0-6 8-12 14-16

Grammar & Punctuation

AC9E6LA06

Future tenses – going to/will

The future tense describes actions that are going to take place in the future. This can be both the near future and the faraway future! There are various ways in English to refer to a future time. One way is to use 'going to'.

Examples: Pat **is going to meet** the teacher. (auxiliary verb 'be' + going to + base form of the verb)

They **are going to do** some baking in class today.

Another way to refer to a future time is to use the auxiliary verb (helper verb) will as shown in the table.

Simple future	Future continuous	Future perfect	Future perfect continuous
auxiliary verb (will) + base form of the main verb	auxiliary verb (will) + be + main verb+ing	auxiliary verb (will) + have + past participle form of the main verb (-ed)	auxiliary verb (will) + have + been + main verb+ing
Sam **will wait** for Pat at the gym.	Sam **will be waiting** for Pat at the gym.	It's now 8 am. Sam **will have waited** for Pat at the gym for one hour.	It's now 8 am. Sam **will have been waiting** for Pat at the gym for one hour.

Practise future tense! Change the past tense sentences into future tense.

Going to:

1. Pat **brought** a recipe to school. Pat **is** ____________ ______ ____________ a recipe to school.

Simple future:

2. Sam **wrote** a story for Mr Wilson. Sam ______ ____________ a story for Mr Wilson.

Future continuous:

3. Pat **came** home for the holidays. Pat ______ ______ ____________ home for the holidays.

Future perfect:

4. Sam **left** school. Sam ______ ____________ ____________ school by now.

Future perfect continuous:

5. Pat **studied** for four hours. By 8 pm, Pat ______ ____________ ____________ ____________ for four hours.

Present continuous tense

Besides the five forms of the future tense with 'going to' and 'will', the present continuous tense can be used to talk about plans for the future or what is happening now.

Examples: Sam **is meeting** Pat at the gym tomorrow. (future)

Pat and Sam **are doing** their homework. (happening now)

The present continuous tense is made with the auxiliary verb 'be' + verb+ing.

Use present continuous tense to complete these sentences.

Example: Pat and Sam (walk) **are walking** home after the gym.

6. Pat (look) ______ ____________ forward to visiting the gym.
7. Mr Wilson (think) ______ ____________ about giving Sam an A for the story.
8. Sam's parents (wonder) ______ ____________ how to reward Sam for an A.
9. Sam (wish) ______ ____________ for lots of ice-cream as a reward.
10. Sam's parents (consider) ______ ____________ giving him a book voucher as a reward.
11. Sam (plan) ______ ____________ how to leave subtle hints about an ice-cream reward.
12. Sam's parents (pick) ______ ____________ up a book voucher tomorrow.
13. Sam (lay) ______ ____________ out a bowl and spoon ready for tomorrow.

Score 2 points for each correct answer! SCORE  /26 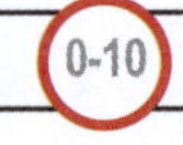 0-10  12-20  22-26

TERM 3

TARGETING ENGLISH HOMEWORK YEAR 6 © PASCAL PRESS ISBN 978 1 925726 63 3

AC9E6LY08, AC9E6LY09

The 's' sound in 'sc' words

The text is about science in the kitchen. The word **sc**ience has the letter pattern 'sc' which makes the 's' sound.

Write the 'sc' words next to their meanings.

adolescence, ascend, resuscitate, effervescent, fascinate, susceptible, rescind, scenario, reminiscence, scent

1. An adjective to describe when a drink has bubbles or froth, like a can of soda ______________________
2. To take away ______________________
3. An outline of the plot of a dramatic work such as a play ______________________
4. A time between childhood and adulthood ______________________
5. The noun for talking or thinking about things that happened in the past ______________________
6. A smell ______________________
7. To go up ______________________
8. Easily influenced or harmed by something ______________________
9. To revive someone from unconsciousness ______________________
10. To cause (someone) to be very interested in something or someone ______________________

Words with 'sc' and 'sk'

The letters 'sc' can also make a 's-k' sound. Because the letters 'sc' and 'sk' can both make the 's-k' sound, how do you determine which one to use?

'Sc' is the most common way to spell the 's-k' sound. 'Sc' can occur at the start, middle or end of words and usually before the vowels 'a', 'o' and 'u'. *Examples:* **sc**are, ab**sc**ond, mollu**sc**

'Sk' usually appears at the end of words but can also start words.

Unjumble the 'sk' words in the following sentences and write them on the lines. Use context clues to help you work out each word.

11. In the kitchen, I used a (khiws) ______________ to whip up the cream.
12. I love coconut water, but I believe the coconut shell or (kush) ______________ is very hard to break into.
13. The captain of a boat is sometimes called a (prisekp) ______________.
14. Another name for a water bottle is a (klafs) ______________.
15. A symbol on a keyboard that looks like a star is an (treaikss) ______________.

'sk' or 'sc'? Circle the correct spelling for each word.

16. cheapskate / cheapscate
17. scheme / skeme
18. scetching / sketching
19. scrumptious / skrumptious
20. scewer / skewer

Score 2 points for each correct answer!

SCORE | /40 |

TERM 3

Imaginative text – Narrative

Mars

The rockets fired, and I was drilled back into my seat, the harness cutting a painful path into my shoulders. We had come so far, and now it was within reach. With a thud, the spaceship landed and the rockets died. An eerie stillness wrapped around the ship. Mars!

Mars, named after the Roman God of war, was ours to explore. The three of us who manned the spaceship eagerly donned our spacesuits, tightening them like a second skin. The large iron door of the ship waited for us, sitting on its hinges, daring us to leave the ship. It groaned as it swung open into a Martian atmosphere and watched as we clambered slowly down the ladder to the surface.

Just before stepping off the ladder, I hesitated. A tingling sensation ran through my body. I felt excited and nervous all at once. With one last push, I landed on the dusty surface. A spray of fine particles drifted slowly from where I had landed. Our first mission, which I agreed to, was to collect soil samples from different depths on the surface and from different locations.

I took the large Mars Rover, or Mars-mobile as I called it, to a dark patch I saw in the distance. I wanted to be the first to discover something unique and different – little did I know. As I drove up to the patch that I had seen in the distance, I was surprised at how different it was to the rest of the planet.

I tapped the hard crust and noted that it had a slight lustre or sheen to it. It was smooth and rather slippery, but it cracked when I hit it with force. I scraped some of it into a sample bag and started to walk towards the vehicle so that I could store it securely. That's when it happened. My foot slipped into one of the cracks that had widened and opened into a fissure or crevice. A sticky ooze grabbed my foot and held me fast. Panic swept over me like a fire, and the more I struggled, the more I was dragged down into the thick, sticky layer.

For a second, I felt the tension around my leg release, so I started to pull back with all my might. Just as I started to feel hopeful, my free foot slipped on the hard surface, and I collapsed into the ooze once again. As my vision cleared, my heart leapt into my throat and almost choked me with fear. My visor was cracked! My space helmet had a large fragment missing from the front visor and the ooze was trickling in, coiling around the inside surface of my visor like a snake. I could smell it, and I was astonished.

The aroma was enticing and hypnotic. I tried to move my head away from the ever-encroaching ooze, but it was relentless. Something inside me wanted to give in to it and let it envelope me. I tried to scream, but the ooze filled my mouth. Wow, I could not believe the wonderful creamy taste. I wanted more. All thoughts of escape left me, and I felt content. Then the strong arms of my fellow astronauts lifted me from the grasping ooze.

We were doing our last checks before blasting off from Mars to return to Earth. We had taken large samples of the ooze to study when back on Earth. I couldn't help thinking that there was another way to use our discovery. I'm sure many people of Earth would like to sample a piece of Mars.

TARGETING ENGLISH HOMEWORK YEAR 6 © PASCAL PRESS ISBN 978 1 925726 63 3

Reading & Comprehension

Write your answers on the lines provided.

1. Who is the planet Mars named after?

2. What was the aim of the mission to Mars?

3. Why did the narrator hesitate before stepping off the ladder?

4. Why did the narrator head towards a dark patch on the surface?

5. What happened to change the narrator's initial panic about being trapped to wanting to surrender and stay?

6. A sentence from the text: I tapped the hard crust and noted that it had a slight lustre or sheen to it. Using context clues, what does lustre mean?

7. What figurative language device is used in this passage? The large iron door of the ship waited for us, sitting on its hinges, daring us to leave the ship. It groaned as it swung open into a Martian atmosphere and watched as we clambered slowly down the ladder to the surface.

8. Use the same language device to talk about your classroom door or front door of your house. Write two sentences describing the door's observations and how it may feel about what it sees.

9. A sentence from the text: Something inside me wanted to give in to it and let it envelope me. What was the narrator giving in to?

10. What could the narrator mean by, I'm sure many people of Earth would like to sample a piece of Mars?

TERM 3

Score 2 points for each correct answer! SCORE /20   

Grammar & Punctuation

Precise verbs

Precise verbs give the reader a clear image of what is happening in a story.

Read the following sentences from the text. Replace the bold precise verbs with simple verbs. Notice how the sentences lose their descriptive quality with simple verbs.

Example: The rockets **fired**, and I **was drilled** back into my seat.

The rockets **started**, and I **was pushed** back into my seat.

1. With a thud, the spaceship landed and the rockets **died**.

____

____

2. An eerie stillness **wrapped** around the ship.

____

____

3. The three of us who manned the spaceship eagerly **donned** our spacesuits.

____

____

4. Just before stepping off the ladder, I **hesitated**.

____

____

5. A sticky ooze **grabbed** my foot and held me fast.

____

____

6. Panic **swept** over me like a fire.

____

____

7. I **collapsed** into the ooze.

____

____

Use of commas

The following sentences from the text each have a comma for a specific purpose. Match the role of the comma, listed in the table, with each sentence. Write the appropriate letter a–e on the lines provided.

a used in a complex sentence after a dependent clause
b used in a compound sentence to separate two independent clauses joined by and, but, or, so, yet
c used around an embedded clause
d used around an explanation
e used after an introductory word or phrase

8. I felt the tension around my leg release, so I started to pull back with all my might. _____
9. As I started to feel hopeful, my foot slipped on the hard surface. _____
10. Our first mission, which I agreed to, was to collect soil samples from different depths on the surface and from different locations. _____
11. Mars, named after the Roman God of war, was ours to explore. _____
12. I took the large Mars Rover, or Mars-mobile as I called it, to a dark patch I saw in the distance. _____
13. As I drove up to the patch that I had seen in the distance, I was surprised at how different it was to the rest of the planet. _____
14. Wow, I could not believe the wonderful creamy taste. _____

TERM 3

Score 2 points for each correct answer! SCORE /28   

TARGETING ENGLISH HOMEWORK YEAR 6 © PASCAL PRESS ISBN 978 1 925726 63 3

Greek and Latin prefixes

Match the words in the list with their description. Write the words on the lines.

monologue, bilingual, bimonthly, monotonous, trilogy, bifocals, triathlon, monotone, bisect, monolingual

1. A group of three related novels
2. A long speech by one person
3. To cut into halves
4. Glasses that have lenses with two strengths
5. When something is boring, dull and repetitious
6. When an event occurs every two months or twice in one month
7. When a person only speaks one language
8. An athletic competition split into three parts
9. When a person can speak two languages well
10. When a sound is continuous and does not change in pitch

Silent letters and mnemonic strategies

Mnemonic strategies help you to spell difficult words or to remember the hardest part of the word. *Examples:* You **fri** the end of your **fri**end. / There is a **rat** in sepa**rat**e.

Strategies can also be used to remember which homophone to use. *Example:* Principal or principle? Think of your princi**pal** as your **pal** or friend.

Work out a strategy to learn each of the following words with silent letters. Write the strategy next to the word. At the end, have a friend test you on spelling the words.

11. asthma
12. subtle
13. mnemonic
14. honest
15. conscience
16. psychology
17. pneumonia
18. silhouette
19. disguise
20. biscuit

Spelling test – cover the words above and have someone test you.

What is your score out of /10?

How successful do you feel your strategies were?

Score 2 points for each correct answer!

SCORE /40    

TERM 3

AC9E6LY04, AC9E6LY05

Imaginative text – Narrative

The Visitor

The mosquitoes hummed and danced around Eve's face as she sat quietly in the backyard after dinner. Unexpectedly, a fiery meteorite streaked across the sky and landed behind the shed. Eve immediately covered her head, waiting for the impact, but there was no Earth-shattering explosion. Just silence. The insects that had been noisily chatting in the backyard a second ago became silent. Even the wind died down, making the night very still.

Curiosity overtook Eve as she cautiously approached the shed, listening and watching. A faint glow and mechanical noise followed by a thud brought Eve to a halt. It was as if something or someone had jumped down from a height. A figure emerged from the side of the shed and faced Eve. It felt as though she was looking into a mirror – two identical figures, standing face to face and toe to toe. Surprise stole the air from Eve's lungs, leaving her breathless.

As she slowly turned her head, so did the alien, mimicking her every move. From the side, you would think a mirror had been placed in front of Eve. Slowly, Eve moved her hand forward and so did the alien until at the very last moment they touched. Instantly, an electrical surge went through Eve's body, and the alien seemed to disappear. Or did they?

Somehow, Eve understood immediately that the alien yearned to be back home, but to get there the alien's spaceship needed to be refuelled. What on Earth could be collected easily to provide enough biofuel for the return trip? An image formed in Eve's mind – seaweed! It was readily available and free for the taking. The only problem would be convincing Eve's mother to let her go to the beach to collect it.

Eve thought through strategies that she could use to persuade her mother to visit the beach. She rehearsed a rhetorical question in her head, "Have you ever had the desire

to just go to the beach and bring back some seaweed?" That just sounded awkward. She needed something stronger, something that would gather a reaction from her mother. She next thought of using emotive language. There's nothing better than to pull at the heart strings.

Eve approached her mother and gave a large sigh. "You know what, Mum?" she asked in a flat and sad tone of voice. "I feel low and rather tired at the moment. I have a lot on my plate with school, and all I want is some time out at the beach." Eve then slumped onto the lounge, waved her hand across her face and gave another loud sigh. For added emphasis, Eve decided to use a metaphor. "The beach is medicine without a prescription."

Eve's mother studied her for a moment and then burst into laughter. "Oh, for heaven's sake, go to your room and do your homework!" Eve gasped in surprise but was more unsettled that she seemed to have lost her pester power. Was she that unconvincing?

When in her room, Eve looked into the mirror. There was a shadow behind her eyes, another voice within her head. She was the only one in the room, but she was not alone. Eve's mother knocked on the door. "Are you really feeling a bit worried about school?"

A slow smile spread across Eve's face, and she nodded to something reflected in the mirror. "Nothing a trip to the beach wouldn't fix," they replied.

TARGETING ENGLISH HOMEWORK YEAR 6 © PASCAL PRESS ISBN 978 1 925726 63 3

Write the answer or shade the bubble next to the correct answer.

The answers to these questions are in the text.

① **At what time of day does the story begin?**

- ◯ morning
- ◯ afternoon
- ◯ sunset
- ◯ evening

Write a sentence to explain why you think that.

____

____

② **Eve expected a meteorite behind the shed. What was actually behind the shed?**

____

③ **What could the alien use for fuel?**

____

Think about these questions and search for the answers in the text.

④ **Eve used persuasive devices with her mother. Name the two devices she used.**

____

⑤ **In paragraph two, why would Eve feel like she was looking onto a mirror?**

____

____

Use inferencing skills to answer these questions. The answers are not in the text. Think about what you know and what the author says.

⑥ **Find mimicking in the third paragraph. Using context clues, what do you think it means?**

- ◯ laughing at
- ◯ watching
- ◯ ignoring
- ◯ copying

⑦ **The beach is medicine without a prescription. What does this metaphor mean?**

____

____

____

Use your experience and opinions to answer these questions. The answers are not in the text.

⑧ **Why do you think Eve's mother laughed at her when she asked to go to the beach?**

____

____

____

⑨ **There was a shadow behind her eyes, another voice within her head. She was the only one in the room, but she was not alone. What do you think this passage means?**

____

____

____

⑩ **Why do you think the author purposely used the last two words in the text?**

____

____

____

Comprehension Reflections

Look at the top of the opposite page. This text is an I__________ text – N__________

Write one thing you learned or found interesting:

____

Write one question you have or something you want to find more information about:

____

____

Rating   

Score 2 points for each correct answer! SCORE /20 

TERM 4

Grammar & Punctuation

AC9E6LA08

Figurative language – Personifications

A few examples of figurative language have been used in the text. The passages below are personifications where something non-human is given human actions or qualities.

After each personification, write what has been given the human qualities and what qualities/actions they have been given.

1. The mosquitoes hummed and danced around Eve's face.
   What: ____________________
   Qualities/Actions: ____________________
   ____

2. The insects that had been noisily chatting in the backyard a second ago …
   What: ____________________
   Qualities/Actions: ____________________
   ____

3. Even the wind died down, making the night very still.
   What: ____________________
   Qualities/Actions: ____________________
   ____

4. Surprise stole the air from Eve's lungs.
   What: ____________________
   Qualities/Actions: ____________________
   ____

Similes, metaphors and hyperboles

Other types of figurative language include similes where comparisons are made using the words like or as and hyperbole which is a form of exaggeration. The text also contains a metaphor comparing the beach to medicine using the word is.

Read the following sentences and circle what type of figurative language is being used.

5. The sun played hide and seek with the clouds.
   simile / metaphor / hyperbole / personification

6. I've told you a million times to listen.
   simile / metaphor / hyperbole / personification

7. He is as happy as a pig in mud.
   simile / metaphor / hyperbole / personification

8. I move fast like a gazelle.
   simile / metaphor / hyperbole / personification

9. This classroom is an icebox.
   simile / metaphor / hyperbole / personification

Alliteration

Alliteration is another form of figurative language. It is the repetition of the same sound or letter at the beginning of each or most of the words in a phrase/sentence. The easiest way to use alliteration would be to repeat the starting letter of the words.
Example: **A**nxious **a**nts **a**void the **a**lien's **a**dvances.

Write alliterations for characters from the text.

10. Eve ____________________
    ____

11. Alien ____________________
    ____

12. Mum ____________________
    ____

This tongue-twister nursery rhyme, first published in 1813, is an alliteration. Practise reading it aloud until you can repeat it twice without mistakes.

13. Peter Piper picked a peck of pickled peppers.
    A peck of pickled peppers Peter Piper picked.
    If Peter Piper picked a peck of pickled peppers,
    Where's the peck of pickled peppers Peter Piper picked?

    Have you repeated it twice without mistakes?
    Yes / No

Score 2 points for each correct answer! SCORE /26

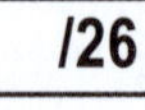
0-10

12-20

22-26

TERM 4

TARGETING ENGLISH HOMEWORK YEAR 6 © PASCAL PRESS ISBN 978 1 925726 63 3

AC9E6LY09

Greek-derived words with 'rh'

Many English words that come from Greek use the 'rh' spelling for the 'r' sound. *Example from the text:* rhetorical

Write the 'rh' words from the list below next to their meaning in the table.

rhapsody, rheumatism, rhododendron, rhetoric, rhombus, rhizome, rhythm, rhubarb, rhinoceros

	Word	Definition
1		A pattern of sounds or movements that repeats.
2		A piece of music or a feeling of elation/ great happiness.
3		A special shape with four equal sides where opposite sides are parallel.
4		A medical condition that causes pain, stiffness or swelling in the muscles, joints or connective tissues of the body.
5		A long, red-stemmed vegetable that is often thought of as a fruit.
6		A plant with beautiful flowers and glossy leaves.
7		An underground plant stem that sends up shoots to the surface.
8		A large, plant-eating mammal with thick skin, short legs and one or two horns on its nose.
9		The art of using words to persuade or influence others.

Loan words from Spanish

English has many loan words from the Spanish language. *Example from the text:* mosquito

Mosquito comes from the Latin word musca meaning 'fly'. The Spanish suffix ito meaning 'small' is added to it, making it 'small fly'. Other words we have borrowed from the Spanish language include tomato, alligator, avocado, banana, canoe, cockroach, crimson, hurricane, plaza and tornado.

Use seven Spanish loan words from the list above to complete the text. Use context clues to help you.

I had a pet (10) _______________, but I had to give it to the zoo when it grew too large. I thought it would eat me. I used a (11) _______________-coloured leash to walk it around the (12) _______________ in the shopping centre. However, it was like a mini- (13) _______________ and crashed into many shopfronts. I used to feed it lots of (14) _______________, and it ate the yellow skins as well. I also fed it an (15) _______________ once, but it nearly choked on the stone inside. I did find out it loved to eat (16) _______________, and that meant it also loved pizzas.

Score 2 points for each correct answer!

SCORE /32    

0-14 16-26 28-32

TERM 4

Persuasive text – Discussion

Cricket Sandwiches and Mealworm Pizza?

"Sam!" Mum called. "What do you want on your sandwich for school? I have ham in the fridge."

Sam considered the question and finally responded, "No, thanks. I'll have the crickets, please."

With that, Sam's mum folded the crickets into the sandwich, making sure the legs did not hang over the sides. Once the sandwich was made, she took mealworm flour out of the cupboard and proceeded to make the dough for the pizza base she was preparing for dinner that evening.

***

Is this 'Sam of the future', or for that matter, your family of the future? Insects could replace meat as our main source of protein. Should we move meat to one side and help ourselves to insect products?

On the one hand, insects are rich in vitamins and high in protein. A big reason for farming and eating insects is that the farm-to-fork process is much better for the environment than farming meat. Less land and water are used, and fewer gases are produced in the process. Many people in the world already consume insects as a major source of protein in their diets. Could Australians also eat insects?

However, the farming of insects is not as easy as you might think. Edible insects can be a source of biological hazards, including bacteria that can cause diseases. Foods that use insect products can become contaminated at all stages of production, delivery and consumption.

Meat, on the other hand, has always been a big part of the Australian diet. Just look at the meat counter at the supermarket. Meat is how most Australians obtain their protein, which is essential for a healthy diet. Insects are a valuable source of protein as well, but the main problem is the 'yuck' factor. Put simply, it may be hard to convince some Australians to eat insects rather than meat-based products. Western diets are not used to insects as food, so there's a concern that people in Australia would not accept the idea. Could you crunch down on a crispy cricket – legs and all?

Although meat eating is very popular with Australians, the meat industry causes many environmental issues. The hard hooves of cattle, sheep and goats damage the surface of the land, often leading to soil erosion. With many animals grazing on the land, native grasses do not have a chance to grow. This means that many small animals, birds and insects lose their food source and habitat.

Moreover, farmed animals, including pigs and poultry, give out various gases during digestion when they burp and fart. Further emissions are released during the processing and transportation of the animals, causing more air pollution. The entire chain from farm to fork in the meat industry contributes to many environmental issues affecting climate change and our water quality.

In summary, there are points for and against the idea of consuming insects as a source of protein rather than relying on meat. It basically depends on whether Australians would accept the change.

***

Later that evening, Sam's family sat down at the table to eat the pizza which was made from mealworm flour and topped with roasted crickets. Would you make the change for the environment?

TARGETING ENGLISH HOMEWORK YEAR 6 © PASCAL PRESS ISBN 978 1 925726 63 3

Reading & Comprehension

Write the answer or shade the bubble next to the correct answer.

The answer to this question is in the text.

① **What are the two kinds of insects that Sam's family eats?**

____

Think about these questions and search for the answers in the text.

② **Name one problem that the meat industry causes in Australia.**

____

____

③ **Name one potential problem with introducing insects as a source of protein in Australian diets.**

____

____

④ **Name one reason why introducing edible insects would be a good idea for Australians.**

____

____

Use inferencing skills to answer these questions. The answers are not in the text. Think about what you know and what the author says.

⑤ **List two reasons why, in your opinion, eating insects could cause the 'yuck' factor.**

____

____

⑥ **The text mentions the farming of insects. Why do you think we can't just eat the insects out of our gardens? Name two reasons.**

____

____

____

____

Use your experience and opinions to answer these questions. The answers are not in the text.

⑦ **After reading points for and against consuming insects for protein instead of meat, would you be willing to change to an insect-based diet?**

◯ Yes ◯ No

⑧ **Write a sentence to explain your answer.**

____

____

____

____

Your task is to produce two foods that contain edible insects that you could convince your family to eat (different to the ones in the text). Remember, edible insects can be fried or ground into products such as flour.

What are these products? Why did you choose them?

⑨ **Product 1** ______________________________

Why chosen? ______________________________

____

⑩ **Product 2** ______________________________

Why chosen? ______________________________

____

Comprehension Reflections

Look at the top of the opposite page. This text is a P__________ text – D__________.

Write one thing you learned or found interesting:

____

Write one question you have or something you want to find more information about:

____

____

Rating   

Score 2 points for each correct answer! SCORE  /20 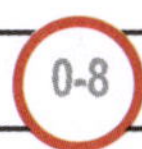

TERM 4

Grammar & Punctuation

AC9E6LA05

Commas – Embedded clauses

As we have seen in previous units, commas are used in compound and complex sentences to separate clauses such as embedded clauses.

An embedded clause is inserted within a main clause with commas either side of it. Embedded clauses are subordinate, so they cannot stand on their own as a sentence. *Example:* Insects, **as we already know**, are full of vitamins and protein.

Insert the commas in these sentences that contain embedded clauses.

1. Pat although she was ravenous was reluctant to try a cricket-packed sandwich.
2. Even Mr Wilson because he was late for a meeting was reluctant to try a cricket sandwich.

Relative clauses

Relative clauses often begin with a relative pronoun such as that, which, who, whom or whose and follow the noun/s that they are referring to in a sentence. *Example:* Sam and Pat, **who were best friends**, could not agree on the taste of fried crickets.

The relative clause (who were best friends) gives us more information about Sam and Pat, so it follows directly after. Commas are used before and after the relative clause because it is embedded in the main clause.

Insert the commas in the following sentences that contain relative clauses.

3. Sam whose sandwich was being discussed could not see what all the fuss was about.
4. Mr Wilson who sat quietly at his desk was hoping Sam would not offer to bring him a cricket sandwich for lunch the next day.

Essential relative clauses

If the relative clause is essential to the meaning of the main idea of the sentence, you do not use commas to separate it from the rest of the sentence. *Example:* The person **who is standing by the door** is a well-known chef.

In this case, the relative clause (who is standing by the door) is essential because it tells us which person is being talked about.

The following sentences all have relative clauses. Add commas where necessary.

5. The sandwich that held the crickets was sitting in front of the chef.
6. The chef who was dressed in white looked with disdain at the sandwich.
7. Sam's mum bumped into the chef who was studying her sandwich.
8. The sandwich which was feeling important continued to sit in silence on the table while being studied.
9. Sam's mum who was standing at the back of the room was waiting impatiently for the chef's point of view.
10. The chef believed that children who ate insects were helping the environment.
11. Sam's mum who couldn't help herself gave a shout of approval.
12. The cricket sandwich that was recommended by the chef made the school newsletter.
13. Parents who read the newsletter were reluctant to take on the idea of cricket sandwiches for lunch boxes.

Score 2 points for each correct answer! SCORE /26

TERM 4

TARGETING ENGLISH HOMEWORK YEAR 6 © PASCAL PRESS ISBN 978 1 925726 63 3

AC9E6LY09

Latin root word 'cept'

The word accept is made from the Latin root word 'cept' meaning 'take'.

Example: The edible insect industry in Australia will need Australians to **accept** the possibility of eating insects.

① – ⑳ Using the table below, make as many words as possible using the root word 'cept'. Write your words on the lines provided. Can you get to 20?

Prefix	Root word	Suffix
inter		tion – You may need to drop a letter.
per		ive
con		ed
sus		ible
ac	cept	able
de		tional – You may need to drop a letter.
ex		ing
		ual

20 – genius level, 18 – very good, 15 – good

Write your words here:

Example: **ac**cept

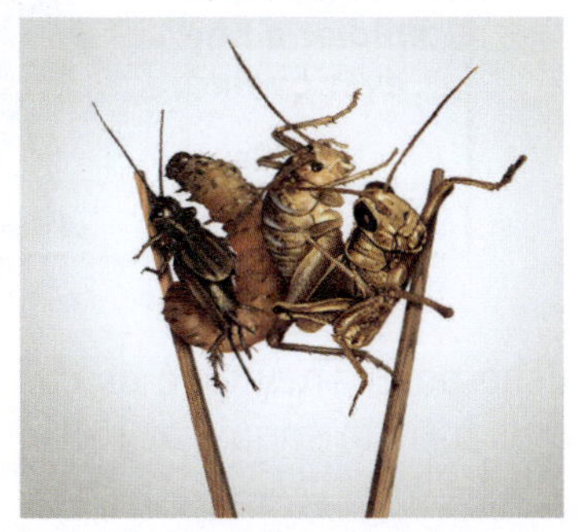

Word building by adding letters

You can make words by adding one new letter to an existing word. You can switch the letters around to build new words.

Example:

is
sir ← add r
rids ← add d
birds ← add b

Follow the previous example to build these words from the text. Use the starting words below and add one letter at a time. Some letters have been given to help you. Remember, you can switch the letters around.

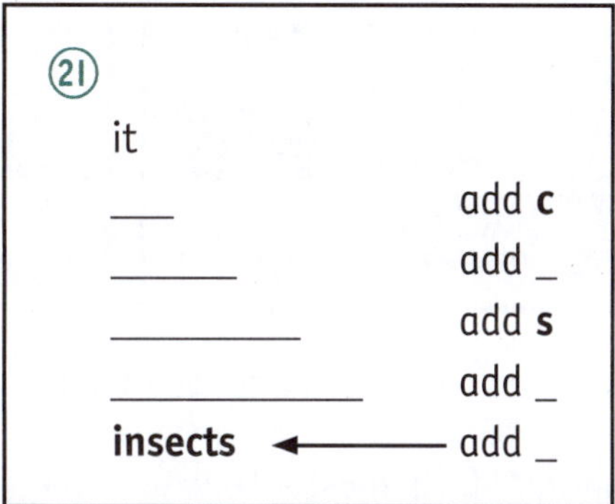

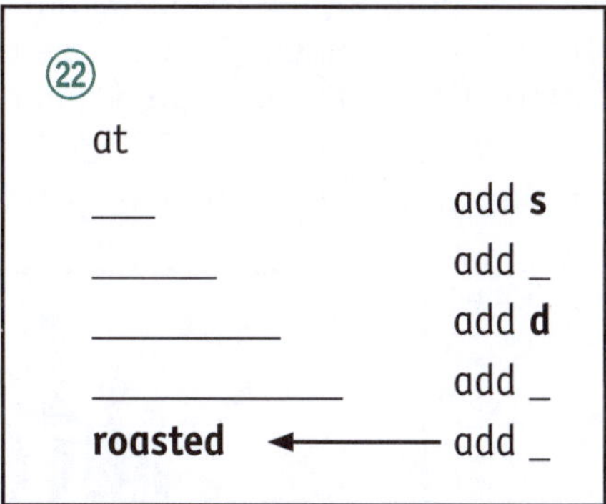

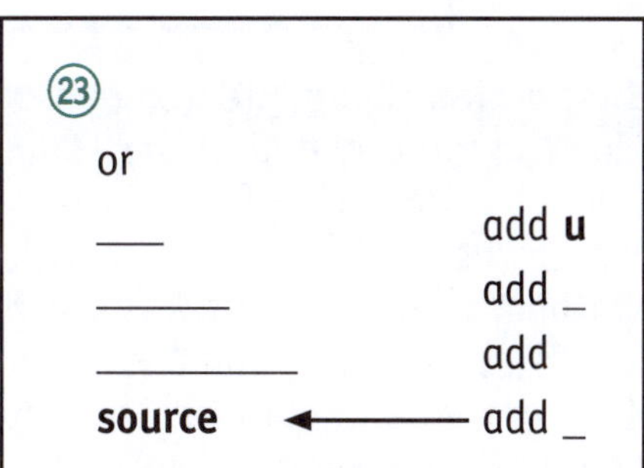

Score 2 points for each correct answer!

TERM 4

Informative text – Report

Advertisements - Snapshots in Time

Advertisements, or ads, can be annoying at times, but they do give us information about available products and services. Their main job is to persuade us to buy or use the products being displayed, but is that all they do? Looking at advertising can give us a lot of information about the time in history that an ad was created. This is called the context.

One form of advertising that you will certainly have noticed is ads for the latest gadgets. These ads tell you what is popular or trending and try to persuade you to buy these items or at least pester your parents for them. However, these ads can also give a snapshot in **time**. From the ads below, you can see the progression of technology from the 1980s to more recent ads in the 2020s. You can see what was considered popular and the 'must-haves' for that time in history. You may not recognise some of the items, but your parents probably would. The ads give a context of time. What technology will the ads display 10 years from now?

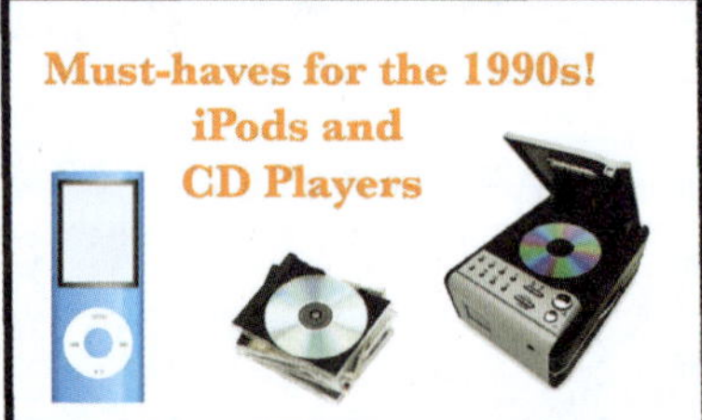

Looking at toy ads is one way to look at context. Let's look at specific toys, such as Barbie® dolls and G.I. Joe® action figures. Most dolls before Barbie® were old-fashioned or modelled on babies. Girls mostly tended to play with the baby dolls by pretending they were mothers.

The ads for Barbie® below show that the idea of a doll has changed from being a replica of a baby to being modelled on people and professions that girls could one day think about becoming. The doll was created and advertised to appeal to girls. There is also a further change from the 1960s Barbie® doll being a fashion model to the 2016 version of the doll where girls or Barbie® can be anything they imagine.

The first action figure, created and advertised for boys, was G.I. Joe®, a military doll in the 1960s. It was not advertised as a 'doll' but an action figure. The ad at the right for G.I. Joe® from the 1960s shows that with G.I. Joe® boys could play at being soldiers. This was a very popular game back in the 1960s as American and Australian military forces were involved in the Vietnam War. This toy represents what was happening in the world at that time.

G. I. Joe ®
is the greatest
soldier a boy
ever owned.
1960s

Ads can tell us more than just what was available to buy in the past. They give us context of the period in history in which they were created and give us a little snapshot in time!

TERM 4

TARGETING ENGLISH HOMEWORK YEAR 6 © PASCAL PRESS ISBN 978 1 925726 63 3

Write the answer or shade the bubble next to the correct answer.

The answers to these questions are in the text.

① What does the **context** tell you about an advertisement?

② Before **the 1960s**, what were dolls modelled on and what games were girls restricted to playing?

Modelled on ______

Games played ______

Think about these questions and search for the answers in the text.

③ Why were **military dolls** popular in the 1960s?

④ **How has** Barbie® changed in the way it advertises what girls can do?

In the 1960s ______

In 2016? ______

Use inferencing skills to answer these questions. The answers are not in the text. Think about what you know and what the author says.

⑤ Using context clues, what does **replica** in the fourth paragraph mean?

- ◯ doll
- ◯ picture
- ◯ copy
- ◯ replacement

⑥ Why would your parents know some of the items in the ads that you might not know?

Use your experience and opinions to answer these questions. The answers are not in the text.

⑦ Why do you think Barbie® and G.I. Joe® have this symbol ®?

⑧ G.I. Joe® was advertised as an **action figure** and not a doll. Do you think G.I. Joe® is a doll?

◯ Yes ◯ No

Why do you think that?

⑨ Why do you think G.I. Joe® was advertised as an **action figure** and not a doll?

⑩ The toys that will be popular ten years from now possibly have not been invented yet. What toy would you like to invent that could be made in the future and why?

Toy ______

Reason ______

Comprehension Reflections

Look at the top of the opposite page. This text is an I__________ text – R__________.

Write one thing you learned or found interesting:

Write one question you have or something you want to find more information about:

Rating   

Score 2 points for each correct answer! SCORE  /20  0-8  10-14  16-20

TERM 4

Grammar & Punctuation

AC9E6LA05, AC9E6LA06, AC9E6LA09

Adverbial clauses

An adverbial clause explains why, how, where or when a particular action occurred. As it is a clause, it has a subject and a verb. Adverbial clauses can make a sentence more interesting and add more information to the action or subject they are describing.

An adverbial clause is a dependent clause which means it doesn't make sense on its own. Therefore, a comma is used when it starts the sentence because it is part of a complex sentence.

Examples: **Until it was bedtime,** Sarah **played** with her doll. (adverbial clause tells 'when' Sarah played)

Emma **played** with her action figure **where the mud is very sloshy.** (adverbial clause tells 'where' Emma played)

Read the following complex sentences. Write whether the adverbial clause explains why, how, where or when about the action.

1. Fred would not call G.I. Joe® a toy because it was an action figure. ____________
2. When it was dinnertime, Fred had to pack up his toys, including G.I. Joe®. ____________
3. Fred started to pack his action figure away so that it would not get lost. ____________
4. As though it was on a mission, the dog unfortunately grabbed the figure. ____________
5. The dog ran behind the shed where it's dark and scary. ____________

Commas and adverbial clauses

Adverbial clauses are dependent clauses, so they need a comma after them when:

- they start a sentence. *Example:* **When all his friends are hanging out,** Fred goes to piano lessons. (tells 'when')
- they are embedded in a sentence. *Example:* Fred, **when he is at home,** does not practise the piano. (tells 'where')

Add commas where necessary in these complex sentences with adverbial clauses.

6. Because it still had the action figure in its mouth Fred walked towards the sleeping dog.
7. The action figure was wedged in its mouth where all the slobber was pooling.
8. So that the dog wouldn't wake up Fred very carefully curled his fingers around the figure.
9. Fred pulled the figure from the dog's mouth while a deep growl came from its throat.
10. Fred because he loved his G.I. Joe® grabbed it and ran away quickly.
11. The dog and Fred stared eye to eye when the dog stood up.
12. So that the dog wasn't upset anymore Fred gave it a big, juicy bone.
13. Because they both had what they wanted Fred and the dog were best friends again.

Score 2 points for each correct answer! SCORE /26   

0-10 | 12-20 | 22-26

TERM 4

TARGETING ENGLISH HOMEWORK YEAR 6 © PASCAL PRESS ISBN 978 1 925726 63 3

AC9E6LY09

Australian and American spelling

The word recognise, spelt with an 's', is used in this unit's text. However, you may often see the American spelling of the word with a 'z' – recognize.
Australian English follows British spelling very closely, but many common words are spelt differently in American English. Despite being spelt differently, the meaning of these words is the same.
The three main differences in spelling between Australian/British and American spelling are outlined in the table below.

British/ Australian spelling	American spelling
Australian 'ise' American 'ize'	In **Australian** spelling, many Greek-derived words end in -yse or -ise. In American spelling, they end in -yze or -ize. *Example:* **recognise** / recognize
Australian 'our' American 'or'	In **Australian** spelling, many Latin-derived words end in -our. In American spelling, they end in -or. *Example:* **favour** / favor
Australian 're' American 'er'	In **Australian** spelling, some French-, Latin- or Greek-derived words end in -re. In American spelling, these same words end in -er. *Example:* **litre** / liter

Write the Australian spelling of the following words. Use the information in the previous table to help you.

1. meter / metre: ______
2. centre / center: ______
3. organization / organisation: ______
4. realise / realize: ______
5. recognize / recognise: ______
6. analyze / analyse: ______
7. behaviour / behavior: ______
8. labor / labour: ______
9. favour / favor: ______
10. favorite / favourite: ______
11. colour / color: ______
12. honour / honor: ______
13. theater / theatre: ______
14. litre / liter: ______
15. fiber / fibre: ______

Practise your Australian spelling. Unscramble these words that come from the previous activity.

16. tteerah ______
17. cringeeos ______
18. eiaoutvfr ______
19. vabiheruo ______
20. roolcu ______

Score 2 points for each correct answer!

SCORE /40  0-18   20-34   36-40

TERM 4

Reading & Comprehension

AC9E6LY04, AC9E6LY05, AC9HS6K03

Imaginative text – Recount

Brian's Diary

Between 1945 and 1981, over a million Britons immigrated to Australia, and I am proud to say that I am one of them. The majority of us, like my family, came on the Ten Pound Pom scheme. I was reminded of this when I had to clean out the spare room and I came across an old diary of mine that I had kept as a child. When I sat down and read the diary, I felt myself transported back to a time when I was an eleven-year-old in England.

Dear Diary (DD) – February 1953. It's been eight years since the war ended – not that I remember much of it – yet we still have rationing and shortages of food. Mum still has to queue for food at the shops. But I've heard that chocolate rationing will end soon. And later in the year we can buy as much sugar as we like when rationing of sugar finishes. Oh boy! I can't wait to stuff my face full of chocolate and get Mum to bake trillions of cakes.

DD – April 1953. A kid up the block has got a new appliance called a fridge! No more ice to keep food cold. Imagine that! They must be rich because they're talking about going away to a holiday camp. We can't afford that. In fact, Dad says he wants a better job, and both Mum and Dad have said they want a better life with better weather. How can they get that?

DD – December 1953. Mum came into my bedroom and started talking about surfing. She gave me a picture of a surfboard and said that I could learn how to surf. And I could sit on the beach all day. Then she said something about migrating to a place called Australia or Austria – one of the two. A friend at school said I would be snow skiing, not surfing, if I went to Austria. I like the thought of skiing. Not sure why I have a picture of a surfboard though.

DD – January 1954. Well, things move quickly around here. Before I knew it, Mum and Dad packed up what little belongings we have and have taken me and my brother onto a big ship called the Orcades. Mum says it's a liner not a troop carrier. I think that means that it has more luxuries than other ships. Talk about a bit posh. We have waiters and dining rooms, and we can eat soup, a main meal and dessert for lunch and for dinner. I wonder what's for dinner this evening. I can't remember. Anyway, I have rumbles in my tummy just thinking about it.

DD – March 1954. Sorry diary, I've been too busy to write. It's been five weeks at sea. The adults have been getting a little bored, and lots of them have been seasick in the bad weather. But us kids have been running around the whole ship and swimming in the pool. The best thing ever is the stopovers. While the ship stops at ports to restock on fuel and food and water, we get to go on land. I saw snake charmers in Colombo and Mum bought leather sandals in Port Said. We will soon dock in Melbourne. It's Australia, not Austria, so no skiing. I still have my picture of a surfboard. I'm going to learn how to surf, and I'm going to sit on the beach all day.

This is where the diary finished, which is a pity as I would like to be reminded of my thoughts back then. Today, I think how brave my parents were to come to a place where they knew no-one. But life in Australia has been good, very good. But no surfing, or skiing for that matter.

TARGETING ENGLISH HOMEWORK YEAR 6 © PASCAL PRESS ISBN 978 1 925726 63 3

Reading & Comprehension

Write the answer or shade the bubble next to the correct answer.

The answers to these questions are in the text.

1. How many Britons **immigrated to Australia** between 1945 and 1981?

____

2. What **scheme** did the majority of Britons use to come to Australia?

____

3. Why did Brian think his parents were brave?

____

Think about these questions and search for the answers in the text.

4. Why did Brian's parents decide to immigrate?

____

5. Why did Brian think the *Orcades* was **posh**?

____

Use inferencing skills to answer these questions. The answers are not in the text. Think about what you know and what the author says.

6. Using context clues, what does **rationing** mean in paragraph two?
   - ◯ too much food
   - ◯ food causing rashes
   - ◯ shortages of people
   - ◯ shortages of food

7. Why would Brian think he was going to Austria?

____

8. Brian's mum said the *Orcades* was a **liner not a troop carrier**. What do you think this means?

____

Use your experience and opinions to answer this question. The answer is not in the text.

9. What if your family immigrated to a different country where you have no relatives or friends? Write two sentences to explain **two difficulties** you may encounter.

____

10. If you could choose where your family was immigrating to, what country would you choose? Write a sentence to explain your choice.

Country: _______________

Reason: _______________

Comprehension Reflections

Look at the top of the opposite page. This text is an I__________ text – R__________.

Write one thing you learned or found interesting:

____

Write one question you have or something you want to find more information about:

____

Rating   

Score 2 points for each correct answer! SCORE /20 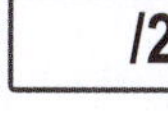  

TERM 4

Grammar & Punctuation

AC9E6LA01, AC9E6LA06

Formal and informal language

In Unit 23, we looked at formal and informal texts. The text for this unit is an informally written diary entry. Brian, the author, uses slang or informal words, so it sounds as if he is speaking to us. *Examples:* oh boy; stuff my face; kids; rumbles in my tummy

Writing compound sentences

Brian has also written some simple sentences starting with 'but' or 'and' which make his diary sound informal. *Example:* But I've heard that chocolate rationing will end soon.

We usually would not start sentences with 'but' or 'and' when we write more formally. Instead, we combine simple sentences to make compound sentences using co-ordinating conjunctions (joining words), such as and, but, or, yet, so.

Example: Mum still has to queue for food at the shops. **But** I've heard that chocolate rationing will end soon.

We can combine these two simple sentences to make one compound sentence with the conjunction 'but'. Use a comma before the conjunction in a compound sentence. *Example:* Mum still has to queue for food at the shops**,** **but** I've heard that chocolate rationing will end soon.

TERM 4

Join the simple sentences to make a compound sentence. Choose a co-ordinating conjunction that fits the meaning of the sentence: and, but, or, yet, so. Use each one only once!

1. I'm leaving for Grandma's house now. I'll be back home tomorrow.

____

____

2. Grandma is very old. I do jobs for her around the house and yard.

____

____

3. We might make pizzas for dinner. We could buy them from the pizza shop.

____

____

4. I love pineapple on my pizza. I also like heaps of stringy cheese.

____

____

5. Grandma always says she's tired. She can stay up later than me!

____

____

The following passage has lots of simple sentences and some start with a conjunction. Circle all the conjunctions and then rewrite the whole paragraph to make 5 compound sentences. Add commas where needed.

I went to a sleepover at Grandma's house on the weekend. But I really would have preferred to stay over at my friend's house. I wasn't allowed. So I just made the best of it. Grandma and I made pizzas. And we ate them in front of the TV. I was very full. Yet I still had room in my belly for ice-cream. Next time, we're going to make burgers. Or we could just practise our pizza making!

6. _______________

____

7. _______________

____

8. _______________

____

9. _______________

____

10. _______________

____

Score 2 points for each correct answer! SCORE /20   

0-8 10-14 16-20

TARGETING ENGLISH HOMEWORK YEAR 6 © PASCAL PRESS ISBN 978 1 925726 63 3

Phonic & Word Knowledge

AC9E6LY09

Understanding the differences – immigrate / emigrate / migrate

This unit's text is about Britons moving to Australia to live, and the verb immigrate is used to describe this. When people move from one place to another to live, various verbs can be used to describe the process.

Immigrate is a verb that means to move to another country to live that is not your country of origin. It is often used with the word 'to' because you immigrate to a new place. *Example:* Britons **immigrated to** Australia.

Emigrate is a verb that means to leave your country of origin and live someplace else. Emigrate is usually used with the word 'from' because you emigrate from a place you already live. *Example:* Britons **emigrated from** Britain.

Migrate is a verb that means to move/relocate. It doesn't have to be a permanent move, but migrate is more than just a weekend away. People who migrate from one place to another are called migrants. *Example:* Britons **migrated to** Australia for a new life.

Quiz – Circle the correct answer.

1. When you emigrate from a country, what are you doing?
   a leaving
   b visiting
   c working
   d arriving
2. When you immigrate to a country, what are you doing?
   a leaving
   b visiting
   c working
   d arriving
3. If Michelle was living in New Zealand, but now lives in Australia, which of the following sentences is correct?
   a Michelle emigrated from New Zealand.
   b Michelle immigrated to New Zealand.
   c Michelle emigrated to Australia.
   d Michelle immigrated from Australia.

Read the sentences below and circle the correct word for each sentence.

4. Brian's parents **immigrated / emigrated** to Australia under the Ten Pound Pom scheme.
5. Brian's parents decided to **immigrate / emigrate** from Britain for a better life.
6. Australia's **immigration / emigration** policy at that time focused on bringing British people to Australia.
7. **Immigration / Emigration** from Britain was seen as important for Australia's future defence.
8. Brian is an **immigrant / emigrant** from Britain.
9. Brian's dad was an **immigrant / emigrant** looking for a fresh start and better opportunities for the family in Australia.
10. The **immigration / migration** of people to Australia increased after WW2.
11. British **immigrants / migrants** often found Australia's weather challenging.
12. Each year, humpback whales **immigrate / migrate** from Alaska to Australia's warm waters to give birth to their young.
13. Brian's family **emigrated / migrated** to Australia for a better life.

Score 2 points for each correct answer! SCORE /26  0-10 12-20  22-26

TERM 4

Reading & Comprehension

AC9E6LY04, AC9E6LY05, AC9HP6P01

Informative text – Explanation

Positive Image

I rushed under the tree and heard the birds squark their dislike of having a human so close. I ignored it and rushed inside. I only had a minute to get ready before Mum took me to the shops to buy new shoes. As I glanced in the mirror, I saw it. Those birds had had their revenge on me as they had left a rather large sign on my shoulder. I hadn't noticed it until I looked in the mirror. That's when I remembered what my teacher had talked about the day before. I passed the 'mirror test'.

My teacher had been talking about self-awareness and self-concept. For humans, self-awareness includes what we think in terms of thoughts and emotions. This is what makes us different from other animals and controls our behaviour. A basic level of self-awareness is thought to be present in animals that pass what is called the 'mirror test', but it is unclear if these animals have internal thoughts and emotions.

The 'mirror test' is where the skin of an animal is marked while it is asleep or sedated. It is marked in such a way that the animal cannot see it directly, but it is visible in a mirror. The animal is then allowed to see its reflection in a mirror. If the animal starts grooming or cleaning itself to get rid of the mark, that is taken as a sign that the animal is aware of itself. It can understand that the mirror image belongs to its own body. Until recently, it was thought that only mammals with large brains, like apes and elephants, would show some sign that the image in the mirror was them. However, scientists have found that magpies and pigeons pass the 'mirror test', as well as dolphins and killer whales.

Humans, it seems, start to build a concept of self from four months onwards, and at 18 months we can recognise that the face in the mirror belongs to us. This is where the teacher told us not to conduct experiments on our younger siblings, but I couldn't resist. Mum wondered how the mark appeared on my little brother's face. Anyway, he failed. As yet, he is not as smart as a pigeon, but he is still a baby. Self-awareness develops as we grow, and it becomes self-identity. The tricky bit for humans is to make sure our sense of self is a positive one.

Our sense of self includes our thoughts and emotions, and lots of things can influence these. Our family and friends influence us, as well as what we see online and in the media. With all this going on, how do we maintain a positive sense of self? Positive messages from family and friends are very important and so is positive self-talk. If you catch yourself making negative talk in your head, take a breath and think of one positive thing you can say about yourself or the situation, such as, "This may be hard, but I will try" or "I know it's okay to make mistakes".

Being positive about yourself leads to more positive actions and behaviours. You will recognise that face in the mirror as yours, but, unlike animals, your thoughts can help you see yourself as worthy and happy. Oh, and don't get caught putting marks on your younger siblings even if you want to see whether they are as smart as a pigeon.

Reading & Comprehension

Write the answer or shade the bubble next to the correct answer.

The answers to these questions are in the text.

1. What is it that makes us different from other animals and controls our behaviour?

2. What is **self-awareness** in humans?

3. Animals that pass the 'mirror test' definitely have internal thoughts and emotions.

   ○ True ○ False

4. Until recently, it was thought that only apes and elephants would pass the 'mirror test'. What other animals have now been included?

Think about this question and search for the answer in the text.

5. How would you conduct a 'mirror test' on a **younger sibling**? Outline the steps involved in a 'mirror test'.

Use inferencing skills to answer these questions. The answers are not in the text. Think about what you know and what the author says.

6. Why would scientists think that only **mammals with large brains** would pass the 'mirror test'?

7. Why would a **ten-month-old baby** crawl around a mirror after seeing a reflection of themselves in it?

Our family and friends, as well as what we see online and in the media, influence our thoughts and emotions and sense of self.

8. Write one sentence to explain how family and friends can positively influence your sense of self.

9. Write a sentence to explain how online and media sites can negatively influence your sense of self.

Use your experience and opinions to answer this question. The answer is not in the text.

10. If you were a scientist, how would you go about putting a mark on the body of a killer whale for the 'mirror test'? You can be creative.

Comprehension Reflections

Look at the top of the opposite page. This text is an I__________ text – E__________.

Write one thing you learned or found interesting:

Write one question you have or something you want to find more information about:

Rating

Score 2 points for each correct answer! SCORE /20 0-8 10-14 16-20

TERM 4

Grammar & Punctuation

AC9E6LA08

Figurative language and positive self-identity

We are all guilty of being a little too hard on ourselves sometimes, especially if we have made a mistake or think we could do better at something. Using figurative language to describe the positive aspects of ourselves helps to create a better and more positive image of ourselves in our minds.

Similes

Similes are used to compare the characteristics of two things using the words like, as, as if or as though. *Example:* I am **as popular as** a family pizza at a sleepover.

Write four similes that describe you in a positive way. Do not use ones you have heard before. Form your own original similes like the example above.

1. ______________________________
2. ______________________________
3. ______________________________
4. ______________________________

Hyperboles

Hyperbole is a form of exaggeration, often with humour. Turn a negative hyperbole into a positive one. *Example:* I'm so stupid I won't pass any tests this year. / My brain is so large it hurts to frown.

Rewrite these sentences into positive statements using hyperbole (with humour if possible).

5. I can't do anything right.

____

6. I'm so unattractive even the mirrors won't look at me.

____

7. No-one wants me in their group.

____

Write two more hyperboles to describe yourself in the most positive and exaggerated way you can.

8. ______________________________
9. ______________________________

Personifications

Personification is when the writer gives human characteristics, actions or feelings to non-human things, such as objects or animals. *Examples:* The sun kissed my cheeks. The camera loves me. The last piece of cake set itself aside and waited impatiently for me.

Write four personifications that describe you in a positive way. How do non-human things react to you?

10. ______________________________
11. ______________________________
12. ______________________________
13. ______________________________

Score 2 points for each correct answer! SCORE  /26  0-10  12-20  22-26

TERM 4

TARGETING ENGLISH HOMEWORK YEAR 6 © PASCAL PRESS ISBN 978 1 925726 63 3

Phonic & Word Knowledge

AC9E6LY09

Tricky words – Effect or affect?

Positive thoughts and self-talk have an effect or an affect on your self-identity. Which word is correct in this sentence?

Effect is usually used as a noun, meaning the result of a change or an outcome. If there is a/an/the in front of it, it's an 'effect'. The sentence above should read: Positive thoughts and self-talk have **an effect** on your self-identity.

Affect is a verb. It means to change or influence something. *Example:* Passing the 'mirror test' **affects** scientists' opinions about certain animals.

Circle effect or affect in each sentence.

1. The 'mirror test' had an **effect / affect** on Sammie as he gave the test to his little brother.
2. In fact, the **effect / affect** of the test was felt throughout the entire family.
3. Sammie did not want his brother's test results to **effect / affect** his self-confidence even though he was only eight months old.
4. The results did not **effect / affect** Sammie's opinion of his brother.
5. Sammie's little brother failing the 'mirror test' was not the **effect / affect** Sammie wanted.
6. Sammie hated to think that pigeons had more self-awareness, but of course, his brother's age certainly **effected / affected** the outcome.

Allot or a lot?

Allot is a verb and is often confused with 'a lot'. To allot means to parcel out. *Example:* **Allot** one slice of cake per student.

A lot, on the other hand, is always two words. The word 'lot' on its own means 'a plot of land' or a 'group of something'. Often 'a lot' is used to mean 'very much' or 'a large amount'. *Examples:* If you like whipped cream, ask for **a lot**. (a large amount)

If you follow a band, you like their music **a lot**. (very much)

Circle allot or a lot in each sentence.

7. Your parents **allot / a lot** you only fifteen minutes to get ready in the morning.
8. You have **allot / a lot** of things to do in the morning.
9. You use **allot / a lot** of butter on your toast at breakfast.
10. At school, the teacher **allots / a lots** a space for you to store your bag.
11. Unfortunately, you have a large bag, and it takes up **allot / a lot** of space.
12. During the day, you have **allot / a lot** of things to learn about identity and 'mirror tests'.

Conscious or conscience?

These two words are pronounced very similarly and can be confusing to say and write.

Conscious (pronounced KON-shuhs) means being aware of yourself or the world around you. It also means being sensitive to something or being awake. *Example:* The injured man was barely **conscious** on the way to hospital.

Conscience (pronounced KON-shuh**n**s) is a moral understanding or an inner feeling of what is right and wrong. *Example:* My **conscience** was clear when I returned the money I found.

Circle conscious or conscience in each sentence.

13. Ed bumped his head really hard, but luckily he managed to stay **conscious / conscience**.
14. After losing his friend's book, Fred had a guilty **conscious / conscience**.
15. The teacher often wonders if Fred is awake and **conscious / conscience** during class.
16. Sam questioned Fred's **conscious / conscience** after he ate Sam's lunch.

Score 2 points for each correct answer! SCORE /32  0-14  16-26  28-32

TERM 4

AC9E6LY04, AC9E6LY05, AC9HS6K07, AC9E6LA07

Informative text – Explanation

Homework - My Form of Government

Hi Mr Wilson,

Our homework assignment is to show our understanding of Australia's three levels of government. I hope you see the connections I have made.

I want three things: **1** – New shoes for sport; **2** – More PE with the teacher and my classmates; **3** – Safety from bullies in the schoolyard.

How can I make these things happen? Who is responsible for these things? How can I tell them what I want?

1 – New sport shoes

This decision is made at home, so my home is like the local council/ government.

Local government	My home
Leader – Mayor or Shire President	**Leaders** – Mum & Dad
Councillors or aldermen represent the people to form a council.	The family all have some input, but the younger you are, the less say you have. I am the youngest.
Responsibilities: local roads, garbage collection, public parks, building regulations etc.	Responsibilities: provide food, clothing, a place to live, medical care, protection, love etc.

The adults are in charge of the finances in my local government or home, and although I do have some input, the decision is going to rest with Mum and Dad. As a council member, I assess the needs of the community, **me**, and I see that it's in the public's interest to supply new shoes to **me**. I have conducted research and chosen the brand that reflects the community's values, which of course are **my** values. I look forward to our next council meeting at the kitchen table. I am quite confident in my ability to win over the council.

2 – More PE

This decision is made in the classroom, so my classroom is like the state government.

State government	My classroom
Leader – Premier	**Leader** – My teacher
Two decision-making bodies (except QLD): • House of Assembly • Legislative Council	Two decision-making bodies: • Class meeting with students • The teacher
Responsibilities: health, education, public transport, main roads etc.	Responsibilities: teach the curriculum, plan lessons, write reports, have fun, do PE etc.

In our next class meeting, I will introduce a bill for more PE. As a class, we will discuss the benefits of sport for students and the benefits for teachers of a happy, active class. I believe the bill is reviewed by you, Mr Wilson, before it is passed. Either way, can we please have more PE?

3 – Safety from bullies

This decision is made at school, so my school is like the federal government.

Federal government	My school
Leader – Prime Minister	**Leader** – My principal
Two decision-making bodies: • House of Representatives • The Senate	Two decision-making bodies: • Teachers at staff meetings • Decision-making committee
Responsibilities: foreign affairs, defence, trade, immigration, currency etc.	Responsibilities: delivery of education, providing a safe environment to learn etc.

When I talk to you, Mr Wilson, about the bullying problems I see in the schoolyard, you then talk to other teachers in staff meetings and to the committee who deals with schoolyard behaviour. As you see in my table above, the school is responsible for a safe environment for students. This includes the sharing of the oval during breaks and how you can make sure my friends and I get what we want.

So, Mr Wilson, that is how I see the three levels of government for me and for all Australians. The only thing is, I did not vote for any of you as my leaders. Can I vote Mum and Dad out?

TARGETING ENGLISH HOMEWORK YEAR 6 © PASCAL PRESS ISBN 978 1 925726 63 3

Reading & Comprehension

Write your answers on the lines provided.

The answers to these questions are in the text.

1. What are the **three levels** of government?

2. What is the leader of the **local council** called?

3. Name three responsibilities of local government.

Think about these questions and search for the answers in the text.

4. What decision-making body is the **House of Assembly** compared to in the classroom?

5. What decision-making body is the **House of Representatives** compared to at school?

6. Which level of government would you approach for the following concerns?
   - ◯ the buses in your area
   - ◯ permission to add an extension to your house
   - ◯ applying for a passport

Use inferencing skills to answer these questions. The answers are not in the text. Think about what you know and what the author says.

7. What are two ways the roles of the Prime Minister and the principal of your school the same?

8. What are two ways the roles of the Prime Minister and the principal of your school are different?

Use your experience and opinions to answer these questions. The answers are not in the text.

9. What bill would you like to introduce at a classroom meeting for your class?

   Why this bill?

10. What bill would you like to introduce in your own home?

    Why this bill?

Comprehension Reflections

Look at the top of the opposite page. This text is an I__________ text – E__________.

Write one thing you learned or found interesting:

Write one question you have or something you want to find more information about:

Rating

Score 2 points for each correct answer! SCORE /20 0-8 10-14 16-20

TERM 4

Participial phrases

One way to join sentences to improve your writing is to use participial phrases formed with a present participle.

These two sentences can be joined to form one sentence by using a participial phrase.

Example: Sam **crept** up behind Chris. He was able to scare him.

Creeping up behind Chris, Sam was able to scare him. (creep + ing = creeping)

'Creeping up behind Chris' is a participial phrase and 'creeping' is a present participle. Note that there is a comma after the phrase.

A present participle is formed from the base form of the verb + ing. It is also used to form continuous tenses. *Examples:* writing, speaking, running

Combine the following sentences by using a participial phrase. Change the verb in the first sentence to a present participle like the example above.

1. Sam **heard** the council's decision. Sam jumped for joy.

2. Sam **ran** to the oval. Sam expected to argue for space.

3. Mr Wilson **placed** Sam's oval proposal on the table. Mr Wilson smiled wearily.

4. Sam **felt** proud. Sam told his friends about the proposal.

Combine the following sentences by using a participial phrase. Change the verb in the second sentence to a present participle. You may need to leave out some words.

Example: Mr Wilson left the classroom. He **took** Sam's proposal with him.

Mr Wilson left the classroom, **taking** Sam's proposal with him.

5. Mr Wilson talked to the principal about Sam's oval proposal. He **thought** it was a bold request.

6. Mr Wilson passed on the decision. He **tried** to hide his smile.

Participial phrases and conjunctions

Look at these three sentences: The class had a meeting. They discussed the benefits of sport. They decided they needed more PE.

These sentences can be combined by using subordinating conjunctions such as: when, after, as, while, before and coordinating conjunctions such as: and, but, or, yet, so.

Example: When the class had a meeting, they discussed the benefits of sport and decided they needed more PE. (note the comma after the dependent clause)

Or you can use a **participial phrase**.

Example: When the class had a meeting, they discussed the benefits of sport **deciding** they needed more PE.

Combine the following sentences by using a subordinating conjunction and/or a participial phrase. Use one coordinating conjunction in each sentence.

7. The class celebrated the idea of more PE. Mr Wilson added a condition. He asked for more homework. (Suggestion: start the sentence with **as**.)

8. The class heard Mr Wilson's condition. They looked in horror at Sam. They decided against the proposal of more PE. (Suggestion: start the sentence with **after**.)

Score 2 points for each correct answer! SCORE /16

TARGETING ENGLISH HOMEWORK YEAR 6 © PASCAL PRESS ISBN 978 1 925726 63 3

AC9E6LY09

Spelling generalisation – Drop the 'e'

The final 'e' of a word is dropped if the suffix begins with a vowel. *Example:* cut**e** + '**e**st' = cutest

Also drop the 'e' when adding 'y'. *Example:* slim**e** + 'y' = slimy

Keep the final 'e' if adding a suffix starting with a consonant. *Example:* plac**e** + '**m**ent' = placement

There are always exceptions to these generalisations. *Example:* argue + 'ment' = argument (drop the 'e')

Adding 'ion'

The final 'e' of a word is dropped if the suffix begins with a vowel. *Example:* immers**e** + '**i**on' = immersion

However, sometimes the root word changes when you add the suffix 'ion'. For verbs ending in 'd' or 'de', you change the 'd' or 'de' to an 's' and add 'ion'.

Example: colli**de** + 'ion' = collision

Complete the table by adding the 'ion' suffix to the words listed.

	collide	ion	*e.g.* **collision**
①	diffuse		
②	persuade		
③	supervise		
④	revise		
⑤	extend		
⑥	allude		
⑦	tense		

⑧ – ㊲ You are marking Sam's homework about root words and adding suffixes. Tick all the words that are correctly spelt. If the word is incorrect, write it correctly. There are 30 words to check!

Hi Mr Wilson, I have completed my spelling homework where we added suffixes. PS: I think I got them all right!

Spelling homework *Sam*

expand = expandsion ______

comprehens = comprehension ______

paste = pasting ______

argue = argument ______

provide = provision ______

slime = ~~slimey~~ slimy ______

invade = invassion ______

erode = erosion ______

paste = pastey or ~~pasty~~ ______

case = casement ______

base = basement ______

exploode = explosion ______

suspend = suspension ______

hope + ing = hopping ______

late = latest ______

Score 2 points for each correct answer! SCORE /74 0-34 36-68 70-74

AC9E6LY04, AC9E6LY05, AC9HP6P09

Persuasive text – Argument

Making Healthy Choices

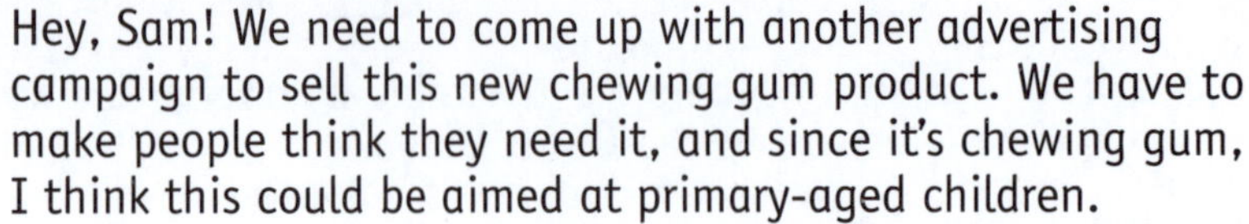

Hey, Sam! We need to come up with another advertising campaign to sell this new chewing gum product. We have to make people think they need it, and since it's chewing gum, I think this could be aimed at primary-aged children.

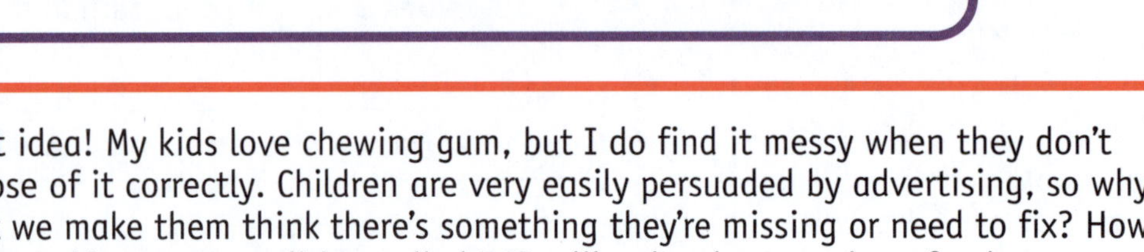

Great idea! My kids love chewing gum, but I do find it messy when they don't dispose of it correctly. Children are very easily persuaded by advertising, so why don't we make them think there's something they're missing or need to fix? How about making up a condition called PJS – like the short version of pyjamas, pronounced 'pea jays'? Only this stands for Poor Jaw Strength.

Oh, dear. Do I have it? Do my kids?

Relax, I made it up. We could say that, because teachers don't allow students to talk through class, students have an underdeveloped or poor jaw due to lack of use. They would rather text than talk or watch a screen than interact with each other. Teachers may disagree, but we could persuade children that they don't talk enough and need to exercise their jaws. What better way to do that than chewing our brand of gum because it provides the right amount of tension for the jaw muscles to get a workout.

That's brilliant! I do know for a fact that chewing gum increases your saliva production, which is good for oral health. A healthy flow of saliva helps wash away harmful sugars and food particles and protects the teeth from decay. So, our health information is that chewing our gum prevents children from developing PJS and helps prevent tooth decay. This will persuade children and their parents that making good healthy choices involves purchasing our gum.

Exactly. We persuade children and their parents to purchase our gum so that they can develop better jaw strength and oral health.

I might get my kids to start chewing the gum tomorrow. Maybe I should too, just in case. I don't want PJS.

Oh, Chris!

TARGETING ENGLISH HOMEWORK YEAR 6 © PASCAL PRESS ISBN 978 1 925726 63 3

Reading & Comprehension

Write your answers on the lines provided.

The answers to these questions are in the text.

① What does **PJS** stand for?

② How does chewing gum help with **oral hygiene**?

Think about these questions and search for the answers in the text.

③ According to Sam, name two causes of PJS.

④ How does chewing gum help PJS according to Sam?

⑤ Name two reasons why Sam thinks it is a good idea to aim their advertising campaign at children.

Use inferencing skills to answer these questions. The answers are not in the text. Think about what you know and what the author says.

⑥ Why does Sam say, **"Oh Chris!"** at the end of the email?

Students have PJS because they are not allowed to talk in class and they prefer to text than talk to their friends.

⑦ Write one sentence to convince someone that PJS is a real condition.

⑧ Write one sentence to convince someone that PJS does not exist.

Use your experience and opinions to answer these questions. The answers are not in the text.

The idea behind the campaign is to make people think that there is a problem that needs fixing. In this case, it is poor jaw strength. Make up a problem that you could invent a product to solve, e.g. a special comb to use at school to fix 'PE hair' or alarms that go off if someone opens your lunch box to stop 'lunch theft' etc.

⑨ Problem:

⑩ Product to solve the problem:

Comprehension Reflections

Look at the top of the opposite page. This text is a P__________ text – A__________.

Write one thing you learned or found interesting:

Write one question you have or something you want to find more information about:

Rating

Score 2 points for each correct answer!

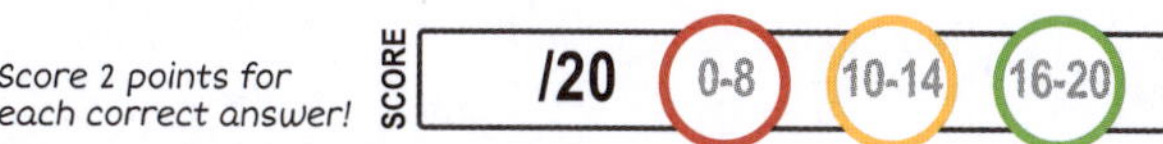

TERM 4

Grammar & Punctuation

AC9E6LA08

Active and passive voice in advertising

Advertising uses the active voice to capture and hold an audience's attention. The active voice makes it clear who did the action, and the information in the sentence is delivered more concisely with fewer words.

Passive voice is useful for making writing sound more formal. It also makes the sentence more objective by focusing on the result of an action rather than on the person/thing doing the action. If you do not know who did the action, or it is not very important who did the action, use passive voice.

To be able to switch between active and passive verbs, you need to know the subject and verb in a sentence.

Active voice – Advertising targets children. (The subject is doing the action.)

Passive voice – Children are targeted for advertising. (The subject is NOT doing the action.)

To make the passive verb, use the verb 'to be' + the past participle of the main verb. *Example:* **targets** (active verb) – **are targeted** (passive verb)

Read each sentence and tick whether it is active or passive voice. Is the subject doing the action or is it having something done to it?

		Active The subject is doing the action.	**Passive** The subject is having something 'done' to it.
1	Kids love chewing gum.		
2	Chewing gum prevents PJS.		
3	Chewing gum is loved by kids.		
4	PJS is prevented by the new chewing gum product.		
5	Chris and Sam are making an advertisement.		
6	An advertisement is being made by Chris and Sam.		

TERM 4

7 **Circle the active voice sentences that Chris and Sam need to use for their advertisement.**

This tooth was eaten away because of PJS.

PJS causes tooth decay!

Our gum needs to be chewed daily.

Kids, chew our gum today!

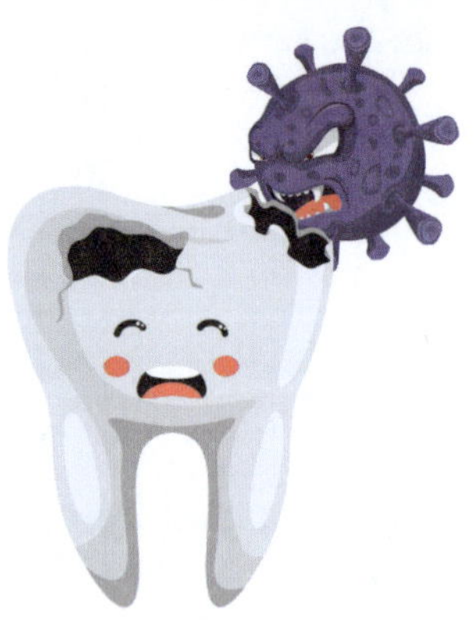

Lack of talking causes PJS.

Parents, buy this product for your children!

PJS is caused by lack of talking.

Children need their parents to buy this product.

Score 2 points for each correct answer!

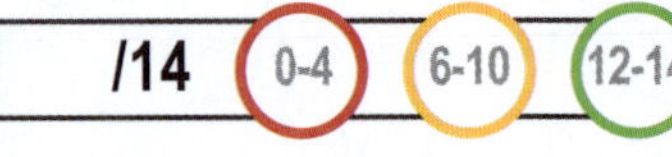

TARGETING ENGLISH HOMEWORK YEAR 6 © PASCAL PRESS ISBN 978 1 925726 63 3

Phonic & Word Knowledge

AC9E6LY09

Greek and Latin affixes

Knowing Greek and Latin affixes can help you understand the meaning of words.

In the text is the word interact which is made from the root word 'act' and the Latin prefix 'inter' meaning 'between'. To interact with each other means to communicate with or react to each other.

Read the following prefix meanings and word definitions. Circle the correct word in the last column.

	Prefixes	Word definitions	Choose which word
Example	inter – means between	to interrupt a conversation	interfere; (interject); international; interact
1	inter – means between	the portion of time between acts of a play or concert	interact; intermission; international; interplay
2	crede – means to believe	when you believe someone, they have this	credibility; incredible; credit; creditor
3	dict – means to speak	a person's manner of speaking	dictation; dictionary; diction; dictaphone
4	tract – means to drag	the act of drawing or pulling a thing	traction; attractive; interactive; traceable
5	audi – means to hear	when you hear something clearly	laudable; audit; audible; audacity

Match these words that have Greek and Latin prefixes with the correct definition. Write the words on the lines.

uneasy, impede, irregular, illicit, antiseptic, nonsensical, immobile, nonentity, irreparable, disposition

6. making no sense, illogical ____________
7. something that stops disease or infection ____________
8. impossible to repair ____________
9. not moving, still ____________
10. not permitted by law ____________
11. feeling uncomfortable ____________
12. prevent by blocking, obstruct ____________
13. something or someone that is not interesting or important ____________
14. a person's mood or attitude ____________
15. abnormal, unnatural ____________

Read the conversation above. Unjumble the bold words which come from the previous activity. The words are:

16. ____________
17. ____________

Score 2 points for each correct answer! SCORE /34   

TERM 4

AC9E6LY04, AC9E6LY05, AC9HS6K04

Informative text – Description

Winner! Winner!

CONGRATULATIONS! You have just been chosen to represent your school in a reality TV show called *Student Survivor Alone*. Your teacher has nominated you to be a contestant on the show, and your family have willingly agreed to let you take part.

How lucky you are to have such a chance! It is a once-in-a-lifetime opportunity. Many of your classmates will be envious of you and want to hear all about your adventures, as indeed will all of Australia. You will become a national identity.

You will be dropped onto an island somewhere in Asia with a survival pack and a camera. Your task is to survive two weeks without any outside help, filming all your experiences. Don't bother asking if you will be near any villages, towns or cities. And there is no point thinking you will come across any people as the island is uninhabited.

Do you want more specific information about your location? Most of Asia lies north of the equator. As you know, the equator is a giant circle around the Earth like a belt. Above that line is the Northern Hemisphere and below it is the Southern Hemisphere. You will be going to a part of Asia which is south of the equator. To find out how far south you are going, you need to know about lines of latitude. These are imaginary lines that circle the Earth below and above the equator. They are measured in degrees starting at the equator and ending at the South and North Poles. The equator is a line of latitude of 0° and your island is 8.4794° south, so it is still close to the equator. I suggest you bring lots of sunscreen.

Found it on a map yet? You need the line of longitude. Lines of longitude are imaginary, long lines that run from the North Pole to the South Pole. The first line, or prime meridian, is in England, and you can go east or west from that location. These lines meet at the International Date Line 180°, which is the boundary line between one calendar day and the next. Your island is 113.3466° east of the prime meridian. Bali is 115° east of the prime meridian, so it is close to Bali but not as far east from the prime meridian.

Hopefully, you have now located your island. It has beautiful sandy beaches, so practise up on your surfing and survival skills. You may need to learn how to make a fire, build a shelter, and find water and food. To make sure you find your base camp every night, you need to think of how you will remember your camp's location. You will need to use natural navigation aids like the sun, stars and landmarks to determine direction and location. Remember, it's an honour to be offered this opportunity, so enjoy the experience!

We will see you soon on Student Survivor Alone. On the Island of B _ _ _ _ _

Executive Producer
(Don't worry about the fine print.)

The station takes no responsibility for any accident or injury the contestant may endure while on the island.
The station also reserves the right to change the length of stay, lengthening the duration on the island to one month if ratings are good.
A contestant may leave the island early if they feel they cannot cope.

TARGETING ENGLISH HOMEWORK YEAR 6 © PASCAL PRESS ISBN 978 1 925726 63 3

Reading & Comprehension

Write the answer or shade the bubble next to the correct answer.

The answers to these questions are in the text.

① **What is the reality TV show called?**

____

② **When you are dropped off you will be given:**

- ◯ food and water.
- ◯ a survival pack and camera.
- ◯ directions to the nearest village.
- ◯ a national identity.

Think about these questions and search for the answers in the text.

③ **Where do the lines of latitude start and finish?**

____

____

④ **What is the name of the line of longitude of 180°? What is it?**

____

____

____

⑤ **Name three natural navigation aids that you will need to find your way back to camp again.**

____

Use inferencing skills to answer these questions. The answers are not in the text. Think about what you know and what the author says.

⑥ **The equator is a real line that rings the Earth. You will feel a bump as you pass over it.**

◯ True ◯ False

⑦ **Why would you need lots of sunscreen for the island?**

____

____

____

⑧ **Locate the island using the coordinates.**

The island is ______________________________.

Use your experience and opinions to answer these questions. The answers are not in the text.

⑨ **Why would the Executive Producer not want you to read the fine print?**

____

____

____

____

⑩ **If the island is close to other islands in Indonesia which have large populations, why do you think your island is uninhabited?**

____

____

____

____

TERM 4

Comprehension Reflections

Look at the top of the opposite page. This text is an I__________ text – D__________.

Write one thing you learned or found interesting:

____

Write one question you have or something you want to find more information about:

____

____

Rating    

Score 2 points for each correct answer!

SCORE 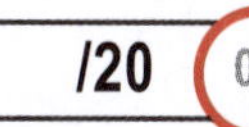 /20  

UNIT 32

Grammar & Punctuation

AC9E6LA09

Punctuation in a conversation

The last contestant on the program *Student Survivor Alone* was interviewed about being stranded in the desert. Their experiences were turned into a book. Part of the book has been copied here, but unfortunately, some of the punctuation is missing.

Add the missing punctuation which could include: , ! ? . " "

1. The interviewer approached Eve and put the microphone under her chin. Now tell me Eve she said with enthusiasm how was it?
2. In an exhausted tone Eve replied well it was certainly an experience.
3. Fantastic the interviewer retorted in an exaggerated tone. I think we all want to know about how you survived without water or food.
4. Eve looked uncomfortable and mumbled well I did know the producer of the show
5. What asked the interviewer in surprise do you mean you cheated?
6. This was when the film crew started to look more interested and Eve more nervous
7. No! I did not cheat! replied Eve. I just had some help, that's all.
8. What type of help the interviewer inquired
9. Eve looked into the camera and said I happened to run into some camels that had supplies.
10. The interviewer turned to the camera and said, we thank Eve for her explanation. We hope the next contestants find some help on their uninhabited island.

TERM 4

Commas and why they are used

As we have seen in previous units, commas are used in a number of different ways, such as in lists, after introductory words and phrases, in direct speech, between clauses in compound sentences, after dependent clauses when they are first in a sentence, and before and after embedded clauses.

Read the sentences below. Write why the comma has been used in each sentence.

11. The first line or prime meridian is in England, and you can go east or west from that location.

    ____

12. Once you have located your island, you can research what it will be like to live there.

    ____

13. As you know, the equator is a giant circle around the Earth.

    ____

14. Your teacher, when they had some spare time, nominated you to be a contestant.

    ____

15. Your family, friends and teacher all wish you well.

    ____

16. "I am so proud of our student," said Mr Wilson. "We will all be watching the outcome."

    ____

Score 2 points for each correct answer! SCORE /32

TARGETING ENGLISH HOMEWORK YEAR 6 © PASCAL PRESS ISBN 978 1 925726 63 3

AC9E6LY09

Latin root word 'tude'

In the text are the words latitude and longitude. The root word 'tude' is Latin and means 'a state/condition or quality'. Many words are made from this root word.
Examples: gratitude, attitude, solitude

While on the island, you find a note written on parchment paper hidden in a cave. The missing words happen to be derived from the Latin root word, 'tude'. Using context clues, fill in the missing words from the list provided below.

gratitude	longitude
extrude	solitude
latitude	altitude
aptitude	multitude
attitude	

If anyone finds this, then be warned. I was stranded on this island for many a year. It was the loneliness, the ① s__________ that drove me mad. I don't know what ② l__________ and ③ l__________ this island is, but I hope someone will navigate themselves here. I would certainly show my ④ g__________ to anyone who rescues me. I have climbed the highest mountain hoping the high ⑤ a__________ would help me see further out to sea. I have the ⑥ a__________ and skills to build structures for protection. I can ⑦ e__________ liquid from the coconuts on the beach. There is a ⑧ m__________ and abundance of fruits, but I am lonely. So, my ⑨ a__________ is one of frustration.

How I long to be saved.

Comparative and superlative adjectives

While on the island for the TV program, you have to record your thoughts. However, you are having trouble working out which adjectives to use when making comparisons.

You know you use comparative adjectives with 'er' and 'more' when comparing two things.

Examples: The cave is **warmer** than the tent.

Surfing is **more fun** than fishing.

You use superlative adjectives with 'est' and 'most' when comparing more than two things.

Examples: The **biggest** coconuts are high on the tree.

The **most beautiful** view is from the top of the mountain.

This is the first draft of your diary. Edit your work by crossing out the 6 mistakes. Write the correct comparative or superlative adjectives on the lines below.

Here I am on the more isolated island I have ever been on. I was the most excitedest I have ever been to find a handwritten note from someone who might still be stranded on the island.

The kinder thing I could have done was notify the authorities to search for this person, but that would have knocked me out of the competition. Perhaps it would be most good if I ignored the note. However, my conscience has got the betterer of me, and I have decided to contact the authorities. I hope this person is more happy than me to be off the island.

⑩ __________

⑪ __________

⑫ __________

⑬ __________

⑭ __________

⑮ __________

Score 2 points for each correct answer! SCORE /30

TERM 4

Imaginative text – Narrative

Mission for KAC

Lia peered carefully out the window, leaning close to the wall so as not to be seen from outside. The street was busy as usual for a Saturday morning. The neighbours were chaotically organising carloads of children to be driven to the various sporting grounds in the area, and along the street were the sights and sounds of lawnmowers chugging along untidy yards. Many a dog owner was forcefully pulled along by their pet prompting one to question which one was in charge. After surveying the street, Lia moved away from the window. You never knew who might be watching you. You had to be very careful in the spy business.

Lia's family, her mum, dad, grandma and herself, were recruited by the government agency KAC – Keep Australia Clean. They had found out that a large company was planning on dumping chemical waste into one of the country's largest rivers, but they needed to find out how this was going to happen. As a professional spy kid, Lia had been assigned the task. A school excursion to the chemical company in question had been organised for the next school day. Lia was to sneak away and take pictures of documents that would prove the company's wrongdoing. Easy in theory, but more difficult in practice.

During the lunch break on the day of the excursion, Lia carefully inched away from her classmates and shuffled behind a large container. No-one had noticed, or so she thought. A surveillance camera swung around on its mounted position on the wall and followed Lia's every move like a large, unblinking eye. It followed her to the director's office and watched as she picked the lock. It then noted her entry into the office. The camera inside the office picked up her image from there.

As Lia made her way around the director's desk, the director strode in followed by two security guards. In a cold tone she asked, "Can I help you?"

Lia stood up quickly and responded, "Yes, you can. I'm here to interview you on behalf of my classmates. I was just going to sit in your chair. It's cheeky of me, I know. I apologise."

The director eyed her suspiciously and commanded, "Sit! Ask me your questions now and they'd better be good!" Lia could feel her palms begin to sweat and her breath come out in little gasps. Did the director also notice her nervousness? Lia racked her brain for good questions that she could ask. She knew Mr Wilson, her teacher, had talked about asking open questions rather than closed questions to get information.

Just as Lia was stammering a response, Mr Wilson walked in followed by the rest of the class. With a knowing look to Lia, he said in a rush, "Oh, Lia! Here you are. I was worried we had lost you."

Mr Wilson explained to the director that they had to catch the bus back to school or risk being late, all the while guiding Lia past the security guards and the fuming director.

Once outside, Lia could breathe. She looked at Mr Wilson who quietly told her, "You are not the only one who works for KAC." A smile spread across his face like a little secret.

TARGETING ENGLISH HOMEWORK YEAR 6 © PASCAL PRESS ISBN 978 1 925726 63 3

Reading & Comprehension

Write your answers on the lines provided.

① What does KAC stand for?

② What day of the week did Lia's class attend the excursion to the factory?

③ According to the text, how many people were **recruited** into KAC?

④ What task was Lia assigned?

⑤ How did the director know Lia was inside the office?

⑥ In the first paragraph is the clause, **After surveying the street ...**
Use context clues to determine what it means.

⑦ **Mr Wilson walked in followed by the rest of the class. With a knowing look to Lia, he said ...**
What does **knowing look** mean?

⑧ Why was the director **fuming**?

⑨ If you were recruited to KAC, how would you gather evidence on the company without going to the director's office?

⑩ Should children be used as spies?

Write one sentence saying why you think they should.

Write one sentence saying why you think they should not.

Score 2 points for each correct answer!

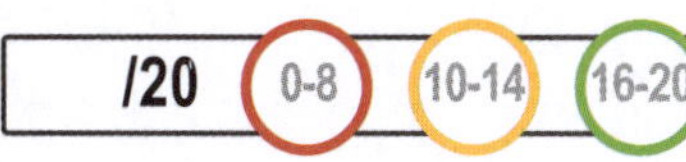

TERM 4

Grammar & Punctuation

Figurative language

① **Read the following passage from the text. Name two forms of figurative language used in the description.**

A surveillance camera swung around on its mounted position on the wall and followed Lia's every move like a large, unblinking eye. It followed her to the director's office and watched as she picked the lock.

____

____

② **Read the following sentence from the text. Circle the type of figurative language it is.**

A smile spread across his face like a little secret.

a hyperbole

b simile

c metaphor

d personification

③ 	In the space below, describe the action of the crane using personification.
④  	In the space below, describe the sneeze using a hyperbole.
⑤	In the space below, describe how your classmates dance using a simile (like or as).

Commas

Commas help us create meaning in what we read.

For example, "Let's eat Fred!" is very different from, "Let's eat, Fred!"

Add commas to the following sentences where needed.

⑥ Lia's parents when they found out were not very surprised by her actions. (embedded clause)

⑦ As the director watched Lia left quickly with her class. (dependent clause)

⑧ The class had no idea that Lia and Mr Wilson were spies but the director suspected they both were. (two independent clauses)

⑨ The director snarled "We will keep an eye on them!" (dialogue)

⑩ "Let's eat Grandma!" (to make sense)

⑪ The student said the teacher is a delight. (to change the meaning)

Score 2 points for each correct answer! SCORE /22   

TARGETING ENGLISH HOMEWORK YEAR 6 © PASCAL PRESS ISBN 978 1 925726 63 3

Phonic & Word Knowledge

Australian spellings

Start with the 2-letter word and add one letter at a time to create the Australian-spelt word at the end. Remember, you can switch the letters around. Record what letters you add and what new word they create.

①

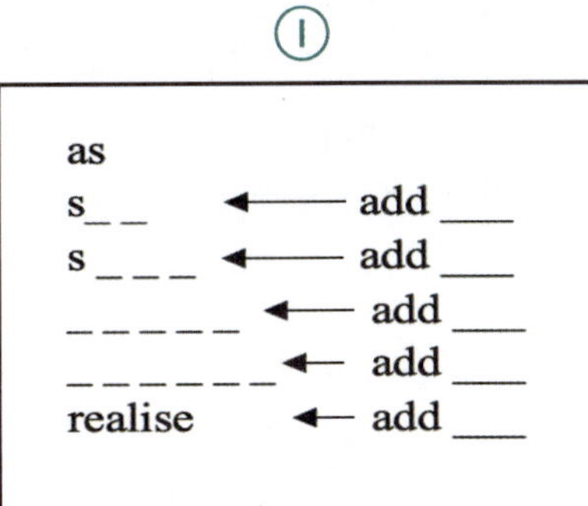

②

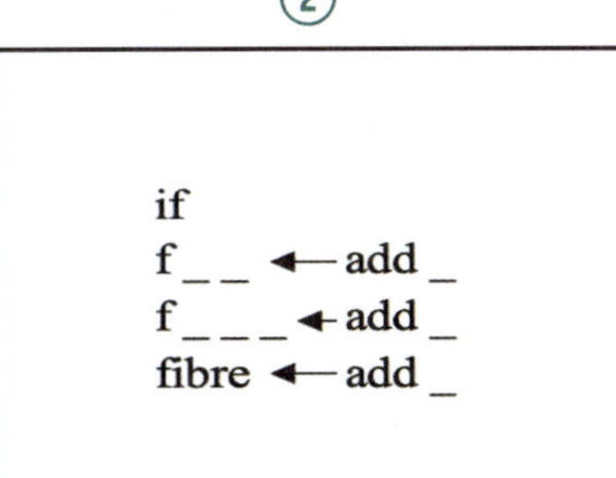

③

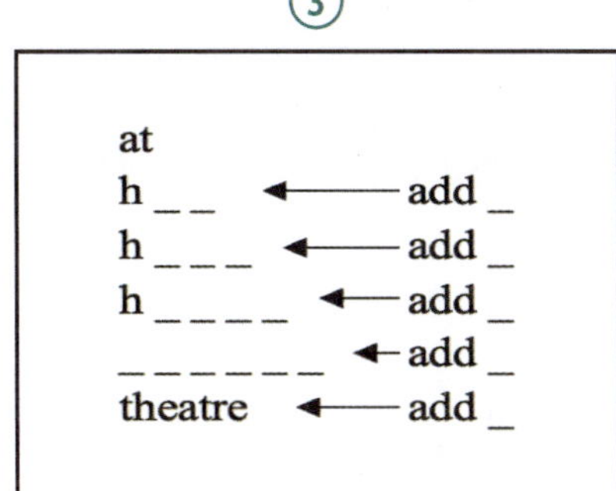

Find a word

④ – ㉒ Use the words listed below in the Word Find. The words are horizontal, vertical and diagonal.

r	j	i	n	t	e	r	c	e	p	t	o	q	i	c	c	o	i	t	x	d	s	p	i	s	t	n	m	d
n	b	b	r	n	c	a	v	j	x	c	p	i	s	i	c	r	c	s	y	a	e	d	o	y	o	y	k	s
g	r	m	o	b	k	d	v	y	o	w	h	d	d	y	e	x	j	j	u	u	r	w	y	j	f	q	b	d
m	z	a	q	h	x	i	m	m	i	g	r	a	t	e	i	l	b	k	f	s	g	g	g	m	o	f	a	l
s	p	r	h	i	n	o	c	e	r	o	s	q	d	b	n	k	r	h	e	q	c	c	u	v	g	u	c	t
d	s	e	n	h	y	r	o	q	z	y	f	w	p	w	x	q	f	n	b	t	v	e	b	m	l	t	j	y
k	m	z	n	t	a	z	r	x	r	t	o	c	g	z	x	p	g	d	z	z	u	w	p	v	e	x	z	k
j	p	i	g	b	a	n	a	l	y	s	e	u	k	z	q	s	b	s	l	z	e	t	l	t	e	n	e	b
k	g	u	v	j	h	m	v	m	x	f	a	c	c	e	p	t	e	d	u	j	o	x	f	u	i	q	t	t
r	u	j	s	k	r	q	a	r	t	n	j	b	q	o	w	x	y	d	s	s	f	a	v	b	a	b	b	v
q	j	p	e	j	u	u	f	h	o	y	p	e	t	r	t	o	s	d	x	a	p	a	t	c	d	u	l	q
y	j	r	h	m	g	b	a	y	v	x	y	u	u	r	n	y	j	o	p	v	f	e	e	t	c	v	u	e
p	o	j	h	z	i	p	n	t	d	b	o	w	g	f	i	c	s	w	n	s	s	o	n	z	r	m	c	w
m	f	e	i	a	x	g	j	h	i	q	x	t	p	c	h	c	d	o	w	v	g	p	a	s	v	d	m	j
g	h	a	z	e	p	u	r	m	y	i	f	k	k	q	o	y	d	h	w	o	n	d	q	p	i	h	s	q
c	o	b	y	z	x	s	a	a	f	c	e	w	c	t	i	u	x	l	x	r	v	z	e	a	m	o	q	y
o	j	r	l	i	n	p	o	c	t	z	z	n	u	u	c	d	j	r	y	f	q	u	f	t	w	i	n	c
l	w	p	c	i	o	u	r	d	m	e	w	a	m	l	a	m	p	l	i	t	u	d	e	a	i	q	s	z
o	p	p	g	y	o	n	t	n	y	u	r	p	t	a	u	j	y	t	r	z	h	r	h	e	q	t	g	y
u	p	t	z	n	n	a	r	p	x	k	z	t	s	t	k	p	a	u	h	m	x	y	x	j	j	t	h	y
r	m	w	s	x	u	h	y	q	a	l	o	n	g	i	t	u	d	e	b	e	p	l	u	t	k	j	h	h
m	s	f	e	n	p	p	x	z	p	t	y	b	m	t	u	j	c	b	s	w	a	m	d	n	m	a	n	j
i	m	b	o	s	z	i	v	v	t	c	i	d	x	u	e	x	g	n	s	p	q	t	r	p	j	d	d	f
j	o	m	k	b	e	h	a	v	i	o	u	r	m	d	a	t	v	b	m	w	t	n	r	o	y	e	t	z
w	z	u	l	d	q	r	i	j	j	w	n	y	q	e	y	y	x	b	k	x	r	d	t	e	z	h	x	e
l	w	t	r	z	w	y	t	d	m	b	w	g	s	s	d	b	a	p	f	y	h	t	c	a	m	k	d	p
p	k	j	p	f	g	f	n	y	a	z	z	p	b	o	g	f	s	b	f	a	v	o	u	r	i	t	e	f
i	r	h	e	b	m	i	o	t	e	x	c	e	p	t	i	o	n	t	i	w	m	p	i	u	u	s	a	w

'rh' words
rhinoceros, rhythm, rhapsody

'cept' words
susceptible, intercept, accepted

Australian spellings
behaviour, colour, theatre, analyse, favourite

'tude' words
amplitude, latitude, longitude

'ion' words
suspension, exception

others
emigrate, immigrate, argument

Score /19

TERM 4

Score 2 points for each correct answer!

TARGETING ENGLISH HOMEWORK YEAR 6 © PASCAL PRESS ISBN 978 1 925726 63 3

MY READING LIST

Name: ______________________

____

	Title	Author	Rating	Date
1			☆☆☆☆☆	
2			☆☆☆☆☆	
3			☆☆☆☆☆	
4			☆☆☆☆☆	
5			☆☆☆☆☆	
6			☆☆☆☆☆	
7			☆☆☆☆☆	
8			☆☆☆☆☆	
9			☆☆☆☆☆	
10			☆☆☆☆☆	
11			☆☆☆☆☆	
12			☆☆☆☆☆	
13			☆☆☆☆☆	
14			☆☆☆☆☆	
15			☆☆☆☆☆	
16			☆☆☆☆☆	
17			☆☆☆☆☆	
18			☆☆☆☆☆	
19			☆☆☆☆☆	
20			☆☆☆☆☆	
21			☆☆☆☆☆	
22			☆☆☆☆☆	
23			☆☆☆☆☆	
24			☆☆☆☆☆	
25			☆☆☆☆☆	
26			☆☆☆☆☆	
27			☆☆☆☆☆	
28			☆☆☆☆☆	
29			☆☆☆☆☆	
30			☆☆☆☆☆	
31			☆☆☆☆☆	
32			☆☆☆☆☆	

TARGETING ENGLISH HOMEWORK YEAR 6 © PASCAL PRESS ISBN 978 1 925726 63 3

Answers

Term 1

Unit 1

Page 3 Reading & Comprehension

1 'She'
2 His feet pads were sticking to the iron surface.
3 night-time
- shards of streetlight penetrated the darkness
- She swayed back and forth in the glow of the streetlights.
- looming out of the darkness was the rust-encrusted fence

4 ... encircling his waist and holding onto him with a vice-like grip, suffocating him and coiling tighter at the end of each breath.
5 snake
- She drew herself up to a terrifying height.
- She swayed back and forth in the glow of the streetlights, a hypnotic and dangerous dance.
- She lunged forward, encircling his waist and holding onto him with a vice-like grip, suffocating him and coiling tighter at the end of each breath.
- slithered back to where she had been hiding

6 She is the dominant predator, attacking those who enter her territory. She considers herself the ruler, and those who enter are victims.
7 The main purpose is to be able to escape predators as in the story.
8 eat greedily
9 The gecko fell heavily, collapsing onto the ground and feeling worse for the experience – bruised and sore. Answers will vary. Descriptions should mean falling heavily.
10 Answers will vary but need to show thought.

Page 4 Grammar & Punctuation

1 overlooked
2 encrusted
3 manoeuvre
4 restoration
5 descended
6 retreated
7 It followed along the path.
8 - its rusty uniform ribs jutting to the sky
- the ravages of time had reduced it to a sad and stooping remnant of its old self

9 - her black eyes were still and glittering like black diamonds
- looming above the startled and increasingly anxious newcomer like a gathering storm
- his short legs working as hard as engine pistons

10 Answers will vary but students need to be able to say what qualities they are comparing, e.g. speed, agility, skill or lack of skill.

Page 5 Phonic & Word Knowledge

1 outmanoeuvre
2 manoeuvrable
3 manoeuvred
4 outmanoeuvred
5 manoeuvring
6 outmanoeuvring
7 manoeuvres
8 outmanoeuvres
9 manoeuvrability
10 unmanoeuvrable
11 aeroplane
12 aeronautic
13 aerodynamic
14 aerobics
15 aerosol
16 pneumatic
17 psychic
18 psychiatrist
19 psychology

Unit 2

Page 7 Reading & Comprehension

1 sidestepped the attacks from the ruler of the path
2 the ruler of the path and Mr G's tail
3 brave and confident
4 dispute
5 shocked
6 **Reason she would** - to find out the local news
- to find out who is new in the area
- to check up on what the geckos are doing
- to check up on stories about herself

7 **Reason she would not** - The reporter, Sally Skink, is a gecko and is reporting from the gecko's point of view.
- It is the Gecko News, so the news would be of interest to geckoes.

8 Mr G disappeared and left the area because his story is false. He has exaggerated his own ability and the outcome of the conflict. He would not be able to take on the role as 'Protector of the Path', so he left the area.
9 Answers may vary but could include: It is intentionally misleading people to believe that events occurred in a way that did not happen, so it is lying.
10 Answers may vary but could include: It is a subjective view of what happened. We are all biased in our own stories. / Mr G exaggerated to save himself from embarrassment in nearly being eaten. / Mr G wanted to make a good impression, so he embellished the truth.

Page 8 Grammar & Punctuation

Adjective – describes noun	Noun – name of person, place or thing
Example: nasty	conflict
(1) menacing	hiss
(2) brutal	onslaught
(3) exhausted	frame
(4) mighty	scream
(5) valiant	effort
(6) large	creature
(7) heroic	efforts

Mr G's adjectives may vary but could include the following:

Reporter's adjectives	Mr G's adjectives	Nouns
round	*Example:* observant	eyes
thin	(8) muscular	legs
chubby	(9) athletic	body
nervous	(10) determined	attitude
meek	(11) deep	voice
dull	(12) lustrous	skin
small	(13) striking	creature
unsteady	(14) confident	walk

Example: cower or back away	shrink
(15) demanded	asked
(16) launched	jumped
(17) hurled	threw
(18) annihilate	beat
(19) seized	took

20 Answers will vary.

Page 9 Phonic & Word Knowledge

1 athletic
2 admiration
3 decision
4 production

Short vowel	Long vowel
Example: wisdom	wise
(5) reduction	reduce
(6) inspiration	inspire
(7) division	divide
(8) president	preside

ANSWERS

Answers

Silent	Sounded	Silent letter
Example: sign	signature	g
(9) design	designate	g
(10) muscle	muscular	c
(11) bomb	bombard	b
(12) resign	resignation	g
(13) doubt	dubious	b

14 resign
15 dubious
16 muscular
17 doubt
18 designate

Unit 3

Page 11 Reading & Comprehension

1. damp, dark and somewhat warm
2. when 'they' started to grow
3. Mould spores are tiny, microscopic fungi that float on every breeze.
4. a sandwich bag
5. a sandwich
   - Answers can include: the making of the sandwich – My new owner took me home and lay me in what I learnt was a kitchen bench. My outer wrapper was opened, and I was spread with delightful ingredients and then put into another wrapper and into total darkness.
   - Mum says, "You have a horrible mouldy sandwich."
6. mould spores
7. This describes the bread aisle of a supermarket where the bread is wrapped in plastic and lined up on the shelves.
8. The narrator was overtaken by mould spores and became a mouldy sandwich. The sandwich became a colony of mould and was consumed in the process.
9. The narrator had had enough. It was the last thing they wanted to happen. It was what lead to the eventual demise of the sandwich.
10. Answers will vary.

Page 12 Grammar & Punctuation

1. Until they started to grow, I did not see them.
2. After we were locked in the prison, the colony started to grow.
3. Before I became part of it, I resented the colony.
4. I missed my old self even though I was part of the colony.
5. I was covered by millions of them once they started to grow.
6. You will create your own colony if you leave your lunch in your bag over the holidays.
7. Because I left a banana in my bag all holidays, there was a horrible smell in my room.
8. Dad made me clean out my bag while Mum gave me a lecture.
9. The teacher makes me leave my bag outside whenever I take it to school.

Page 13 Phonic & Word Knowledge

1 **ob**-ject
2 ob-**ject**
3 dis-**like**
4 **pres**-ent
5 re-**ceive**
6 **de**-sert
7 **fam**-i-ly
8 **ex**-tra
9 **sal**-ad
10 **hea**-ven
11 be-**low**
12 **for**-mal
13 a-**maze**
14 **free**-dom
15 for-**mal**
16 **a**-maze
17 **be**-low
18 free-**dom**
19 doc-**tor**
20 hea-**ven**

Unit 4

Page 15 Reading & Comprehension

1. sponges and worms
2. 75%
3. An asteroid collided with Earth, blotting out the sun which dropped world temperatures. The oceans became more acidic.
4. 3
5. Coastal developments and overfishing cause a loss of ocean life. Pollution from run-off, oil spills and plastic waste is killing species at an alarming rate. Global warming causes the melting of glaciers, and, with that, rising sea levels. The extra carbon dioxide that humans make is dissolving into the water and causing the seas to become more acidic.
6. The sea level dropped because water on land froze to form glaciers. There was therefore less water in the oceans and seas.
7. Most living things on Earth need oxygen to reproduce and grow. When temperatures rise, so does sea temperature and more organisms can develop. Most organisms cannot survive with sea temperatures around freezing.
8. Answers will vary but may include: regular yard clean-ups/each class looks after an area and is awarded more playtime for the cleanest area/research how long it takes for plastic to break down/research the Great Garbage Patch in the Pacific Ocean/have plastic-free days etc.
9. Answers will vary but encourage optimism around the United Nations goal.
10. If plastic disappeared, cars, buses, planes, trains, cell phones, laptops, play stations, credit cards, water pipes and the insulation for electrical wires would be gone. Plastic has become an essential part of our lives. Students need to think at a deeper level and become aware of what around them is made of plastic and how they use it.

Page 16 Grammar & Punctuation

Simple Past	Past Continuous	Past Perfect	Past Perfect Continuous
Example: I **checked** my scuba gear.	I **was checking** my scuba gear.	I **had checked** my scuba gear.	I **had been checking** my scuba gear.
I **watched** for predators.	(1) I was watching for predators.	(2) I had watched for predators.	(3) I had been watching for predators.
I **stayed** clear of danger.	(4) I was staying clear of danger.	(5) I had stayed clear of danger.	(6) I had been staying clear of danger.
I **enjoyed** the dive.	(7) I was enjoying the dive.	(8) I had enjoyed the dive.	(9) I had been enjoying the dive.
I **fought** (fight) for my life.	(10) I was fighting for my life.	(11) I had fought for my life.	(12) I had been fighting for my life.
I **sank** (sink) to the bottom.	(13) I was sinking to the bottom.	(14) I had sunk to the bottom.	(15) I had been sinking to the bottom.
I **pretended** to be lifeless.	(16) I was pretending to be lifeless.	(17) I had pretended to be lifeless.	(18) I had been pretending to be lifeless.
I **threw** (throw) away my gear.	(19) I was throwing away my gear.	(20) I had thrown away my gear.	(21) I had been throwing away my gear.

Answers

Page 17 Phonic & Word Knowledge

1 unlikely
2 antisocial
3 inaccurate
4 inoffensive
5 illogical
6 illiterate
7 immoral
8 impossible
9 irresponsible
10 dismount
11 deconstruct
12 imperfect
13 illegible
14 unhelpful
15 disbelieve
16 unorganised/disorganised (both acceptable)
17 irrational
18 unhealthy
19 dishonest
20 immature
21 unfair
22 nonsense
23 illegal
24 unsuccessful
25 ungrateful
26 unbelievable
27 impossible
28 irresponsible

Unit 5

Page 19 Reading & Comprehension

1 land parts or plates are moved by forces under the crust of the Earth
2 are landmasses that have been divided by people
3 False
4 Asia
5 northern
6 - The Afghan cameleers brought camels to Australia. They began a transportation business.
- The Japanese and Malaysian pearl divers in Western Australia were important in the development of the Australian pearling industry.
- Chinese people came to Australia to look for gold in the 1850s. They set up many small businesses and helped pioneer the banana industry in Queensland.
- Many people from Asia have migrated to Australia, making our country a rich and diverse multicultural place to live.
7 Answers may include: Both continents have land in the Southern Hemisphere. / Both have large deserts. / Both contain large cities, and both have wealth. / Asian people live on both continents. / Both have access to Asian cuisine and festivals.
8 Answers may include: Asia is almost entirely in the Northern Hemisphere, but Australia is in the Southern Hemisphere. / Asia is the world's largest continent by area and population while Australia is the smallest continent in size and almost the smallest in population. / Asia has cities with over 30 million people while Australia's largest city is just over 5 million people.
9 Answers may include: In the times before motorised transport, camels were a vital means of transport in the inland regions of Australia. Horses struggled due to the soft sand and intense heat. Camels could carry more weight than horses and go for many days without needing water.
10 Antarctica is cold and barren and not easily habitable. There are no cities or permanent residents and people cannot survive or make a living there. Those who live on the continent are involved in research bases or stations and the other people are tourists. There are no indigenous people from this continent.

Page 20 Grammar & Punctuation

1 belongs
2 move
3 lives
4 live
5 fly
6 accepts
7 accept
8 plays
9 play
10 loves
11 take
12 bans
13 ban
14 takes
15 wish

16 have (Each family member has their own opinion, so the group is seen as plural.)
17 supports (The family unit is seen as one group [singular] – 'on the whole'.)

Page 21 Phonic & Word Knowledge

1–17
China – bok choy, chopsticks, judo, ketchup, kung-fu, tea, tycoon, typhoon
India – bandana, bangle, cheetah, cot, dinghy, jungle, pyjamas, shampoo, thug, verandah

18 arm**our**
19 col**our**
20 hum**our**
21 flav**our**
22 enorm**ous**
23 fam**ous**
24 hide**ous**
25 jeal**ous**
26 nerv**ous**
27 seri**ous**

28–47

m	h	c	y	q	b	a	r	g	a	i	n	e	u	e
h	p	s	v	i	l	l	a	i	n	a	c	o	s	d
i	a	k	e	d	t	c	u	p	b	o	a	r	d	i
d	a	c	e	r	o	h	m	t	h	f	p	e	x	n
e	s	l	o	m	i	b	o	b	u	a	t	z	w	o
o	t	a	n	l	u	o	w	r	m	m	a	g	u	s
u	r	r	p	e	o	j	u	j	o	o	i	i	n	a
s	o	m	b	y	i	u	c	s	u	u	n	z	e	u
e	n	o	f	x	q	g	r	h	r	s	g	p	r	r
w	a	u	t	w	k	h	h	x	i	s	r	h	v	p
g	u	r	v	w	i	t	y	b	e	n	s	s	o	o
p	t	j	e	a	l	o	u	s	o	h	a	l	u	t
p	k	e	n	o	r	m	o	u	s	u	s	z	s	i
h	n	e	o	t	w	e	x	g	z	b	r	o	m	o
z	l	h	r	a	h	f	l	a	v	o	u	r	l	n

Unit 6

Page 23 Reading & Comprehension

1 Sentosa
2 Malaysia
3 11 159 times
4 Population density is the number of people living in a certain space or land area. In Singapore it means more people live in the same area compared to Sydney. It is 1/17th of the area of Sydney but close in population. Apartments and homes are much smaller, and there are many high-rise buildings in Singapore.
5 The 'Mer' is for sea as Singapore is a major port in the world, and it is made up of many islands surrounded by the sea. The word 'Singapore' means lion city and the story is based on the presumed sighting of a lion.
6 It may be the third-richest country in the world, but there are still poor people. Some people are very wealthy and others are very poor. The difference between them is extreme.
7 Due to population density, there is not enough space for everyone to own their own separate house. Land is very expensive and there is not a lot of it, so one way to fit more people into a space is to build up with apartments.
8 Answers will vary but may include: population density; humidity and climate; access to the coast; type of housing, perhaps houses rather than apartments; food of choice; language; testing in Year 6.
9 Answers will vary. Reasons for – The test is one way to help direct students to high schools. It could create competition and interest in learning.
10 Answers will vary. Reason against – It is like NAPLAN and is based on how you perform on one day but with bigger consequences. It determines where you go to high school and could influence your future career/occupation.

Page 24 Grammar & Punctuation

1 As we drove around Singapore, **I noticed many temples.**
2 **I squealed with excitement** because we went inside the temples.
3 Even though WaterWorld was next, **I was very impatient.**
4 After I took my pictures, **we travelled to WaterWorld.**
5 **I should have taken my phone out of my pocket** before I went down the waterslide.
6 My phone, **although it was dripping with water**, was given to the teacher.

ANSWERS

7 My best friend, **who had followed me down the slide**, found my phone at the bottom of the pool.
8 My parents, **after we had a heated conversation**, understood it was an accident.
9 My teacher, **who knew where to shop**, helped me buy a cheaper replacement phone.
10 The relief on my face, **after I bought the phone**, was clear for all to see.
11 Before we flew home, we visited Universal Studios.
12 The ride, which was very expensive, would test my level of bravery.
13 No commas
14 The ice-cream, which I ate right before the ride, made me feel sick. Oops!
15 Mum and Dad, who usually have a great sense of humour, will laugh about this one day.

Page 25 Phonic & Word Knowledge

1 Portugal – Portuguese
2 Iraq – Iraqi
3 Chile – Chilean
4 Malta – Maltese
5 Peru – Peruvian
6 Finland – Finnish
7 Denmark – Danish
8 Ukraine – Ukrainian
9 Switzerland – Swiss
10 Greenland – Greenlandic
11 genealogy
12 photogenic
13 generations
14 gender
15 generic
16 genuine

Unit 7

Page 27 Reading & Comprehension

1 larger build
2 The bulky form was bundled ...
3 One leg was missing from above the knee. In its place was a thin, wooden stump that tapped along the pavement at each step.
4 Answers may include:
- bulky form
- bundled in a once-elegant red velvet coat that stopped at the knees, but grime and dirt made it look faded and worn
- jet-black hair was tied into a stiff pigtail and topped with a black, triangular hat with a brim that curled in on itself.
- eyes, glittering black and unblinking
- dirty finger with a black, broken nail
- the face was set and expressionless
- Dirty lace was bunched around the throat and protruded at the ends of the sleeves.
- One leg was missing from above the knee. In its place was a thin, wooden stump.
- vice-like grip
- stained and blackened teeth

5 - Fear swept through me like a searing wind.
- I was like a rat caught in a trap.
- A whistle sounded in the distance and a shot echoed through the dark like a thunderclap.

6 The yellow streetlights barely **pushed** back the blackness of the moonless night and **fell** weakly onto the approaching figure.
7 It was a moonless night, so it was very dark and hard to be seen.
8 The captain spoke in an angry, fierce way.
9 Answers may include: The things you want may not turn out to be what you wanted after all, so think before you wish for something.
10 Answers may include: to form a twist in the plot; to challenge people's stereotypical view that only men would/could be pirate captains; to make people stop and think.

Page 28 Grammar & Punctuation

1 S 2 M 3 M 4 M 5 S 6 M 7 S
8 Answers may vary, however, imaginative and clever ideas can be encouraged.
Example – Product: pasta
9 Example – Name using alliteration: **Pl**iable, **Pl**ump **P**asta
10 Example – Sentence using onomatopoeia words: A compliment to the chef is **smacking** lips and **slurping** off your fork.
11 The **bullets** <u>cried out</u> in the still night.
12 The **streetlights** <u>stood to attention</u> when the captain passed by.
13 The **coat** <u>sat stiffly</u> on the captain's shoulders as it was encrusted with years of dirt.
14 The **captain's hat** <u>stared menacingly</u> down at all who gazed upon it.
15 The **night** <u>looked down with sadness</u> at the kidnapping of a new sailor.

Page 29 Phonic & Word Knowledge

1–10

Long vowel sound	Short vowel sound
slave	olive
brave	above
shave	glove
drove	active
drive	native

11 heritage
12 language
13 porridge
14 ledge
15 cringe
16 fridge
17 knowledge
18 cartridge
19 hinge
20 porridge
21 cringe
22 language
23 knowledge
24 fridge

Unit 8

Page 31 Reading & Comprehension

1 Biased is an adjective used to describe someone who has an unfair belief about a group of people based on a stereotype.
2 A stereotype can be a label or a very simple idea about how, in this case, boys and girls should behave.
3 True
4 Babies were generally dressed in white or the natural colour of the fabric that was available at the time. In many western countries, boys and girls wore dresses until about the age of six when they would also get their first haircuts.
5 manufacturers
6 This is not an exhaustive list and students may add some of their own ideas. From: family, friends, school and religious bodies, online when playing online games, watching online videos and communicating with others through comments, photos and even avatars.
7 Answers may vary, however, students need to show some depth of thinking. The poem is describing the difference between boys and girls and is stereotypical in its description. Boys are made of unpleasant things and can be naughty and messy. Girls are made of nice things, meaning they have to be nice and sweet.
8 Coloured clothing means more sales. You have to buy different clothes for boys and girls which means hand-me-downs between siblings would not be ideal.
9 Answers may vary, however, students need to show some depth of thinking and to promote the discussion if their examples are more open or very stereotypical. Discussion can be on how they differ from the original rhyme.
10 Answers may vary, however, students need to show some depth of thinking and introspection.

Page 32 Grammar & Punctuation

1 My great grandfather, <u>who</u> live to one hundred, wore dresses as a very young boy.
2 He wore a dress, <u>which</u> I think is really cool, and leather shoes.
3 The photo of him, <u>which</u> Mum keeps in a frame, shows him with long, curly hair.
4 Great Grandfather did not get a short haircut, <u>which</u> is evident in the picture, until he started school.

ANSWERS

TARGETING ENGLISH HOMEWORK YEAR 6 © PASCAL PRESS ISBN 978 1 925726 63 3

5 My great grandfather, whose picture we were discussing, lived through two world wars.
6 shortest
7 silkier
8 more tangled
9 most expensive
10 the most intelligent

Page 33 Phonic & Word Knowledge

Syllables	Rule
(1) jum-bo	a
(2) flu-id	d
(3) mu-sic	b
(4) re-read	h
(5) fin-ish	c
(6) rain-bow	e
(7) ta-ble	f
(8) na-tion	b
(9) bea-gle	f
(10) dam-age	c

11 con-ver-sa-tion-al
12 di-vis-i-bil-i-ty
13 o-ver-sim-pli-fi-ca-tion
14 bi-o-de-grad-a-bil-i-ty
15 an-ti-dis-es-tab-lish-men-tar-i-an-i-sm

Term 1 Review

Page 35 Reading & Comprehension

1 The intruder was too close to him and his family.
2 early spring
3 The intruder was Sarah, a school student, cycling her way to school.
4 'He' was a male magpie or bird, and he was protecting the nest.
5 by staring at the bird and not breaking eye contact
6 simile
7 alliteration
8 personification
9 metaphor
10 Answers will vary. Students can be encouraged to be creative and even create a design for a device.

Page 36 Grammar & Punctuation

1 **Although** he was wary, he continued to stare her straight in the eyes.
2 She walked under the tree slowly **even though** she was in his territory. (no commas)
3 **As** she walked further away from the tree, Sarah started to feel rather pleased with herself.
4 **After** she arrived at school, Sarah was determined to find a new route that avoided the tree.
5 The students, although they were warned, decided to play under the tree.
6 Sam, who didn't listen to the warning, strode under the tree.
7 The tree, although it was the shortest in the park, was easily about 10 metres tall.
8 Sam, even though she felt nervous, climbed quickly and sturdily.
9 A flurry of feathers and a pecking beak, which would one day give her nightmares, sent Sam crashing to the ground.
10 Sam's friends, who had been laughing, ran from the fierce attack they were under.
11 the easiest
12 the biggest
13 more intelligent than
14 the most terrible
15 the bravest

Page 37 Phonic & Word Knowledge

Down
1 to bend in fear – **cringe**
3 to destroy – **annihilate**
4 to quit or to accept – **resign**
5 to select someone or something – **designate**
8 lung inflammation – **pneumonia**
12 person living next door – **neighbour**

Across
2 garments for sleeping in – **pyjamas**
6 threw with force – **hurled**
7 ugly or disgusting to look at – **hideous**
9 roofed platform on outside of house – **verandah**
10 powered flying vehicle – **aeroplane**
11 relating to muscles – **muscular**
13 facts and information gained – **knowledge**
14 quick in movement – **nimble**
15 the act of giving up – **resignation**
16 a series of moves – **manoeuvre**
17 greatly surprised – **flabbergasted**

Term 2

Unit 9

Page 39 Reading & Comprehension

1 365¼
2 the Earth's tilted axis
3 winter
4 Because of the Earth's tilted axis, different parts of Earth receive the Sun's most direct rays at different times of the year. When the Northern Hemisphere is tilted towards the Sun, it is summer there, and it is winter in the Southern Hemisphere.
5 Answers may differ in the positive or negative deliberation depending on how the students view it.
Positive consequences: There would be no seasons. / You would experience the same temperature all year round. / Tropical regions would be constantly hot and polar regions constantly cold. / You could pick where you want to live with the temperatures you enjoy. / You would need less variety of clothes.
Negative consequences: Experiencing the same temperature can be seen as a negative. / The life cycles of many plants and animals would be affected. / Life as we know it would be negatively affected.
6 The author is on the 'Straighten the Earth' campaign.
7 The author wants you to join the campaign and donate money to the cause.
8 Answers may include: You need to hear both sides to make an informed choice. / You may not be aware of all the consequences. / Everyone has a right to their opinion.
9 Those people are opposing the campaign. They are the opposition. Calling them negative paints them in a poor light.
10 Answers will vary. Reasons may be drawn from the text.

Answers

Page 40 Grammar & Punctuation

1–2

Is winter too cold for you?

Do you want to escape the heat or humidity?

Do you suffer from allergies at certain times of the year?

What if there were no seasons and you could live somewhere that has the same temperature or weather all year round?

In that time, we experience different seasons on Earth, but what causes them?

What if scientists could straighten the Earth on its axis?

What's not to like?

3 Ignore those who **stand in the way of progress.**

4 Join our campaign today for a **better, straighter** Earth.

5 You have to **tolerate** the seasons.

6 **Negative people** only want to **cause drama.** (You could have both or either.)

7 I might/could do my homework every night.

8 You must/have to help; It is essential/vital that you help

9 I must not watch; I will not watch; I shall not watch

10 My teacher could/may/might

11–22

Poor, **suffering** teachers <u>have to</u> take on the **heavy task** of marking homework. Students <u>could</u> <u>possibly</u> help by **selflessly** volunteering to leave homework for a week. Students believe it is <u>essential</u> to do homework every night. However, **hardworking** teachers **struggle** to keep up with the **onerous** marking required.

Page 41 Phonic & Word Knowledge

1 oxygen
2 synthesise
3 symptom
4 typical
5 lyrics
6 pyramid
7 Results will vary.

8–21

One point is awarded for every word with an underlined diphthong spelt correctly.

Unit 10

Page 43 Reading & Comprehension

1 an industry that calls our attention to a product or service

2 to persuade you to do something, buy something or think a certain way

3 so that you know how to make up your own mind without being easily persuaded

4 Answers can include: obesity, heart disease, diabetes and poor dental health.
Long term: anxiety and migraines

5 Pester power is a nagging technique used by children the world over to persuade the adults in their household to do or buy what they want.

6 Children use pester power to influence what they snack on or what they eat at mealtimes. This may be for fast food after being exposed to advertising.

7 Answers can include: Responsible adults make sure that children eat a healthy diet to become healthy adults; are the ones who need to teach children restraint; help children form good habits; make good choices.

8 Answers will vary. Students need to provide a sentence to explain their answer.

9 Answers may include: the need for budgets; the need to learn restraint; to learn patience and not greed.

10 Answers will vary. Students need to provide a sentence to explain their answer.

Page 44 Grammar & Punctuation

1–4

Answers may vary.

5–9

<u>Get</u> on board and <u>join</u> us in the campaign to ban fast-food advertising for children. <u>Improve</u> the eating habits of your family and <u>make</u> better decisions on what to eat. <u>Act</u> now!

10–15

<u>Demand</u> the best by placing your fast-food orders with us. <u>Order</u> over the phone or <u>text</u> and <u>have</u> your food in minutes. <u>Revitalise</u> family meals with our delicious take-away menu. <u>Act</u> now!

16–17

Answers will vary.

Page 45 Phonic & Word Knowledge

Prefixes	Base words	New words
pro	duct	product
de	(1) **duct**	deduct
(2) **in**	duct	induct
aque	duct	(3) **aqueduct**
(4) intro	(5) **duce**	introduce
(6) **de**	(7) **duce**	deduce
re	duce	(8) **reduce**

9 deduct
10 aqueduct
11 deduce
12 induct
13 reduce
14 induct
15 deduce
16 product
17 deduct
18 reduce
19 interference
20 reverence
21 persistence
22 clearance
23 insurance
24 significance
25 dominance
26 reliance

27 To be belligerent is to be aggressive or hostile. Students need to show they understand the word by explaining how they are gentle and nice.

Unit 11

Page 47 Reading & Comprehension

1 Student Identification Chips

2 email

3 finding more information; comparing prices; saving for the future; and questioning if they really need it before buying

4 a play on words

5 Teachers will know who is in class, the school will know where students are located during school hours, and parents and caregivers will be able to track their child's whereabouts at any time of the day.

6 **Protection** – password protection; no-one can hack the chip and track kids without permission. **Access** – schools can only access this chip in school time and parents and caregivers can access it 24 hours a day.

7 Answers will vary. Students need to explain their choice of example.

8–9 Answers will vary. Students need to explain their answer.

10 Answers will vary but may include: keeping track of pets; following celebrities; tracking people on their holidays; monitoring elderly people with dementia; helping people who get lost at sea or in the outback.

Page 48 Grammar & Punctuation

1 Answers may include: Students hate/have hated the idea of SIC.

2 Answers may include: Parents track/are tracking/have tracked/have been tracking their child's route from school.

3 Answers may include: Teachers find/are finding/have found/have been finding the system useful to monitor student absences.

ANSWERS

TARGETING ENGLISH HOMEWORK YEAR 6 © PASCAL PRESS ISBN 978 1 925726 63 3

4 Answers may include: My school monitors/is monitoring/has monitored/has been monitoring student movement during the day.
5 Answers may include: I feel/am feeling/have felt/have been feeling positive about using SIC.
6 have used
7 has been using
8 has been feeding
9 are wondering/have wondered
10 Schools **use/have used** SIC.
11 Students **feel/are feeling** safer while using SIC.
12 Sam's dog **loves** the cookies.

Page 49 Phonic & Word Knowledge

1 a
2 c
3 a
4 frenemy
5 motel
6 smog
7 podcast
8 labradoodle
9 fortnight
10 infomercial
11 internet
12 spork
13 email
14 twirl
15 screenshot
16–19 Answers will vary. Encourage imaginative answers.

Unit 12

Page 51 Reading & Comprehension

1 Energy is the ability to do work.
2 Energy is not a 'thing' because you cannot pick it up or weigh it. It isn't matter.
3 Kinetic energy is an energy of movement, such as with moving objects.
4 Potential energy is stored energy.
5 False
6 Over 200 years ago, scientists had a limited understanding of electrical energy, and they conducted many different experiments. In her book, Shelley used the current thinking around energy for that time.
7 Transferred energy is moving energy from one place to another. Transformed energy is changing from one type of energy to another.
8 Einstein said that energy cannot be created or destroyed.
9 digesting your meal – chemical
using a slippery dip – gravitational
using a rubber band and a ruler to flick paper – elastic
turning on the TV – electrical
a baby crying – sound
the warmth from the sun – heat
10 Answers may include: If this power were in the wrong hands, it could be used in many negative experiments to do with people, such as creating an army of monsters; creating superhumans by putting different parts of people together; overcrowding Earth if people do not die; rich people living forever etc.

Page 52 Grammar & Punctuation

1–6 Answers will vary; however, the sentences need to make sense.
7 I have a lot of homework.
8 My leg really hurts.
9 He talks a lot.
10 It was very funny.
11 They live quite a distance away.
12 Answers can vary; however, originality is encouraged. Possible answers: I waited for days. / I almost died waiting for you. / I started to sprout roots I waited so long.
13 Possible answers: It cost the Earth. / It blew the bank. / I had to take a loan. / I had to sell the family car.
14 Possible answers: Mum will kill you. / Mum will disown you. / Mum will hit the roof. / You'll be banned for life.

Page 53 Phonic & Word Knowledge

-ate	-ise	-ify
① regulate	*Example:* popularise	⑧ falsify
② activate	⑤ computerise	⑨ intensify
③ motivate	⑥ equalise	⑩ simplify
④ validate	⑦ pressurise	⑪ liquify

12 activate
13 intensify
14 liquify
15 validate
16 popularise
17 simplify
18 **al**right
19 **aw**esome
20 **al**ways
21 c**au**tious
22 **au**tumn
23 **al**together
24 w**alk**
25 dr**aw**
26 awesome
27 draw
28 autumn
29 always
30 cautious
31 walk
32 altogether
33 alright

Unit 13

Page 55 Reading & Comprehension

1 False
2 Electrons are found inside atoms.
3 Electricity comes from electrons moving around in a circuit.
4 A conductor lets the electrons move. Usually, this is metal wiring.
5 Examples of bioelectricity include: electric eels; electricity makes the muscles in our heart contract; the human body conducts electricity as nerves in our bodies carry small electrical currents.
6 The first diagram which shows the current moving from negative to positive.
7 When they are turned off, switches break the circuit, causing the electrons to stop moving.
8 Electrons are negatively charged, and two negatives repel. This may not be common knowledge for students unless they have conducted work around magnetism and electric circuits. Students may have misconceptions, and this is an area where teacher intervention is needed.
9 Electricity makes the muscles in our heart contract which in turn causes the heart to pump blood around our bodies. When the heart stops or is out of rhythm, a defibrillator applies an electric charge or current to the heart to restore a normal heartbeat.
10 Encourage students to 'think outside the box' to create diverse answers. Answers may include: flexible battery; portable battery; take camping and use instead of camp stove; swimming pool heaters; swimming pool lights; heat an aquarium; Xmas lights on a tree etc.

Page 56 Grammar & Punctuation

1–2 Drawings try to match the texts. The main idea is to see how punctuation changes the meaning of a text and how important it is to use in writing to create meaning.
3 When a battery is connected to a circuit, electrons flow (or move) from the negative side of the battery.
4 After he got home, Sam started reading about electricity.
5 "Oh, it was okay," said Sam, trying to act relaxed.
6 Dad walked in and said, "I have read a message from your teacher, something about a test."
7 Sam swallowed hard, "Really, I wonder what that could be about?"
OR "Really? I wonder what that could be about?"
8 Dad looked at Sam and asked, "So you know nothing about it?"
9 Sam replied, "I think the teacher sent a message telling you how fantastic I was today." (could use … today!")
10 Sam's mum looked away, rather amused, and said, "I think we have ants in the kitchen." (could use … kitchen!")

Answers

Page 57 Phonic & Word Knowledge

1 mistake
2 mistreated
3 miscalculation
4 mistrusted
5 misconstrued
6 mismanagement
7 misconstrued
8 mistake
9 miscalculation
10 mismanagement
11 mistrusted
12 mistreated
13 biodegradable
14 biochemist
15 biofuel
16 biosphere
17 biogas
18 biopic
19 bioelectric
20 biology
21 biohazard

22–36

```
n c s f q e o x e v l g b b l h t e l b u h n i x d i o t d
z m z q p a u p r r q m w v o i p a y d b i o c h e m i s t
j j y e h b r e i i a i h r p z b h j b d j v t e k g r h j
k x x f p h a h q b m i y u b i o s p h e r e t f r e l q u
j f a l j f l v j v m z o r m t f o k r r q g e j b m q l c
h j p r e f c z f o t t m f e y h z h w r a n y c n t m g q
z y m r r i g m i l n g b t h l l f x x r p q g o m x e f n
h s k i b t t n v m h q m i s m a n a g e m e n t w i m u J
b s w r h z m o b i m u j s k x s q m w x m b d l v f y v w
b q b m v l z m q s o h h m g l n v z q p h d w t x s e z q
i v p i n o z u u t z y s i r r x v o l u m p v z m y k h q
o w s s m x e f q r d d m s h g c w g l o b g c k s o h p y
h t k c h a p d u u c a f c z s b q r y m t j x c b i g g k
a t c a d d q n l s n n s o u t z s j z e i v i k y o t b a
z z f l s a e u q t k c z n t p k q q d o y s h p n h s i o
a n d c y i q u y e o y k s s r g w p h l e t t a a w n o d
r g a u e s p x e d n l c t y w t n n q d k a v r a z i p f
d f x l a j r a h d h d i r b e x e f u h t h f v e v b i b
o f v a b i m r j k b n o u i e w m e a x n u v d k a t c n
n k b t h b x b q s q p e e o n h e a e h d o e a d j t p s
y g k i e z u x b j t f a d d b i o g a s g m b b p c v e z
r e n o h e q c m z f e d h e o y b h j p o i h y r w r n d
t y s n b i o l o g y c q f g y r r u t z l s h f s x e s x
s l d a f z l t q y j c r j r t r g s f x m t r p p l g m j
n f h b i o e l e c t r i c a i n b h h r q a s y s a n h i
q f u k a l q u w d m f z n d c o b w m l z k j r r e k d m
y l y y w t i b p d r s a x a c b m d b f e e u s l f d s k
c v l f j z a c s k e o v j b l x b s y m l d o d p q y m u
m r i y n l v s x j o j e o l p y z a k w d b h z d t x k w
b x m o b i o f u e l n t h e r t i o k k p e d w h b c m m
```

Unit 14

Page 59 Reading & Comprehension

1 Britain or the UK
2 False
3 leather shoes
4 The different taxes and laws for each colony make it hard to do business. Fred finds travelling difficult because each colony has different rail gauges. He hops on and off trains all the time and pays taxes each time.
5 The colonies do not agree on many things. Some of the larger and more populous colonies feel they will lose power, and some smaller colonies feel they will not be listened to if Federation goes ahead.
6 The author is a woman, and not all women had gained the right to vote before Federation. The exceptions were SA in 1894 and WA in 1899.
7 The author sees herself as being less attached to the mother country and developing a sense of belonging in Australia. She sees Australia as her home.
8 The mother country was the place where people originated from, the country of birth for the first settlers. The colonies could be seen as the offspring or children of the original country.
9 The thought of being vulnerable to attack from other nations and the thought of invasion.
10 The correct answers are NSW and Victoria. They were powerful as they had larger populations. They both believed that they were the best colony and so didn't want to federate. Points can be awarded if students show they have thought about the topic and can explain their thinking. If the answers are incorrect then misconceptions need to be addressed; however, thinking around the topic can be rewarded.

Page 60 Grammar & Punctuation

1 "Federation is the next topic of study," the teacher explained to the class.
2 "Sorry, but I already know all about this," stated Sam to the teacher.
3 "I'm sorry, Sam, but I don't think you do," the teacher persisted.
4 "Oh, I do, so I don't need to stay in class for these lessons," Sam said very confidently.
5 "Oh, I just watch YouTube. Don't you?" asked Sam.
6 "Please, tell us what you know!" exclaimed the teacher with a smile.
7 "Oh, how long before recess?" asked Sam, darting a look at the clock on the wall.
8 The teacher beamed and said, "Fantastic Sam, please go on."
9 Sam started to look confused and asked, "You mean there's more?"
10 With an encouraging smile, the teacher asked, "Why did people want Federation?"
11 "Well," started Sam, "there was not a combined army or navy to fight against invaders."
12 "What other reasons," asked Mr Wilson smiling, "were there for Federation?"
13 "That's right!" exclaimed Mr Wilson. "However, some people did not want Federation."
14 "Some powerful people were worried," explained Sam. "They thought they would lose money and power to the smaller states."
15 "I am most impressed, Sam," said Mr Wilson. "I know you'd love to continue after recess."

Page 61 Phonic & Word Knowledge

1	**translation** vibration decoration	donation population
2	confession impression	repression expression
3	omission admission	commission remission
4	admiration examination	determination observation

5 knew
6 insight
7 council
8 elicit
9 too
10 stationery
11 time
12 reign
13 allude
14 lightning
15 wholly

Unit 15

Page 63 Reading & Comprehension

1 all of the above
2 Gravity is an invisible force that pulls objects towards each other.
3 If the Sun suddenly lost its gravitational pull, then the planets in our solar system, including us, would fly off in straight lines away from the Sun to drift in space.
4 It seems Dr G's power came via the comic book – an eerie glow emanated from the comic by the bed, forming a small globe of light that seeped into Pat's sleeping form.
5 Without Earth's gravity, the water from rivers and oceans started to rise upwards. Even the air in the atmosphere began to float into space. No-one would last long if the planet did not have gravity. Life would not be able to exist. Humans would also drift into space where survival is impossibe without life support.
6 Pat was planning to relocate the entire school. The headline would question where the school went.
7 Pat wanted to relocate the school so there would be no school the next day. Pat wanted to see the surprise on the faces of the teachers and perhaps gloat or delight in their surprise and inability to teach the students.
8 Pat's eyes grew large with fear with the realisation of what was happening. He restored gravity as he was afraid of the consequences.

ANSWERS

9 Answers will vary but could include: **Positive** – not limited to our solar system; tour of the galaxy; we would be free and not captured by a sun.
Negative – no sun = no life; it would be cold and we would freeze; we would be lost and float aimlessly in space.

10 Answers will vary. Encourage answers other than what is in the text. Answers could include: lifting a swimming pool from a neighbour's house to yours; stopping car crashes; saving stranded whales or marine life; helping birds when they fall from their nest; getting to places without the traffic; getting rid of rubbish such as the Pacific Garbage Patch.

Page 64 Grammar & Punctuation

1 Answers will vary but could include: The school took off like a lumbering giant; like an old wreck wrenched from its moorings; like a speeding rocket.

2 Answers will vary but could include: The school was as eager as the students to fly away; insignificant as a fly as it flew higher.

3–4 Answers will vary but could include: The school escaped from the students and flew to freedom; The building planted its feet onto the ground, resisting until the last moment.

5 lead balloon

6 uninvited guests

7 deafening silence

8 only choice

9 Answers may vary but can include: sad smile

10 silent scream

11 open secret

12 loud whisper

13 Answers may vary but can include: If Pat is working, then it is not a vacation.

14 In order for a pizza to be in halves, each piece must be equal and not larger than the other half.

15 Pat's brother's opinion is his personal belief, so it cannot be unbiased.

Page 65 Phonic & Word Knowledge

1–18

'i' before 'e'	achieve, brief, patience, pierce, hygiene, priest, friend
except after 'c'	ceiling, receipt, conceit, receive, deceit, deceive, perceive
or when sounding like 'ay'	beige, sleigh, vein, weight, freight, neighbour, feint

19 neither: not the one nor the other

20 caffeine: a stimulant found in tea and coffee

21 counterfeit: a fake or forgery

22 foreign: strange or unfamiliar; outside your country

23 forfeit: to lose or give up something as a consequence of something that you have done

24 leisure: free time or relaxation

25 height: measurement of someone from head to foot

26 their: belonging to or connected to someone

27 weird: very strange and unusual

28 seize: to take something quickly and keep hold of it

29 seize
30 neither
31 ceiling
32 height
33 weight
34 forfeit
35 achieve
36 brief

Unit 16

Page 67 Reading & Comprehension

1 Member of Parliament
2 green
3 House of Representatives
4 a proposal of a new law
5 red
6 the Senate
7 False
8 Lower House; Upper House; committee; amended; Lower House; Upper House; King

9 The bill would be to pay the MPs in Jenkins Street Parliament.

10 Answers will vary. Points are awarded if students give a reason for their bill.

Page 68 Grammar & Punctuation

1 The King's signature is needed.

2 The Senate's colour is red.

3 no apostrophe

4 Sam's bill was passed.

5 In the street, other families' children wanted the same bill.

6 no apostrophe

7 Many kings' signatures have been added to many bills in the past.

8 All the teachers' discussions were about Sam's bill.

9 men's fashion

10 women's fashion

11 people's vote

12 sheep's wool

13 James's

14 Lois's

15–22

Sam's bill caused a lot of discussion. Many **families'** furniture was examined for green and red so that they too could have their own Upper and Lower Houses. The **teachers'** discussions in the staffroom revolved around the bill, and the **school's** homework policy was reviewed. Initially, it had been **James's** idea, but **Sam's** family passed the bill. In the district, many **schools'** discussions and many **classes'** discussions were about homework.

Page 69 Phonic & Word Knowledge

1–12

Generalisations for 'or'	Examples
verbs with more than one syllable ending in 'it'	edit – editor **visitor** **creditor**
verbs with more than one syllable ending in 'ate'	narrate – narrator **educator** **generator**
Verbs ending in 'ct'	act – actor **contractor** **instructor**
Generalisations for 'er'	**Examples**
verbs ending in silent 'e'	bake – baker **organiser** **writer**
Verbs ending with a single consonant (sometimes double last consonant)	bat – batter **reader** **traveller**
Verbs ending with two or more consonants	dust – duster **watcher** **jumper**

13–32

narrator; traveller; contractor; watcher

Term 2 Review

Page 71 Reading & Comprehension

1 They entered the theatre to seek refuge from the storm.

2 They did not see the sign that asked for payment upon entry.

3 The three friends were astonished to see their own images projected in front of them. It was a recording of their entry into the theatre and passage past the ticket booth.

4 The theatre is to be demolished in the next week.

5 Answers may vary but can include the following: the door was open, inviting them inside; a heavy darkness was within; some of the posters on the wall were more recent than others; the sign on the ticket booth that they ignored, asking for payment on entry; the flicker of light on the screen; the smell of popcorn; the sound of music when

that was not possible; the whispering of a non-existent audience; the development of a sense of excitement; the projection of the three friends from an unknown source; the magnified sign asking for an entry fee.

6 They were fascinated.
7 The author meant to warn the reader that something was inside the theatre and that something bad would happen to those who entered.
8 The floors of theatres are sloped so people at the back can see over the heads of those in the seats in front.
9 The children paid for their admission by being trapped in a movie poster and hung on the wall. That is why the poster reads PAID IN FULL.
10 Answers will vary. Encourage students to be creative and think about an alternative ending.

Page 72 Grammar & Punctuation

1–3

Answers may include: The sky frowned down upon them; The wind played and tugged; It enticed them to run for shelter; the sky unleashed its anger; its door was open, inviting them inside; a heavy darkness was within; threadbare seats that sat stiffly facing the front; the mystical camera caught its dance.

4 "Have you finished marking the maths tests yet?" asked Mr Wilson, the class teacher.
5 "Are you kidding?" replied Ms Smith, the maths specialist. "I have four classes to mark!"
6 "Sorry," replied Mr Wilson, "it's just that I'm worried about three of my students." OR "Sorry," replied Mr Wilson. "It's just that I'm worried about three of my students."
7 "Oh, I know who you mean," she answered with a frown. "They have been missing for a week now, haven't they?"
8 Mr Wilson shifted uneasily on his feet and added, "It's just that the street has become so busy since they started knocking down that old theatre that I fear for all students' safety."
9 Ms Smith looked out the window and replied, "Yes, I know what you mean."
At that moment a crash was heard as one of the theatre walls was knocked in.
10 Answers will vary but may include: saving heritage or history of the area; not many theatres left so it could be restored and put to use; it could be used for the community as a whole not just for single homes; residents may be worried how the land will be used as it may devalue their property; they may want to develop the existing building.
11 Answers will vary but may include: it is a danger and attracts rodents etc; the land could be put to better use since it is valuable; people need housing, and the land could be used to help with the problem by building high density housing; getting rid of an eyesore may bring property values up.
12 Answers will vary but there need to be two reasons with some emotional language and use of personal pronouns. May include emotional language about families being missed and being missed by families; the loss of a child would be devastating; we are innocent; we did not see the sign; there could be a trade-off where students bargain for themselves only and use the others as payment.

Page 73 Phonic & Word Knowledge

1 caesar salad – Restaurateur **Caesar** Cardini created the **salad** that now bears his name.
2 diesel – Rudolf **Diesel**, a German–French mechanical engineer, invented the **diesel** engine that bears his name. **Diesel** is a type of fuel that was developed to work inside the **diesel** engine.
3 Fahrenheit – The **Fahrenheit** temperature scale is named after German physicist Daniel Gabriel **Fahrenheit**. **Fahrenheit** was the first person to use mercury in a thermometer.
4 Disneyland – Walt **Disney** was an American pioneer, cartoonist and animator.
5 Barbie™ – A doll named after **Barbera**, the daughter of Ruth Mosko who created the doll in 1959.
6 friend
7 weigh
8 belief; neighbourhood
9 received
10 sufficient
11 weird
12 inconceivable
13 veil
14 weight
15 believe
16 awesome
17 draw
18 cautious
19 altogether
20 autumn

Term 3

Unit 17

Page 75 Reading & Comprehension

1 a ghostly snake
2 The fire plan was to fall to the floor where the smoke is not as thick and feel along the wall for the door.
3 Mr Quibb
4 Mr Quibb had no cape, superpowers or rippling muscles.
5 Mr Quibb was different to the other neighbours. He was bald and shuffled more than walked. He was rarely seen outside of his house.
6 Jess realised that heroes do not need capes and superpowers but need to make a difference through their actions.
7 Jess wanted to publicly thank Mr Quibb and let others know that he was a hero despite not looking like a hero on TV.
8 After the rescue Jess might treat Mr Quibb with greater respect.

9–10

Answers will vary but need to include two sentences to explain their thinking.

Page 76 Grammar & Punctuation

1 Chris and Jess watched transfixed **as** the heroes saved humanity from evil once again.
2 Jess stiffened **as** she smelt the smoke and saw it enveloping the room. OR Fear gripped them **as** they fought the panic that bubbled underneath and threatened to paralyse them.
3 **As** the heroes saved humanity from evil once again, Chris and Jess watched transfixed.
4 **As** she smelt the smoke and saw it enveloping the room, Jess stiffened. OR
5 **As** they fought the panic that bubbled underneath and threatened to paralyse them, fear gripped them.
6 Answers may vary but can include: Mr Quibb was not considered a hero **because** he did not look like a superhero. OR **Since** Mr Quibb did not look like a superhero, he was not considered a hero.
7 Answers may vary but can include: **After** Mr Quibb saved the two children from the fire, he was considered a hero. OR Mr Quibb was considered a hero **when** he saved the two children from the fire.
8 Wherever – place and location
9 Because – cause and effect
10 after – time related
11 Since – cause and effect

Page 77 Phonic & Word Knowledge

1–18

Answers may include:

a – aisle, head, basically
b – lamb, doubt, subtle
c – science, muscle, scene
d – bridge, edge, Wednesday
e – on the end of words like kite, debate, name / in a vowel group like breathe
f – not ever silent
g – sign, high, gnome
h – echo, honest, spaghetti
i – business, suit, heir
j – marijuana
k – knife, know, knit
l – salmon, almond, walk
m – mnemonic (already given)
n – autumn, column, hymn
o – colonel, leopard, tough
p – receipt, pneumonia, coup
q – lacquer (already given)
r – February (already given). Another possible example is iron.
s – aisle, island, debris
t – buffet, castle, whistle
u – guitar, tongue, biscuit
v – not ever silent

ANSWERS

TARGETING ENGLISH HOMEWORK YEAR 6 © PASCAL PRESS ISBN 978 1 925726 63 3

w – wrist, answer, who
x – faux (already given)
y – prayer, prey / y can have an 'i' or 'e' sound: system, cycle
z – rendezvous (already given)

19 f & v
20 basically
21 French
22 t
23 Rendezvous is a French way to say 'meeting' or 'date'.
24 Answers will vary but can include: breaking into parts/ chunking – ren dez vous
25 Points can be a warded for following the instructions and trying to recall the number.

Unit 18

Page 79 Reading & Comprehension

1 Subjective language reflects a person's opinions and emotions. It can also be biased.
2 Objective language tends to be based more on fact, observation and logical argument.
3 Neither is better than the other.
4 subjective
5 objective language – You need the facts and not the opinions about what happened.
6 subjective language – You want to base your decision whether to see it or not on others' recommendations and opinions.
7 The shop owner was biased against the school kid who wore a hoodie. They may have been biased because of what may have occurred in the past and associate a hoodie wearer with vandalism.
8 Answers may vary but could include: times when facts are needed such as information reports for school assignments; giving evidence in court; giving flight or travel details; writing procedures or explanations on how things work etc.

9–10
Answers will vary but need to contain an attempt to write a main idea and opinion of a film.

Page 80 Grammar & Punctuation

1 Sally **has brought** money to buy a birthday present for her brother.
2 However, it **has been raining**, so Sally **has worn** the hoodie to stay dry.
3 She **slides** on the shop floor due to the puddle and **crashes** into the baked beans display.
4 She **freezes**, horrified at what she **has done**. She **flees** the scene in embarrassment.
5 Baked beans **are** a dish that **contains** white common beans
6 According to scientists, baked beans **provide** fibre that **supports** our health.
7 However, baked beans **prove** to be a dish that **has** high levels of sugar and salt.

Page 81 Phonic & Word Knowledge

	Original word	Word with suffix added	Silent consonant now sounded
	Example: solemn	solemnity (soh-lem-nuh-tee)	n
1	crumb	crumble	b
2	column	columnist	n
3	debt	debit	b
4	condemn	condemnation	n
5	assign	assignation	g

6 t
7 assignation
8 solemn
9 debt
10 columnist
11 condemnation
12 crumb
13 autumn
14 honest
15 knife
16 often
17 write
18 assign
19 gnat
20 castle
21 island
22 muscle
23 solemn
24 wrong
25 talk
26 Christmas
27 debt
28 knee
29 listen
30 whistle
31 design
32 haste

			a			d	e	b	t								w
h		i	t	u	c	a	s	t	l	e							h
	o		s	a	t					a	s	s	i	g	n		i
		n		l	l	u											s
	k	o	e		a	k	m	c	h	r	i	s	t	m	a	s	t
		n	f	s		n		n		h	a	s	t	e			l
			i	t	t		d		m	u	s	c	l	e	w		e
				f	e	k	n	e	e						r		
					e	n			l	i	s	t	e	n	i		
		s	o	l	e	m	n								t		
								g	n	a	t				e		
	w	r	o	n	g				d	e	s	i	g	n			

Unit 19

Page 83 Reading & Comprehension

1 ants
2 A ballad tells a story.
3 A refrain is a line that keeps recurring throughout the poem.
4 The refrain in this ballad is **'Cos ants are aware and act**.
5 Anna has six legs. Ants are insects which have six legs.
6 The ballad is recited to all the young ones to show that heroes come in all shapes and sizes.
7 Old Lizard's smile was not genuine. As the ballad says **Old Lizard wanted ants for lunch.** Therefore, he was a danger to the young ants.
8 Old Lizard wanted to eat Adam and Anna's family and friends.
9 Old Lizard was faster, but his size meant that he could not dart around the rocky terrain as well as the smaller and more nimble young ants.
10 Anna is an ant, and ants are capable of lifting objects many times their own weight.
11 Answers will vary.

Page 84 Grammar & Punctuation

1 shows
2 does
3 works
4 believe
5 gather
6 patrol
7 are
8 avoid
9 avoids
10 is
11 takes
12 have
13 are
14 train
15 feels
16 supplies
17 use
18 train

Page 85 Phonic & Word Knowledge

1 mbidextrous – able to use the right and left hands equally well
2 ambiguous – not clear or decided
3 ambience – the atmosphere or mood of a place
4 ambivalent – uncertain if you like something or what you should do about something
5 ambition – a strong desire to achieve something
6 Results will vary, but students need to show they have conducted the test and have come to a conclusion with a sentence to explain their thinking.

7 a neat
8 s past
9 t site
10 r tire
11 o stop
12 n line
13 a boat
14 u spun
15 t sits
16 The mystery word is **astronaut.**

ANSWERS

Answers

Unit 20

Page 87 Reading & Comprehension

1 The grandmother came to live with the author's family because she was not able to cope at home on her own as she had the beginning of dementia.
2 A suffragette is a woman seeking the right to vote through organised protests.
3 False
4 Early 1900s – Women campaigned for equal pay for equal work.
1901 – Federation
1902 – Women won the right to vote in Australia.
1972 – Women were granted equal pay with men.
1984 – The government passed the Sex Discrimination Act to protect people from unfair treatment.
5 Initially, the author resented Grandma and found her dementia hard to put up with.
After finding out that there was more to Grandma than they initially thought, they found a new respect for her.
6 registered
7 The clippings brought back memories which were special as they involved a fight for equality. It brought back something that Grandma could remember and talk about since she played a role in the protest movement.
8 Answers will vary. Students need to provide a reason for their decision.
9–10 Answers will vary. Students need to provide a reason for their strong feelings on the issue they raise.

Page 88 Grammar & Punctuation

1 Kate and **George's** mum was in hospital.
2 **Kate's and George's** offices are in different buildings.
3 You're
4 It's, they're
5–17 **Grandma's** pictures from the **'70s** were starting to fade. I offered to frame them and hang some in **Mum's** and **Grandma's** bedrooms. However, the pictures **weren't** large enough to be seen properly. It **wasn't** ideal. I realised that it was important to enlarge the pictures as **Grandma's** eyesight was not the best. I borrowed Kate and **George's** printer to make larger prints. I value **Mum's** and **Grandma's** opinions about the presentation of the pictures. I would award myself several **A's**, but **that's** just my opinion.
Score /12

Page 89 Phonic & Word Knowledge

1–17 In the **modern** world, **sport** has become very important. Some sports are considered an art form such as **ballet**. However, it can cost a lot of **money** to join a sports team, and it can require a lot of **energy**. Many children are **opting** out of sport and turning to **restaurants** and **cafés** to learn how to cook. Simple **omelette** or **soup** recipes are easy to follow and could be added to any **menu**. Making a **soufflé** or rich cake, called a **gateau**, would be a much more difficult task and require a **magnificent** occasion like a party on the **terrace**. So, many children are saying **bon voyage** to their sporting clubs and picking up kitchen **utensils** instead.
Score /17
18 Six-letter words: change; glance; encage; enlace ...
Five-letter words: glean; eagle; angle; leech; clang; angel; legal; clean; lance; hence ...
Four-letter words: glee; heel; heal; gall; gale; hang; lace; lane; hell; gene; call, cane; cage; elan; acne; ache, lean; glen; clan; each; cell; hall ...
19 challenge

Unit 21

Page 91 Reading & Comprehension

1 Alchemists believed they could turn base metals such as lead into gold.
2 It is a chemical change. No, this is not reversible.
3 chemical change
4 Alchemists believed everything was made of four basic elements: air, earth, fire and water. Since lead and other metals are not composed of fire, air, earth, and water, it's not possible to turn them into gold. You can't make gold through ordinary chemical reactions.
5 The particles (parts inside atoms) of which it is made and the numbers of particles remain unchanged.
6 No. Alchemists believed lead was a lower form of gold, not modern scientists of today. Alchemists believed that lead hadn't fully matured so that means all lead had the ability to eventually become gold. Scientists today know that you can't make gold through ordinary chemical reactions.
7 Answers will vary but may include: Both have conducted experiments, used chemical reactions and investigated properties of metals.
8 Answers will vary but may include: Alchemists believed everything was made of four basic elements: air, earth, fire and water while today's scientists know about atoms and particles. Alchemists would need to learn the difference between physical and chemical changes.
9 Answers may include: baker, chef, restorer of metals, firefighter sports trainer.
10 Answers may include: gardener who prunes; ice maker; harvester of sea salt; toffee maker.

Page 92 Grammar & Punctuation

1–15 Sam, a student at school, is hoping to turn collected pencil shavings into gold.
Mr Wilson, our teacher, explained, "Sam, you will not be able to turn the contents of your sharpener into gold."
Mr Wilson went on, "Gold, which is a precious metal, was created in the explosion of stars and not changed from something else."
(8 commas so far; another 7 to go!)
Wow, that's amazing! I never knew gold came from the debris of dead stars, and I never knew you could not create it from something else. I'm sure I read a story about spinning straw into gold. After much debate, I think Mr Wilson is wrong, and I am going to collect the whole class's pencil shavings from now on. Gold, which is something I desire, will be my secret project. The class may think I am mad, but they will think differently when I fill each pencil sharpener with gold.
16–17
Answers may vary and could include: ICED LICE; C ICE LIED (stretch of the imagination); DECI LICE, C DELI ICE

Page 93 Phonic & Word Knowledge

1–14

Greek micro = small	Greek mega = great
microwave microcosm microbe	megaphone megalopolis megadose
Latin super = over or above	**Greek hyper = over or above**
supermarket superhero superego	hypercritical hyperactive hyperventilate hyperbole hypersensitive

15–26

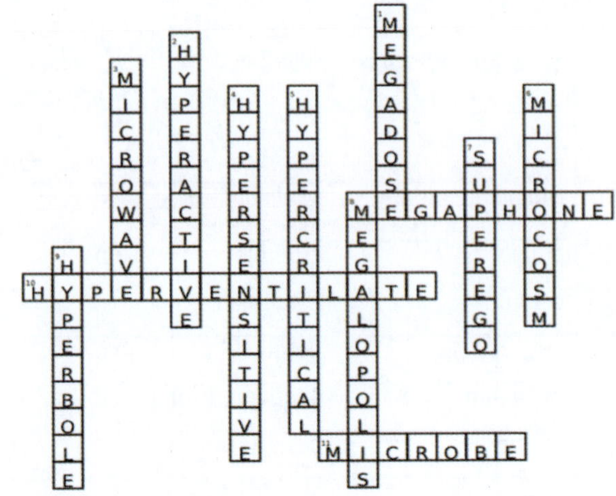

Answers

Unit 22

Page 95 Reading & Comprehension

1 Australia became very nervous after the war as they were nearly invaded by the Japanese and so felt unprotected during WW2. Because of this, the government decided they needed more people to live here.
2 Melbourne, Victoria
3 When the Communists came to South Vietnam where Vi lived, his family had to leave for fear of being put in goal. His family had fought in a war against the Communists.
4 Adults paid ten pounds each while children were free.
5 Maria brought her mother's cooking pot from Italy because it reminded her of Italy. It represents the flavours that are her heritage, and she still uses it to cook food for her family in Australia as a way of passing on the heritage.
6 Brian treasured the picture as a boy and keeps it as a reminder of what inspired the family to come to Australia in the first place – a place he is glad the family moved to.
7 All three stories explain how things were tough in their homeland and how they are happy to be in Australia. They identify as Australians.
8 Vi explained how his family had to leave as they were in danger, meaning they became refugees. Maria and Brian's families wanted a better life and made a choice to leave. They were not forced to leave.
9–10 Answers will vary.

Page 96 Grammar & Punctuation

1 known
2 thought
3 seen
4 predicted
5 struck
6 done
7 found
8 shaken
9 given
10 driven
11 swung
12 written
13 brought

14–20

Verb	Past tense	Past participle
forbid	forbade	forbidden
forget	forgot	forgotten
begin	began	begun
hide	hid	hidden
sing	sang	sung
shrink	shrank	shrunk
stink	stank	stunk

Page 97 Phonic & Word Knowledge

1 6
2 3
3 100
4 9
5 8
6 4
7 1000
8 2
9 5
10 7th
11 1
12 200
13 12
14 deca 10
15 octo 8
16 milli 1000
17 viginti 20
18 penta 5
19 centi 100
20 septi 7
21 tetra 4
22 dodeca 12
23 uni 1
24 hexa 6
25 nona 9
26 tri 3
27 undeca 11
28 di 2

Unit 23

Page 99 Reading & Comprehension

1 Poland has banned homework for Years 1–3 and made it optional for other primary year levels.
2 Pat has a great memory.
3 There are different levels of government, and the Prime Minister is not at the level that governs schools or homework policies.
4 The Prime Minister believes it is an issue Pat needs to discuss with the school principal.
5 Local council
6 It means that everybody wins and gets what they want. Homework can be set by teachers who want students to practise what they have learnt during the day. Students do not have to do the homework. Those who like homework can complete the tasks.
7–10 Answers will vary; however, students need to select the correct level of government for the change they wish to bring about.

Page 100 Grammar & Punctuation

I want the Prime Minister to (1) **consider** my proposal for homework as it affects (2) **numerous** (3) **children** from all over Australia. Homework has its place; (4) **however,** I have an idea to make it better for everyone. (5) **Additionally,** I like the idea that I can (6) **contact** the leader of our country. How wonderful is that? It is not that I (7) **oppose** homework, I just think we need to (8) **ascertain** what other countries are doing. (9) **In conclusion,** I would like my bill to be law and (10) **commence** (11) **as soon as possible.**

12–18

Answers will vary but could include: I **gulped down** my lunch as I was going to meet the head. Oops, I mean the Prime Minister. My little brother **snickered** at me, so I **glared back** at him and **dashed** out to the waiting car. I **wrestled with** the seat belt, and then **slouched** back into the seat, **clutching** my speech.

Page 101 Phonic & Word Knowledge

1–17

Down
1 define
2 distribute
5 declare
8 combine
11 habit
12 social
13 reside
15 incline
17 narrate

Across
3 contribute
4 migrate
5 deprive
6 organise
7 compete
9 prohibit
10 mobile
11 hesitate
14 preside
16 ignore
18 relate

Score /17

Unit 24

Page 103 Reading & Comprehension

1 two days
2 Gas is produced during a chemical change, such as baking a cake. Inside each bubble is a little bit of gas. This gas is made when the ingredients change each other. The bubbles help make the baked food fluffy.

Answers

Chemical change	Physical change	Explain why this answer
(3) Baking a cake		Cooking food is an irreversible, chemical change. During cooking, the molecules that are present in food change to form new substances. Cooked food cannot be reversed back to its raw state.
	(4) Melting chocolate	There is a change in the state of matter. This is a reversible change. Chocolate is still chocolate even when it changes from one state of matter (solid) to another (liquid).
	(5) Cutting up strawberries (6) Mashing strawberries	The appearance of the strawberries changes but the particles remain as strawberries. No new substances are formed. This is considered reversible, but like the cutting up of paper into tiny pieces, restoring the original paper or strawberry can be difficult.
(7) Toasting marshmallows		The toasting is actually burning the outside of the marshmallow. This is an irreversible chemical change.

8 Answers will vary but can include freezing or evaporating liquid, crushing and heating but not cooking. For example, making a flavoured milk drink with crushed ice or chocolate. Jelly is tricky. It is seen as a change in state from liquid to solid. However, the powder itself has gone through a chemical change to become the jelly crystals. This could be an interesting question to ask students.

Page 104 Grammar & Punctuation

Going to:
1 Pat **is going to bring** a recipe to school.

Simple future:
2 Sam **will write** a story for Mr Wilson.

Future continuous:
3 Pat **will be coming** home for the holidays.

Future perfect:
4 Sam **will have left** school by now.

Future perfect continuous:
5 By 8 pm, Pat **will have been studying** for four hours.

6 is looking
7 is thinking
8 are wondering
9 is wishing
10 are considering
11 is planning
12 are picking
13 is laying

Page 105 Phonic & Word Knowledge

1 effervescent
2 rescind
3 scenario
4 adolescence
5 reminiscence
6 scent
7 ascend
8 susceptible
9 resuscitate
10 fascinate
11 whisk
12 husk
13 skipper
14 flask
15 asterisk
16 cheapskate
17 scheme
18 sketching
19 scrumptious
20 skewer

Term 3 Review

Page 107 Reading & Comprehension

1 the Roman God of war
2 The mission was to collect soil samples from different depths on the surface and from different locations.
3 The narrator was feeling a tingling sensation because they were excited and nervous all at once.
4 The narrator wanted to be the first to discover something unique and different.
5 The ooze changed the narrator's feelings about being trapped. It forced its way into the helmet, and its smell was enticing and hypnotic. When the narrator tasted the wonderful creamy ooze, they wanted more. After that, all thoughts of escape left them, and they felt content.
6 sheen or shine
7 personification
8 Answers will vary.
9 Answers will vary.
10 Students may see the references to an actual Mars bar in the narrative – the dark patch of shiny crust and creamy ooze.

Page 108 Grammar & Punctuation

1–7 Answers will vary but may include:
1 With a thud, the spaceship landed and the rockets **stopped**.
2 An eerie stillness **came** around the ship.
3 The three of us who manned the spaceship eagerly **put on** our spacesuits.
4 Just before stepping off the ladder, I **stopped**.
5 A sticky ooze **held** my foot and held me fast.
6 Panic **came** over me like a fire.
7 I **fell** into the ooze.
8 b
9 a
10 c
11 d
12 d
13 a
14 e

Page 109 Phonic & Word Knowledge

1 trilogy
2 monologue
3 bisect
4 bifocals
5 monotonous
6 bimonthly
7 monolingual
8 triathlon
9 bilingual
10 monotone

11–20
Answers will vary but may include: seeing smaller words in the large word as in con-science; sounding the word as it looks, for example, chem-ist or sub-tle; ways to target specific letters for example, 'm' comes before 'n' in the alphabet and in mnemonics.

Term 4

Unit 25

Page 111 Reading & Comprehension

1 Evening. Answers may include: It was after dinner. / It was a still and clear night. / The meteorite was fiery against the sky. / The mosquitoes were out.
2 an alien spacecraft
3 seaweed
4 a rhetorical question and emotive language
5 Two identical figures stood face to face and toe to toe.
6 copying
7 A metaphor is a way to compare. Eve is saying that the beach is what could cure her feeling of being low. It is a natural cure and does not need to be prescribed by a doctor.
8 Answers may vary but could include: Eve was being very dramatic which her mother saw through. / Her mother did not believe her and thought it was a way to get out of doing homework. / Her mother thought her choices of persuasion were insincere and comical.
9 Answers may vary but can include: This passage shows that both the alien and Eve are in one body. There are two beings but only one body.
10 The last two words are 'they replied' which implies that Eve and the alien have become one and are working together.

Answers

Page 112 Grammar & Punctuation

1 the mosquitoes; hummed and danced
2 the insects; noisily chatting
3 the wind; died down to make a still night
4 surprise; stole air
5 personification
6 hyperbole
7 simile
8 simile
9 metaphor
10–12
Answers will vary.
13 The tongue-twister needs to be read aloud.

Page 113 Phonic & Word Knowledge

	Word	Definition
①	rhythm	A pattern of sounds or movements that repeats.
②	rhapsody	A piece of music or a feeling of elation/great happiness.
③	rhombus	A special shape with four equal sides where opposite sides are parallel.
④	rheumatism	A medical condition that causes pain, stiffness or swelling in the muscles, joints or connective tissues of the body.
⑤	rhubarb	A long, red-stemmed vegetable that is often thought of as a fruit.
⑥	rhododendron	A plant with beautiful flowers and glossy leaves.
⑦	rhizome	An underground plant stem that sends up shoots to the surface.
⑧	rhinoceros	A large, plant-eating mammal with thick skin, short legs and one or two horns on its nose.
⑨	rhetoric	The art of using words to persuade or influence others.

10 alligator
11 crimson
12 plaza
13 tornado or hurricane
14 bananas
15 avocado
16 tomatoes

Unit 26

Page 115 Reading & Comprehension

1 crickets and mealworms
2 Answers may vary but will include the following: The meat industry causes lots of environmental issues. / The hard hooves of cattle, sheep and goats damage the surface of the soil often leading to soil erosion. / Native grasses do not have a chance to grow due to overgrazing. / Loss of grasses means that many small animals, birds and insects lose their food source and habitat. / Livestock gives out various gases. / The entire chain from farm to fork in the meat industry contributes to many environmental issues affecting climate change and our water quality.
3 Answers may vary but will include the following: Tradition or habit in that meat has always been part of the Australian diet. / The 'yuck' factor is the main problem to introducing insects. / It may be hard to convince some Australians to eat insects rather than meat-based products. / We are not used to insects as food, so there's a concern that people in Australia will not accept the idea. / The farming of insects is not easy. / Edible insects can be a source of biological hazards, including bacteria that can cause diseases. / Foods that use insect products can become contaminated at all stages of production, delivery and consumption.
4 Answers may vary but will include the following: Insects are rich in vitamins and high in protein. / The farm-to-fork process is much better for the environment. / Less land and water are used, and fewer gases are produced in the process.
5 Answers may vary but may include: the thought of eating them / the texture in the mouth and how they would feel / the taste / getting legs of insects caught in your throat or between your teeth / the visual aspect – just the look of them / being repulsed or frightened of insects
6 The farming of insects is not easy. Edible insects can be a source of biological hazards, including bacteria that can cause diseases. Foods that use insect products can become contaminated at all stages of production, delivery and consumption. / Pesticides used in the garden and animals in the garden could cause contamination of the insects.
7–8
Answers will vary.
9–10
Answers will vary. An example could include: Product – Peanut butter ants. My family loves peanut sauce and peanut-flavoured spreads.

Page 116 Grammar & Punctuation

1 Pat, although she was ravenous, was reluctant to try a cricket-packed sandwich.
2 Even Mr Wilson, because he was late for a meeting, was reluctant to try a cricket sandwich.
3 Sam, whose sandwich was being discussed, could not see what all the fuss was about.
4 Mr Wilson, who sat quietly at his desk, was hoping Sam would not offer to bring him a cricket sandwich for lunch the next day.
5 No commas are necessary.
6 The chef, who was dressed in white, looked with disdain at the sandwich.
7 No commas are necessary.
8 The sandwich, which was feeling important, continued to sit in silence on the table while being studied.
9 Sam's mum, who was standing at the back of the room, was waiting impatiently for the chef's point of view.
10 No commas are necessary.
11 Sam's mum, who couldn't help herself, gave a shout of approval.
12 No commas are necessary.
13 No commas are necessary.

Page 117 Phonic & Word Knowledge

1–20
Answers may include any number of the following. Students score one point per word.
intercept; interception; intercepted; interceptible; intercepting; percept; perception; perceptible; perceptual; concept; conception; conceptional; concepting; conceptual; susceptive; susceptible; accept; accepted; acceptable; accepting; deception; deceptive; decepted; deceptible; except; exception; excepted; exceptional; excepting

21	22	23
it	at	or
tic	sat	our
cite	seat	sour
cites	dates	scour
nicest	trades	source
insects	roasted	

Unit 27

Page 119 Reading & Comprehension

1 Context is information about the time in history that an ad was created.
2 Most dolls before Barbie® were old-fashioned or **modelled on babies**. Girls tended to play with the baby dolls by **pretending they were mothers.**
3 In the 1960s, American and Australian military forces were involved in the Vietnam War. This toy represents what was happening in the world at that time.
4 In the 1960s – a fashion model
In 2016 – girls or Barbie® can be anything they imagine

ANSWERS

5 copy
6 Your parents are older and would have seen these forms of technology that are not used today.
7 Barbie® and G.I. Joe® have a trademark which means that no other toy company can use that name for their product. It is used to protect a brand from competitors.
8 Answers will vary. There are varying responses online. The question brings up gender stereotyping and gender-specific language.
9 In the early 1960s, it was generally considered that boys would not play with dolls and parents would not buy their sons dolls as they were seen as a girl's toy. So action figure was an acceptable term. It has since become the generic description for any doll intended for boys.
10 Answers will vary.

Page 120 Grammar & Punctuation

1 why 2 when 3 why 4 how 5 where
6 Because it still had the action figure in its mouth, Fred walked towards the sleeping dog.
7 No comma necessary.
8 So that the dog wouldn't wake up, Fred very carefully curled his fingers around the figure.
9 No comma necessary.
10 Fred, because he loved his G.I. Joe®, grabbed it and ran away quickly.
11 No comma necessary.
12 So that the dog wasn't upset anymore, Fred gave it a big, juicy bone.
13 Because they both had what they wanted, Fred and the dog were best friends again.

Page 121 Phonic & Word Knowledge

1 metre
2 centre
3 organisation
4 realise
5 recognise
6 analyse
7 behaviour
8 labour
9 favour
10 favourite
11 colour
12 honour
13 theatre
14 litre
15 fibre
16 theatre
17 recognise
18 favourite
19 behaviour
20 colour

Unit 28

Page 123 Reading & Comprehension

1 over a million
2 Ten Pound Pom scheme
3 They came to a place where they knew no-one.
4 Brian's father wanted a better job, and his Mum and Dad said they wanted a better life with better weather.
5 The *Orcades* had more luxuries than other ships; waiters and dining rooms; lots of food as Brian's family could eat soup, a main meal and dessert for lunch and dinner. The ship offered comforts Brian had not experienced back in Britain.
6 shortages of food
7 Brain confused the similar spelling of Austria and Australia.
8 Many liners were converted during the war to troop carriers which were very basic. After the war, these ships were again used for passengers with only some modifications, so amenities were still basic. The *Orcades* was a specifically built liner after the war, so it had swimming pools and dining rooms that Brian mentions. Liners are associated with passenger travel.
9 Answers will vary but could include the following: isolation; difficulty with the language, food and climate; being accepted
10 Answers will vary.

Page 124 Grammar & Punctuation

1 I'm leaving for Grandma's house now, **but** I'll be back home tomorrow.
2 Grandma is very old, **so** I do jobs for her around the house and yard.
3 We might make pizzas for dinner, **or** we could buy them from the pizza shop.
4 I love pineapple on my pizza, **and** I also like heaps of stringy cheese.
5 Grandma always says she's tired, **yet** she can stay up later than me!
6 I went to a sleepover at Grandma's house on the weekend, **but** I really would have preferred to stay over at my friend's house.
7 I wasn't allowed, **so** I just made the best of it.
8 Grandma and I made pizzas, **and** we ate them in front of the TV.
9 I was very full, **yet** I still had room in my belly for ice-cream.
10 Next time, we're going to make burgers, **or** we could just practise our pizza making!

Page 125 Phonic & Word Knowledge

1 a
2 d
3 a
4 immigrated
5 emigrate
6 immigration
7 Emigration
8 emigrant
9 immigrant
10 migration
11 The preferred word is 'migrants', but often the words are used interchangeably.
12 migrate
13 migrated

Unit 29

Page 127 Reading & Comprehension

1 Self-awareness is what makes us different from other animals and controls our behaviour.
2 For humans, self-awareness includes what we think in terms of thoughts and emotions.
3 False
4 Magpies and pigeons pass the 'mirror test' as well as dolphins and killer whales.
5 **Mark the individual** on their body in a place they cannot see without a mirror. This can be done while they are asleep if it is a sibling. **Let them see their reflection.** Note whether they **make attempts to remove the mark.** This signals whether they recognise that the reflection is them.
6 Large-brained animals are considered more intelligent.
7 We start to build a concept of self from four months onwards, and at 18 months we can recognise that the face in the mirror belongs to us. At 10 months, the child is looking for the other child reflected as they do not see it as a reflection of themselves.
8 Answers may vary but can include: giving praise; giving supportive comments; being there for you; helping stop your negative thoughts; helping create more positive thoughts; providing a sense of fun; providing a sense of security etc.
9 Answers may vary but can include: providing a way for you to compare yourself to others in a negative way; giving a false sense of what is considered 'normal' or appropriate in looks, dress, behaviour etc.; following negative influencers; giving continuous advice on improving yourself; can be materialistic and beauty-centred
10 Answers will vary.

Page 128 Grammar & Punctuation

Answers will vary in these activities. Students need to show imagination and originality in what they write.

Page 129 Phonic & Word Knowledge

1 effect
2 effect
3 affect
4 affect
5 effect
6 affected
7 allot
8 a lot
9 a lot
10 allots
11 a lot
12 a lot
13 conscious
14 conscience
15 conscious
16 conscience

Unit 30

Page 131 Reading & Comprehension

1 local, state and federal
2 Mayor or Shire President
3 local roads, garbage collection, public parks, building regulations

ANSWERS

4 class meeting with students
5 teachers at staff meeting
6 buses – state; extension – local; passport – federal
7 Answers will vary but may include: both are leaders; both have committees to help run their school/country; both deal with providing a safe environment; there is no limit to the amount of time that somebody can be PM or principal; both answer to the communities they serve; both have two main decision-making bodies
8 Answers will vary but may include: One is elected and the other is not. / The PM influences all Australians, while a principal only has influence over the students and families at the school. / The PM is the leader of a country while a principal is the leader of a school.

9–10 Answers will vary.

Page 132 Grammar & Punctuation

1 **Hearing** the council's decision, Sam jumped for joy.
2 **Running** to the oval, Sam expected to argue for space on the oval.
3 **Placing** Sam's oval proposal on the table, Mr Wilson smiled wearily.
4 **Feeling** proud, Sam told his friends about the proposal.
5 Mr Wilson talked to the principal about Sam's oval proposal, **thinking** it was a bold request.
6 Mr Wilson passed on the decision, **trying** to hide his smile.

Answers may vary in the following sentences as long as they make sense. The sentences may start with an independent/dependent clause.

7 As the class celebrated the idea of more PE, Mr Wilson added a condition and asked for more homework.
As the class celebrated the idea of more PE, Mr Wilson added a condition asking for more homework.
8 After the class heard Mr Wilson's condition, they looked in horror at Sam and decided against the proposal of more PE.
After the class heard Mr Wilson's condition, they looked in horror at Sam deciding against the proposal of more PE.

Page 133 Phonic & Word Knowledge

1 diffusion
2 persuasion
3 supervision
4 revision
5 extension
6 allusion
7 tension

8–37

expand ✔ = expandsion x **expansion**
comprehens x **comprehend** = comprehension ✔
paste ✔ = pasting ✔
argue ✔ = arguement x **argument**
provide ✔ = provision ✔
slime ✔ = slimey x **slimy**
invade ✔ = invassion x **invasion**
erode ✔ = erosion ✔
paste ✔ = pastey x **pasty**
case ✔ = casement ✔
base ✔ = basement ✔
exploode x **explode** = explosion ✔
suspend ✔ = suspension ✔
hope + ing ✔ = hopping x **hoping**
late ✔ = latest ✔

Unit 31

Page 135 Reading & Comprehension

1 Poor Jaw Strength
2 Chewing gum increases your saliva production, which is good for oral health. A healthy flow of saliva helps wash away harmful sugars and food particles, so it protects the teeth from decay.
3 Answers can include: Poor jaw strength is due to a lack of use. / Students rather text than talk or watch a screen than interact with each other. / Children do not talk enough and need to exercise their jaws.
4 The chewing gum provides the right amount of tension for the jaw muscles to get a workout.
5 Kids love chewing gum. / Children are very easily persuaded by advertising.
6 Chris has been persuaded by their own advertising campaign to believe that PJS exists.

7–8 Answers will vary but may include anecdotal evidence about their own experiences; what they have observed; expert opinions if they have researched information.

9–10 Answers will vary. Encourage imaginative responses.

Page 136 Grammar & Punctuation

1 active
2 active
3 passive
4 passive
5 active
6 passive
7 PJS causes tooth decay!
8 Kids, chew our gum today!
9 Lack of talking causes PJS.
10 Parents, buy this product for your children!
11 Children need their parents to buy this product.

Page 137 Phonic & Word Knowledge

1 intermission
2 credibility
3 diction
4 traction
5 audible
6 nonsensical
7 antiseptic
8 irreparable
9 immobile
10 illicit
11 uneasy
12 impede
13 nonentity
14 disposition
15 irregular
16 antiseptic
17 impede

Unit 32

Page 139 Reading & Comprehension

1 Student Survivor Alone
2 a survival pack and camera
3 Lines of latitude circle the Earth below and above the equator. They are measured in degrees starting at the equator and ending at the South and North Poles.
4 International Date Line at 180°. It is the boundary line between one calendar day and the next.
5 Natural navigation aids like the **sun**, **stars**, and **landmarks** determine the direction and location of your camp site.
6 False
7 Answers may include: The island is close to the equator which means hotter temperatures and more sunshine than lower or higher latitudes.
8 Barung Island 8.4794° S, 113.3466° E
9 The producer wants the best ratings on TV and does not want to be sued for injuries. They do not want you to know that they can change the length of stay to one month. They also do not want you to know that they take no responsibility for your injuries or that contestants have the right to leave early if they feel they cannot cope.
10 Answers will vary but may include: too mountainous to be lived on; too small; no fresh water; no way to make a living on the island; no utilities such as electricity, water, sewerage etc.; rising sea level may make the island vulnerable to disappearing in the near future

Page 140 Grammar & Punctuation

1–10 Answers may vary with the use of exclamation marks etc. Some form of punctuation is needed before quotation marks and direct speech must be punctuated.

1 The interviewer approached Eve and put the microphone under her chin. "Now tell me, Eve," she said with enthusiasm. "How was it?"
2 In an exhausted tone, Eve replied, "Well, it was certainly an experience."
3 "Fantastic!" the interviewer retorted in an exaggerated tone. "I think we all want to know about how you survived without water or food."
4 Eve looked uncomfortable and mumbled, "Well, I did know the producer of the show."

5 "What?" asked the interviewer in surprise. "Do you mean you cheated?"
6 This was when the film crew started to look more interested and Eve more nervous.
7 "No! I did not cheat!" replied Eve. "I just had some help, that's all."
8 "What type of help?" the interviewer inquired.
9 Eve looked into the camera and said, "I happened to run into some camels that had supplies."
10 The interviewer turned to the camera and said, "We thank Eve for her explanation. We hope the next contestants find some help on their uninhabited island."

11–16
Answers may vary in language used but understanding needs to be evident.
11 Between two independent clauses in a compound sentence. The comma goes in front of the co-ordinating conjunction.
12 after a dependent clause in a complex sentence
13 introductory word or phrase
14 embedded clause
15 list
16 direct speech or dialogue

Page 141 Phonic & Word Knowledge

1 solitude
2 latitude/longitude
3 latitude/longitude
4 gratitude
5 altitude
6 aptitude
7 extrude
8 multitude
9 attitude

10–15
Here I am on the (10) **most** isolated island I have ever been on. I was the (11) **most excited** I have ever been to find a handwritten note from someone who might still be stranded on the island.
The (12) **kindest** thing I could have done was notify the authorities to search for this person, but that would have knocked me out of the competition. Perhaps it would be (13) **best** if I ignored the note. However, my conscience has got the (14) **better** of me, and I have decided to contact the authorities. I hope this person is (15) **happier** than me to be off the island.

Term 4 Review

Page 143 Reading & Comprehension

1 Keep Australia Clean
2 Monday
3 Lia, her mum, dad, grandma and Mr Wilson = 5
4 A large company was planning on dumping chemical waste into one of the country's largest rivers, but they needed to find out how this was going to happen. As a professional spy kid, Lia had been assigned the task.
5 A surveillance camera positioned on the wall followed Lia's every move.
6 Looking around and observing what is happening in the street.
7 Mr Wilson knew what Lia was up to, and he was part of the same organisation.
8 The director was angry/fuming because Lia was escorted out of the office before she could interrogate her.
9 Answers will vary but can include: taking samples at the river; watching the trucks that leave the factory; interviewing workers at the factory.
10 Answers may vary. Children **should be** spies because: Children would not be suspected of being spies. / Children often go unnoticed as they are smaller. / Children are quick and nimble and could sneak into places easily.
Children **should not be** spies because: It is dangerous. / They cannot drive to places when they need to. / They may not make the best choices as they are children.

Page 144 Grammar & Punctuation

1 personification; simile
2 b
3 Answers will vary and could include: The crane grabbed the rocks, curling its claws and holding tight.
4 Answers could include: His sneeze was so strong it caused the maths test next door to be blown away.
5 Answers could include: Fred dances like he has ants in his pants.
6 Lia's parents, when they found out, were not very surprised by her actions.
7 As the director watched, Lia left quickly with her class.
8 The class had no idea that Lia and Mr Wilson were spies, but the director suspected they both were.
9 The director snarled, "We will keep an eye on them!"
10 "Let's eat, Grandma!"
11 The student, said the teacher, is a delight.

Page 145 Phonic & Word Knowledge

1	2	3
as	if	at
sea	fir	hat
sale	fire	heat
lease	fibre	hater
sealer		heater
realise		theatre

4–22

r j i n t e r c e p t o q i c c o i t x d s p i s t n m d
n b b r n c a v j x c p i s i c r c s y a e d o y o y k s
g r m o b k d v y o w h d d y e x j j u u r w y j f q b d
m z a q h x i m m i g r a t e i l b k f s g g g m o f a l
s p r h i n o c e r o s q d b n k r h e q c c u v g u c t
d s e n h y r o q z y f w p w x q f n b t v e b m l t j y
k m z n t a z r x r t o c g z x p g d z z u w p v e x z k
j p i g b a n a l y s e u k z q s b s l z e t l t e n e b
k g u v j h m v m x f a c c e p t e d u j o x f u i q t t
r u j s k r q a r t n j b q o w x y d s s f a v b a b b v
q j p e j u u f h o y p e t r t o s d x a p a t c d u l q
y j r h m g b a y v x y u u r n y j o p v f e e t c v u e
p o j h z i p n t d b o w g f i c s w n s s o n z r m c w
m f e i a x g j h i q x t p c h c d o w v g p a s v d m j
g h a z e p u r m y i f k k q o y d h w o n d q p i h s q
c o b y z x s a a f c e w c t i u x l x r v z e a m o q y
o j r l i n p o c t z z n u u c d j r y f q u f t w i n c
l w p c i o u r d m e w a m l a m p l i t u d e a i q s z
o p p g y o n t n y u r p t a u j y t r z h r h e q t g y
u p t z n n a r p x k z t s t k p a u h m x y x j j t h y
r m w s x u h y q a l o n g i t u d e b e p l u t k j h h
m s f e n p p x z p t y b m t u j c b s w a m d n m a n j
i m b o s z i v v t c i d x u e x g n s p q t r p j d d f
j o m k b e h a v i o u r m d a t v b m w t n r o y e t z
w z u l d q r i j j w n y q e y y x b k x r d t e z h x e
l w t r z w y t d m b w g s s d b a p f y h t c a m k d p
p k j p f g f n y a z z p b o g f s b f a v o u r i t e f
i r h e b m i o t e x c e p t i o n t i w m p i u u s a w

Score /19

ANSWERS

TARGETING ENGLISH HOMEWORK YEAR 6 © PASCAL PRESS ISBN 978 1 925726 63 3

TARGETING ENGLISH HOMEWORK YEAR 6 © PASCAL PRESS ISBN 978 1 925726 63 3